DOWN THE DRAIN

RALPH PENTLAND
CHRIS WOOD

DOWN
THE DRAIN

How We Are Failing To Protect
Our Water Resources

GREYSTONE BOOKS

Vancouver/Berkeley

Greystone Books Ltd.
www.greystonebooks.com

Cataloguing data available from Library and Archives Canada
ISBN 978-1-926812-77-9 (cloth)
ISBN 978-1-926812-78-6 (epub)

Editing by Nancy Flight
Copyediting by Shirarose Wilensky
Jacket and text design by Heather Pringle
Jacket photographs by Martin Kemp and Victor Polyakov / iStockphoto.com
Printed and bound in Canada by Friesens
Distributed in the U.S. by Publishers Group West

We gratefully acknowledge the financial support of the Canada Council
for the Arts, the British Columbia Arts Council, the Province of British Columbia
through the Book Publishing Tax Credit, and the Government of Canada
through the Canada Book Fund for our publishing activities.

Greystone Books is committed to reducing the consumption of old-growth
forests in the books it publishes. This book is one step toward that goal.

Contents

PROLOGUE

All We Have

ONE OF the most powerful photographic images of our time shows the gauzy ball of planet Earth hovering weightless in the velvet dark of space.

That is all we have. This one planet is our Eden, our space capsule, and if we fail to maintain it, will be our species' coffin. iPods and 3-D television do not exempt our big-brained, thumb-wielding race of primates from the laws of biology.

On this planet, water is necessary to everything that matters. In many faiths, water is a sacred essence. In the empirical eye of science, it is the elemental prerequisite of life. Without water, there are no crops. Without water, not one of our modern miracles of technology could be manufactured. Essence of the Creator's spirit, essential molecule of organic chemistry, water is no less the essential solvent, lubricant, and medium of transport for the modern industrial economy. What we do with water affects what it can do for us and for the rest of creation later.

For that reason, when we speak of "water" in the pages that follow, we mean its role in multiple contexts. We cannot discuss the safety of tap water without also discussing the security of the natural climate and ecosystems that are its ultimate source. Correspondingly, the state of water—revealed in qualities such as temperature and oxygen content—is often our best clue to the health of the ecosystems it flows through. Here, we strive to understand water in all its dimensions: the stuff itself, the bi-elemental condensate of two gasses; the company it keeps, its desirable and undesirable "contaminants"; and its network, the veins and currents of its movement over, above, and beneath the surface of the earth. In any of these roles and dimensions, unforeseen changes in water's quantity or condition disrupt human accomplishment, threaten human and wild life, and fray our common habitat.

Our view of "wealth" is similarly inclusive. We do not mean here only the number of digits in an individual's financial worth or a nation's gross domestic product. Rather, "wealth," which derives from the same roots as "well-being" and "wellness," connotes those features as well as a life that is abundant in all the ways that people universally appreciate. The *Shorter Oxford English Dictionary* gives the first meaning of "wealth" as "the condition of being happy and prosperous." Research shows that the determinants of happiness are *enough* money (although beyond a certain point, more becomes superfluous), physical health, rich social connections, meaningful work, and exposure to nature. The value of the last is too easily overlooked in reductionist analyses but shows up in measurably less mental distress among people with regular access to green spaces. There is a reason why gardens have been a feature of cities since Babylon. We take "wealth" to embrace this whole suite of requisites for balanced individual, family, and community well-being.

Another word we will use often that deserves comment here is "Crown." Some readers may find its use precious, quaint, or archaic. It is none of these. In the Canadian context, the word has specific meanings. These are, variously, symbolic (the Crown as embodiment of the nation and public interest), constitutional (the Crown as symbol of the monarch in whose name the public's affairs are nominally conducted), and legal (the Crown holds title to much of our landscape; if you kill your spouse, the Crown will prosecute you for murder).

These different manifestations of the Crown constitute a large part of what distinguishes Canadian democracy and law from that of the republican United States. And as a public resource, water cannot be managed in Canada without engaging (or butting up against) one or more of these embodiments.

We also take it as beyond debate that greenhouse gasses are pushing the Earth's thermal equilibrium into ranges unprecedented in the human experience, forcing its climate into new configurations. How these will affect local weather may or may not conform to broad trends. But extremes and lurching reversals rule. Dry places and times get drier; wet ones, wetter. The measured parade of familiar seasons breaks down into chaotic swings around the weather dial.

The only planet we have is changing. In this context, "security" means more than a steady job, police on the street, or guards at the border. As we begin to face ecological payback for two centuries of human rapine, security comes from a resilient, productive habitat. We are just beginning to recognize that such *natural* security is also essential to our national, economic, and even personal security.

The essence of our argument in these pages is that water is the currency of natural security. Its fate is co-extensive with ours.

Earth has entered a new age, the Anthropocene. This "human age" is characterized by the retreat and vulnerability of nature in the face of human action. It is experienced in the economy as "nature scarcity": looming limits to mineral resources and scarcity of food and other products of living ecosystems.

The overarching challenge for all nations in the coming decades will be to adapt to this new reality with a minimum of suffering while preserving a maximum of wealth (as defined on the previous page). This cannot be accomplished unless we first preserve the remaining ecosystems providing essential natural services. Failure on this front poses existential risk.

Geography endows Canada with great assets in this new world of nature scarcity. Wisely managed, these assets position us to be among the winners of the Anthropocene. It is a role we can play for profit or global influence, or simply to bring relief to more suffering regions of humanity. But most of our citizens are unaware of their own exposure to water stress and contamination. And we cannot manage what we fail to either measure or defend.

National security is a responsibility that the sovereign—in Canada's constitutional semantics, the Crown—owes to the people. *Natural* security is no less an inherent and inalienable sovereign duty. But it is a duty that our leaders have so far failed. In this era of deepening ecological debt on a global scale, Canadians must insist that our national leaders accept and fulfill their duty to safeguard our natural security as vigorously as they do our military security.

The Earth will be blue for some time to come. Whether it will be green, at least in the same places, or continue to support the complex, ravenous form of life that calls itself *Homo sapiens* is more in doubt. This book offers an account of how Canada and Canadians can avoid disaster and prepare our fortunate country to be a resilient refuge of wealth in a troubled century.

ONE

The Last Water
in the World

COVERING 31,000 square kilometres, Great Bear Lake is either the seventh- or eighth-largest lake on Earth, depending on whether you consider Lakes Huron and Michigan to be separate lakes or, as hydrologists do, one. It is bigger than any of Lakes Ontario, Erie, or Winnipeg and is unquestionably the largest freshwater body entirely within Canada's borders. Yet few Canadians are aware that on Great Bear's 2,719-kilometre coast there exists only one permanent human settlement. Even fewer are likely to know the story of that settlement's unusual prophecy.

The community of Déline sits far down on Great Bear Lake's wide southwestern arm. The Slavey word means "where the water goes out"—a reference to the wide-flowing nearby river that empties the lake and shares its name. Déline used to be called Fort Franklin, after British explorer Sir John Franklin. During one of his earlier and less disastrous expeditions, the ill-fated leader and his men spent the winter of 1823–24 here.[1] Later, a trading post and mission school formed the nucleus of a settled community where nomadic Dene, Dogrib, Gwi'chen, and Slavey people had for centuries stopped to trade and fish the abundant shoals at the river's entrance. A few years ago, Déline's eight hundred or so Sahtu ("Great Bear") Dene residents renamed their community, largely to repudiate any association with the band of armed intruders they remember mostly for theft and the rape of local women.[2]

A far more honoured memory in this small settlement is that of a humble trapper. Early in the twentieth century, Dene elder Louis Ayah earned a reputation for unusual insight. He is reputed to have forecast many of the events of the middle and late decades of the century, from world wars and satellites to the discovery of diamonds in the Northwest Territories. He is venerated today beyond the Sahtu Dene. An annual gathering draws people from First Nations across the North to celebrate Ayah's spirit in a replica of his cabin. But for the Sahtu, his prophecies held a particular and specific warning. As Morris Neyelle, Déline's unofficial community historian, tells it, Ayah foresaw "that one day the people of the rest of the world will run out of water, and when they do they will all come here to Great Bear, because this will be the last pure water left on earth."

Three-quarters of a century after Ayah's death in 1940, the last part of his prophecy is well on its way to coming true. Great Bear Lake is the last unpolluted water body of its size remaining in the Western Hemisphere. With Lake Baikal, it is one of the last large pools of pristine fresh water left on the planet (and paper mill effluent now threatens Baikal's purity). Beyond that, Déline and its prophecy are portraits in miniature of the beliefs almost all Canadians hold about ourselves, "our" water, and the wider world.

Canada, most of us are raised to believe, has an abundance of clean water. We cite with pride our possession of a fifth of the world's liquid fresh water, though only a third of that is renewed by rain and snowfall. Other countries are running out of water, and many of us believe that they will eventually want ours. We routinely tell opinion researchers that water is the nation's most important natural resource, an irreplaceable treasure more valuable than all the oil, gas, gold, and diamonds our geography also yields.

We like to see ourselves as outdoorsy people by nature, proud to "stand on guard" for our landscape of iconic lakes—if only by demanding that Parliament pre-emptively declare our refusal to ever, *ever*, share our water with anyone else.

Many Canadians who do not know Déline's name imagine themselves in its moral image: outnumbered but doughty defenders of a liquid treasure. Our daily reality is much closer to the nightmare first part of Louis Ayah's vision. We waste more water than anyone else on Earth, with the possible exception of citizens of the United States. We are more careless than even they with the purity of our lakes and streams. Expanding cities, retreating ecosystems, and a changing climate give southern Canada, where most of us live, far more in common with the increasingly parched and poisoned landscapes of Ayah's bleak vision than with the living web of lakes, forest, rock, and wetland that cradles the crystalline vastness of Great Bear Lake.

Our beliefs about water are riddled with mythology, error, ignorance, smugness, and complacency. Self-delusion is no mere moral failing, however. It is frequently lethal. A few decades after Franklin's winter on Great Bear, Inuit witnesses would later report, the starving remnants of his doomed last crew stumbled past them through the snow, even *in extremis* disdaining to seek the help of "savages."[3]

Yet the ascetic prophet and untouched lake at Déline offer more than just a salutary rebuke to dangerous hypocrisies. The tiny Dene community and the barely more substantial northern territorial population of which it is a part embody a fundamental challenge to the idea of "dominion"—whether of man over nature or, to use a now archaic term, the political Dominion of Canada. They seek to restore a candour about humanity's dependence upon Earth's natural ecosystems, our habitat, that must be grasped by all of us if we are to understand the foundation of wealth in the coming century

Water is implicated in everything human beings do. Without it, no food is grown, no energy captured, no goods made, no activity performed. Without water to drink, you will die within seventy-two hours. For these reasons, in every faith water is equated with life itself.

A reciprocal but underappreciated fact is that *everything that humans do* in our commercial economy, all our military stratagems, our art, recreation, and culture, right down to our most mundane and intimate domestic moments, *has an effect on our water*.

Water really is everything. In this book, however, we will focus on one question: Can Canadians be confident that our water is safe today and secure for the future?

Answering that question requires us to look further than the kitchen tap.

Many writers have examined the future of water's *quantity*. We will focus equally on water's *quality*. Is it clean? Is it healthy? And what do we mean by those terms? As we'll discover, quantity and quality cannot be entirely disentangled in discussing water.

Confidence, former U.S. president Ronald Reagan once remarked, is an amalgam of trust and verification. Much of this book deals with how these apply to Canada's natural security. Many Canadians, especially those returning from a trip to a country like Mexico, might say their confidence in our public water supply is justified. We'll see whether the arrangements to verify that safety in fact deserve Canadians' trust.

Since antiquity, water has been considered a shared public asset. In Canada today, statute, common law, and popular thinking still hold this to be true of water "in the wild." As one result, the number of provincial and federal agencies whose decisions may affect any given body of water quickly runs into double digits. In most of Canada, moreover, both the oversight and functional operation of municipal water supply and waste water systems are in the public sector and under direct political management.

For all of these reasons, we need to consider how we make decisions about such public assets: the place and role of public agencies, the applicable laws and habitual practices that determine the security of any particular water body. We will ask, that is, whether the social and legal infrastructure Canadians have built to defend our water is effective. And if not, what needs to change.

Water is also mobile. The water splashed about the map of Canada is not as much "ours" as we like to think. Our land receives it and sends it on. Hence we cannot think usefully about water on Canadian soil without thinking about our relationships with others—our partners in trade, economic rivals, and hemispheric peers. The experiences of the United States and Europe provide illuminating perspectives on Canada's water security.

Likewise, our choices today are constrained by decisions in the past. From our homes to our metropolises, water is delivered and waste drained through sophisticated, complex, and—in urban areas—vast systems of pipes, tanks, and other facilities that are among our society's biggest investments in fixed physical capital. Much of that physical capital is a century old; modifying it can take years. So too can amending our social capital of laws, regulatory codes, and personal habits in the handling of water.

As we make our choices we are always fleeing an inflexible past toward a contingent future over which we have limited control. We need to look back a century and a half to the founding of our country to understand the shackles and opportunities it faces on the eve of its sesquicentennial. Our discussion, though, will mainly surround today—the decades from the 1970s and looking forward to the 2020s.

Over that time, three global and domestic trends have decisively influenced the security of Canada's water.

First, global economic thinking has been deeply influenced by market fundamentalism, associated with the surrender of considerable sovereignty by nation-states to an emerging class of "world governance" authorities. At the same time, in a second trend, Canada's leaders have become increasingly passive in the face of threats to the ecological assets that constitute our natural security.

The third critical development is wholly unprecedented and unique in the human story. As a result, we are poorly adapted by evolution or experience to deal with it.

Sometime between the early 1980s and today, the supply-demand balance between human consumption of Earth's resources and the planet's biophysical productive capacity (nature) tipped from a condition of *nature surplus* to one of *nature scarcity*. The entirety of human development occurred under the former state of a surplus supply of nature. Consequently, nothing in our experience, habits, or physical and social infrastructure is adapted to the new state of global nature scarcity. In light of forecast growth in the human population from 7 billion to as many as 15 billion bodies over the present century,[4] this shift appears to be permanent. In the next decade, it will emerge as the dominant factor in this century's geo-economic and geopolitical calculus.

After five years of study, the Millennium Ecosystem Assessment calculated in 2005 that two-thirds of the planetary services on which humanity depends for biological existence—from marine fisheries to atmospheric carbon cycling—were being exploited beyond their capacity to regenerate. Every year the Global Footprint Network calculates the date (Earth Overshoot Day) by which our economy will have exhausted twelve months' worth of planetary productivity and begin running through (and down) legacy stocks from previous years or centuries.[5] For 2011, Earth Overshoot Day was calculated to pass on September 27—implying that the global economy was running an *ecological overdraft* 35 percent beyond Earth's capacity to support.

That overdraft has deepened each year since the mid-1980s. Its most pervasive manifestation is the instability of weather patterns as they accommodate the extra energy pent up on the planet by human carbon emissions that exceed the capacity of oceans and biosphere to assimilate. Scientists tracking many of these changes, from vanishing winter precipitation in the eastern Mediterranean to melting permafrost in the Canadian North, have noted that the records began to divert from historical norms in the 1980s.

Humanity's overdraft at what *New York Times* columnist Tom Friedman has dubbed the "Bank of Nature" is the common denominator behind a range of other stressors: volatility in food prices and supply, the rising cost of natural disasters, political instability in many regions of the globe, persistent poverty in others—as well as the much documented pressure mounting on water resources throughout the world and in every settled region of Canada. The implications of this looming nature scarcity are explored more fully in the next chapter.

In the middle of the last century, a Texas geoscientist working for Shell Oil in Houston, M. King Hubbert, calculated on the basis of past experience the date he believed that U.S. production of crude oil would peak and then decline. The event known as Hubbert's Peak duly occurred in 1970.[6] This concept has since been applied to other non-renewable resources, including water.

The idea of "Peak Water"[7] encompasses the observation that a growing portion of the world's water is being removed from useful circulation. In many river basins around the globe, human extraction of water exceeds natural replenishment. The Colorado, Nile, and Yellow Rivers are among those that often no longer reach the sea. Other water, like that left over from oil and gas extraction, is too severely polluted to be reused.

One trouble with passing through a "peak" of water supply (an idea that not all experts accept) into a period of inexorable and intensifying scarcity (which most experts agree we have already entered) is that although substitutes can be imagined for hydrocarbon energy and minerals, we know of none that can replace water's spectrum of economic and environmental services. If water is life and everything valuable within it, then we are at risk of losing everything.

This shift from the condition of nature surplus under which our species developed to our current condition of global nature scarcity may seem remote to Canadians. It appears that we have water in abundance. But this impression is only partly true.

Apparent plenty of water and other ecological assets has made us sloppy, wasteful, and unable to appreciate or exploit the advantages they give us over other parts of the world. Our overdraft at the Bank of Nature, where water may be our most important but is not our only account, is steadily drawing down Canada's "trust fund" of resources. How can we ensure that it is preserved for future generations? For a start, by ensuring that the water underwriting it remains safe and secure.

Water is mobile, its health co-extensive with that of the landscapes it flows through. The safety of the water in our taps can no longer be segregated from the health of the watersheds that provide it.

Watersheds are recursive, nesting within each other, smaller ones emptying into larger ones until a single estuary delivers their combined outflows at last to the sea. Canada has many thousands of small and large watersheds. But our discussion will return repeatedly to two. Both are on the largest scale. And each represents one side of Canada's polarized settlement pattern: most of us live in cities or their suburbs; outside of those, our rural south is less densely populated than comparable parts of the United States, while the rest of the country can seem practically empty.

The Mackenzie watershed represents one face of this reality: a truly vast and still largely functional ecosystem veined with waterways that for the most part still run unchecked and untainted. But it is neither as pristine nor as undeveloped as it seems. Powerful economic forces from Beijing to Houston and Edmonton to Ottawa are intensifying extractive demands on its already bruised natural water systems. Whether Canadians can have confidence that their water's future supply and safety will be secured depends greatly on how issues at play here are decided.

The crudest of these is the question of when to say "when": how to know when the pace or scale of an economic activity threatens essential ecological supports and must be curtailed. But the great northern watershed wrestles with other issues of emerging importance: the challenge of securing water safety across multiple jurisdictions, the no-less-difficult one of placing meaningful estimates on the value to human economies of ecosystems that compete with industry for water, and, not least, what standard we should set when we strive to keep our water "pure" at all.

The second watershed is where nearly two in three Canadians live: the Great Lakes/St. Lawrence basin, which stretches from Ontario's border with Manitoba to the Atlantic Ocean. It is the other face of Canada's water reality.

Around the lower Great Lakes from Chicago to Montreal roughly 20 million Canadians and 24 million Americans share a landscape that bears no resemblance to its pre-colonial appearance, vegetation, or even natural contours. Across their entire extent, from north of Lake Superior to the bottom end of Lake Michigan and the eastern tip of Lake Ontario, the lakes are also among the most elaborately engineered waterways on the planet. This Anthropocene landscape hosts all the problems that beset every fully settled part of the globe. Notwithstanding the huge volume of water contained in the five lakes, what's available to many local communities within the watershed is limited, especially in the high-demand summer season. A variety of factors, from farm practices to climate change, are straining both natural and engineered systems for assimilating waterborne wastes. Water quality is at risk as a result. At the same time, congestion is highlighting the importance of public choices—of how best to weigh the competing economic and ecological values of a contested landscape, or how to wring maximum economic advantage from a locale's water while keeping its citizens and wildlife healthy.

Beyond the international border that runs through the centre of the Great Lakes watershed, the legal, regulatory, and political regime is materially different from Canada's. That presents challenges to cooperation that have equivalents all along our 8,900-kilometre shared border. But U.S. practices, and those farther afield in Europe, also reveal important new possibilities for securing the health and wealth of Canadians.

This country doesn't lack for expertise of its own in managing and protecting water. The past decade has seen numerous informed analyses of the subject from an impressive range of entities: the POLIS Project on Ecological Governance at the University of Victoria; the Sustainable Prosperity initiative housed at the University of Ottawa; the Program on Water Issues at the University of Toronto's Munk School; the independent David Suzuki Foundation, based in

Vancouver, and Edmonton's Pembina Institute; the federal government–sponsored Canadian Water Network and Statistics Canada; NRTEE, the long-running National Round Table on the Environment and the Economy (disbanded by the federal government in 2013), as well as FLOW, the much newer Forum for Leadership on Water; and, most recently, the Blue Economy Initiative, a joint venture of the Canadian Water Network, the Royal Bank of Canada, and the Walter and Duncan Gordon Foundation. This list is not exhaustive. (Disclosure: the authors have contributed to a number of these.) The work these groups have done informs this book. But we will also explore why it is that so much valuable insight remains in the realm of theory and recommendation, and why so little has been implemented.

Determining whether Canadians can have confidence in the safety of our water today and its security tomorrow necessarily takes us into the realm of economics. Laws and marketplaces are both devices for the same purpose: mediating competing interests in society with a minimum of bloodshed—one through fiat, the other through transaction. The boundary between the two spheres of operation is always fluid, is sometimes in tension, and regularly fails to capture every interest impacted by the industrial economy. Health costs resulting from pollution—bizarrely regarded as "external" to the classical economist's world—are but one example. Others, such as our failure to account for the flood protection provided by a meadow, distort how we perceive both problems and opportunities. Either way, they dangerously mislead our choices as a result.

It will become evident how existing water-management practices systematically underprice pollution's first-order damage to ecosystems and second-order damage to human health and economies. Far from enforcing the principle of "polluter pays" that they have ritually invoked, Canadian governments have instead enabled the cancerous growth of a moral hazard, inviting private industrial interests to reap profit while society bears the ecological cost of their activity. The parallel with the incentives that encouraged "too-big-to-fail" banks and taxpayer bailouts cannot be overlooked.

Chapter 2 puts the assumption that Canada's water is well protected under the microscope, in the light of robust trends of climate change and economic innovation.

Chapter 3 examines how we got here: how Canada's leaders have historically defended our water and natural systems in the pursuit of wealth. We pay particular attention to the goals, principles, and assurances that national and provincial leaders have laid out for Canadians over the last twenty-five years.

Chapter 4 looks at what our industrial peers in Europe and the United States have been doing over the same period. Both places have followed a different strategy from ours.

In Chapter 5, we'll begin to look more closely at how Canada's approach of leaving most of the heavy lifting of water protection to the provinces has worked out in practice. In Chapter 6, we'll assess how well the federal Crown has fulfilled its roles—under its own legislation or the Canadian Constitution. In neither case is the reality what we were promised.

Chapters 7 and 8 ask whether abandoning the defence of our water is making us wealthier—or healthier. Only one answer is what you might expect.

Chapter 9 distills the consensus of Canada's water experts, and lessons from the preceding chapters, to identify what needs to happen to secure our country's water wealth today and into the future.

Chapter 10 examines why we haven't seen these necessary changes emerge from federal and provincial authorities. But we also present an idea, long neglected in Canada but with deep roots in our legal heritage and increasingly influential in similar legal cultures abroad, that could break the impasse.

Canada is not the uniformly water-rich place we think it is. Our world-class cities and widely admired "human development" are not as impregnable as we assume. The world is changing in ways that do not assure the survival of our industrial consumer society and, indeed, in ways that will force dramatic change on it. In Chapter 11, we return to the visionary North to find the inspiration and model for a new strategy for the defence of Canada's threatened natural security.

Perhaps Louis Ayah's prophecy was only the rambling of a half-mad trapper. But *habitat,* a short word for all the services that nature provides a species, is neither speculative nor negotiable. Deprived of habitat, species die. Even when their habitat only suffers, so do they. That is the sting in the tail of our ecological overdraft (just as it can be for the financial kind). And nothing reveals the condition of our habitat or impacts it more intimately than the water flowing through it. The health of those ecosystems has a correspondingly powerful role in whether our water is clean.

That is the real treasure embodied in Great Bear Lake's pristine depths, the one that Canadians rightly prize above all other resources: not just water—there's plenty of that around the world—but fresh water, pure and clean enough to nourish a healthy body, vibrant wildlife, and a prosperous society.

That is the natural security that will underwrite all real wealth in the man-made century ahead.

TWO

~~~~~~~~~~~~~~~~~

Not As Safe As
We Think

N THE second week of October 2011, in Montreal's West Island community of Pointe-Claire, Victor Schukov and his wife were easing into the weekend just before supper when a sudden racket erupted beyond their windows. A city works department van, emergency lights flashing and heralded by sirens, was driving up the leafy residential street announcing something over loudspeakers. Unable to make out the garbled amplified message, Schukov, a local columnist and blogger, went online to the Point-Claire website. There he found a dramatic warning not to drink water from his home taps.

In other West Island homes the phone rang: on the line was an automated recording, a message from municipal offices in both official languages, again warning householders that the water in their homes could poison them.

Earlier that day utility workers had noticed a sudden drop in chlorine levels in the civic water supply—indicating that some unknown contaminant was neutralizing the disinfectant much faster than normal. It did no good to add more chlorine; whatever was in the water seemed to be eating up the powerful oxidant. Just before the dinner hour, officials authorized a wholesale alert. Municipal workers fanned out to carry the word to restaurants, apartment buildings, and seniors' homes in person.

At the same time, Pointe-Claire officials began calling counterparts in half a dozen neighbouring communities served by its water treatment plant. By the time word reached residents of Kirkland, Baie d'Urfe, Sainte-Anne-de-Bellevue, and Beaconsfield, more than 130,000 Montrealers had been warned not to trust the most basic service urban Canadians count on: the ready availability of clean, safe water.

The warning, withdrawn after forty-eight hours, created a brief local storm—more over the effectiveness of the alert than the failure to secure the communities' water supply. With the apparent return to normal, most West Islanders doubtless settled back into a complacent confidence in the safety and security of the water flowing from their household taps. Disruptions like the one they had just experienced, Schukov said, "are not that frequent," though "recently, they seem to be more often."[1]

In fact, the early October breakdown in Pointe-Claire was almost routine. Certainly it wasn't the largest urban water warning ever issued in Canada, nor was it the only one in Canada that day. In 2006, seven times as many people, living in Vancouver, had been warned that their tap water was unsafe unless boiled; that warning lasted for nearly two weeks.[2] On any given day, public health authorities report more than 1,500 water advisories in force in Canada. They warn residents of affected homes either to boil or sterilize tap water before they consume it or not drink it at all. Montrealers got off easy when the Pointe-Claire advisory was lifted after days. Many alerts have been in place for months or years—a few, incredibly, for decades.

Canada's water insecurities were exposed to Quebecers again less than three weeks later. In early November, eighty thousand Montrealers in adjoining LaSalle and Lachine[3] were told to boil tap water for at least a minute if they wanted to avoid getting sick.

It's not the picture most Canadians have of our water. In the wake of highly publicized failures at the turn of the century in local utilities in Walkerton, Ontario, and North Battleford, Saskatchewan, provincial and federal politicians alike seemed to realize that water supplies needed better protection from contamination.

In the first incident, a heavy spring rain rinsed animal manure from a pasture into a shallow well that served the farm town's 4,800 residents. Municipal water system operators failed to notice a telltale downtick in chlorine levels of the sort that later alerted the Pointe-Claire utility that it had a problem. Instead, contaminated water flowed through the town's mains for weeks, infecting half its residents with gastroenteritis and sending sixty-five to hospital. Twenty-seven people suffered acute kidney damage. Seven died.

Ten months later, another incident caught headlines halfway across the country. Like Walkerton, North Battleford is a rural service town. In April 2001, a plague of diarrhea struck its fifteen thousand residents, again affecting about half the population. This time, diagnostic tests fingered a parasitic protozoa, cryptosporidium, that attaches itself to the lining of the sufferer's small intestine, causing persistent diarrhea and, in some people, nausea and vomiting. It is seldom more than a gruelling but temporary embarrassment for healthy individuals but can be life threatening for those with a deficient immune system.[4] It is excreted with waste and often transmitted indirectly through contaminated water. This was a known risk of the location of the town's sewage treatment plant outfall on the Battlefords [*sic*] River—three kilometres *upstream* from where another pipe sucked in water from the same river for delivery to North Battleford homes. What the town's water treatment operators apparently did not know was that crypto, as it's called in water treatment circles, is impervious to chlorine. When they removed a mechanical filter for maintenance, the parasite was released on North Battleford.

Both outbreaks prompted intense media coverage and soul-searching inquiries by the provinces involved. The following year, Saskatchewan's government beefed up funding for municipal water treatment and water safety monitoring. Ontario commissioned first a judicial inquiry, then an expert panel. In 2006, the province passed a new Clean Water Act, designed to prevent a repetition of the kind of contamination at the source that had poisoned Walkerton's water. By the tenth anniversary of the two outbreaks, many Canadians seemed ready to accept assurances that whatever vulnerabilities the citizens of North Battleford and Walkerton had been exposed to, they were now corrected.

Early in 2011, shortly after accepting his portfolio as federal environment minister, the Honourable Peter Kent, a former television journalist, assured a Toronto audience that the government in which he served had "a credible plan for addressing our environmental challenges." One of its central pillars was "the polluter-pays principle" that whoever dirties the environment should also foot the bill to clean it up, he said. His staff "shared [a] commitment to developing, implementing and enforcing world-class environmental standards for this country."[5]

Five weeks later, the same minister addressed water directly in a speech to a conference on the subject in Ottawa. "When it comes to the stewardship of water, strong leadership is the key," Kent said, implying plainly that that was what his Conservative government was providing. Its actions, Kent claimed, had "made Canada a world leader in regulating harmful chemicals from industrial and household use and their disposal... Our national waterways are directly protected." Within months, he added, Ottawa would enact "the first-ever national standard for Canada's more than 4,000 wastewater facilities."

Considering such assurances, and the minimal media attention given to water warnings in scores of communities, it's small wonder that more than four out of five Canadians surveyed told a Unilever/ RBC-sponsored Canadian Water Attitudes Study in 2011 that they were either "very" or "somewhat" confident of their drinking water.[6] In fact, they were *increasingly* sure of its quantity and quality, in the wild and the tap, and of government's readiness to protect it. The exception—perhaps understandably—was Quebec, where only about two-thirds of respondents were "very" or "somewhat" confident of their water's safety.

Some national and international assessments seem to support their judgement. In 2010, Environment Canada ranked Canada as having the second-best water quality among ten industrial nations.[7] The following year, Statistics Canada's publication *Human Activity and the Environment* calculated that Canada's natural wealth had more than doubled over the decade between 1999 and 2009, from $1.35 trillion to $3 trillion.[8] From this, the unwary might conclude that Canada's natural assets, from forests to streams, are flourishing.

The same conclusion could flow from the first effort by the World Economic Forum (wEF) to weight its annual global ranking of countries' economic muscle with an index reflecting their environmental stewardship.[9] On that scale, in 2011 Canada ranked just out of the top ten, at number eleven.[10] The accompanying text noted that "Canada... in particular... shows a lack of environmental degradation." Many Canadians will also recall that for six years this country led the charts of the United Nations Human Development Index—another ranking that factors the quality of a country's environment into its standings.[11] In 2011, we still held a respectable sixth place.[12]

Unhappily, our confidence is built on sand. From the warm assurances offered by Minister Kent to those international rankings, the safety, security, and sufficiency of Canadians' water is more desert mirage than deep pool: no oasis in a thirsty world, but an illusion.

Canadians' Panglossian confidence rests on demonstrable ignorance and erroneous beliefs. More than four out of five people surveyed for the Canadian Water Attitudes Study in 2011 asserted that Canada has more water than any other country on Earth. It doesn't. Brazil does, with the Amazon River alone discharging twice as much fresh water to the world's oceans as all of Canada's rivers combined. Similarly, fewer than one Canadian in twenty knew how much water the average citizen uses in a day. Most guesstimated their own use at less than half the typical amount of 329 litres (roughly two standard bathtubs full). Most also believed that households use the largest share of Canada's water. Fewer than one in five knew that farming does.

This could be dismissed as the casual error of ordinary citizens, but even experts complain that they are largely in the dark about the real state of Canada's water resources. A score or more of study panels and inquiries over the last decade[13] have deplored the absence of reliable, consistent information about Canada's water on a national scale, let alone by industrial sector or in its natural geography of river basins. Records to show where our water is, how clean it is, how abundant it is, who's using it for what, how much of it they're using, and what shape they're leaving it in when they're done are in many cases fragmented, incomplete, entirely un-collected, suspect, or inconsistent from one province to the next.

In late 2011, the National Round Table on the Environment and the Economy added a postscript to its previous critical assessment. "In Canada," it wrote in a report on water used by resource industries, "governments at all levels lack the capacity... to evaluate, predict, and forecast future water availability at a watershed scale."[14]

Even the experts, it turns out, are often left guessing about the safety and security of Canada's water. What they do know, however, is generally more disturbing than the sunlit impressions given by ministerial assurances or reflected in ordinary Canadians' high estimation of their water security.

Across the country, in scores of places, Canada's water at the tap is flat-out dangerous. At the time of this writing, British Columbia led the country with 290 active water warnings. Saskatchewan had nearly as many in place: 249. The 169 warnings active in Ontario outnumbered Quebec's 146, and even Prince Edward Island had 3 advisories in force. Many of these were not brief. On November 18, 2011, the small town of Canyon, B.C., tucked into a valley in the Kootenays, between the province's southeastern borders with Alberta and Idaho, had 4 advisories in effect. According to the independent online summary maintained by the www.water.ca website, two had been in place since 1994, the *most recent* since 2003.

Environment Canada's boast that the country's water ranks second-best among ten industrial nations is at best outdated. The United

Nations report supporting that claim was published in 2003. More recently, in 2010, using methods and data developed by the inter-jurisdictional Canadian Council of Ministers of the Environment (CCME), the federal agency itself rated the water collected at more than six out of ten sites monitored nationwide between 2005 and 2007 as no better than "fair" in quality (43 percent of all sites). The water at nearly a fifth of the sites was either "marginal" (14 percent) or "poor" (4 percent).[15]

Other studies reach similarly disquieting conclusions. Nearly one Canadian in three drinks water from in-ground rather than surface sources. A panel of experts assembled in 2009 by the eminently neutral Council of Canadian Academies (a consortium of engineering and science academies endowed with $30 million in 2005 to research questions of science for the federal government) estimated that persistent contamination was present in more than thirty thousand such groundwater sources across the country.[16] And the number was climbing. A 2001 study found that between 20 and 40 percent of all the wells in rural Canada were contaminated with coliform bacteria (typically from sewage) or nitrates (a by-product of the decay of manure or other organic matter) at levels exceeding health guidelines for drinking water.[17] Unlike water in a tank or plumbing system, water dispersed over kilometres underground can be next to impossible to purify once it has become polluted.

These failures of water quality are of more than statistical interest. Although clusters of acute illness on the scale of Walkerton and North Battleford have mercifully been rare, a review by Health Canada shortly after those incidents determined that the country had experienced no fewer than 288 outbreaks of illness traceable to contaminated water over the period from 1974 to 2001—nearly *one a month*.[18]

Meanwhile, there is evidence that unsafe water is responsible for an overlooked national epidemic of gastrointestinal illnesses. A study by Health Canada over a six-year period in Vancouver, a city with one of the most pristine water catchment areas and newest water systems in the country, reported in 2000 that contaminated water had been responsible for 17,500 doctor visits, 138 visits to pediatric emergency rooms, and 85 hospitalizations over that time.[19] If the rate in the rest of the country—much of it with aging water mains and watersheds heavily affected by industry or agriculture—is close to the same,[20] then nearly 200,000 Canadians suffer seriously enough each year from stomach pain, cramps, vomiting, or diarrhea because of something in their water to consult a doctor or visit an ER. In Montreal, another study traced as many as a third of all gastrointestinal illnesses to tainted tap water.

One study, published in 2006 by the Sierra Legal Defence Fund (now Ecojustice), attributes to Health Canada[21] an estimate that contaminated drinking water "causes 90,000 illnesses and 90 deaths *every year*, the equivalent to 13 Walkerton tragedies." (Emphasis in the original.) It's an illustration of our national neglect of the subject, however, that this alarming estimate turns out to be an extrapolation from research actually conducted in the United States. Whether the American findings can fairly be applied to Canada is debatable—as we will learn, the two countries have taken sharply different tacks in protecting their water.

But if the transference of American data to the Canadian context is justified, then other estimates of U.S. deaths due to unsafe water presented in the 2006 paper indicate that as many as 1,300 Canadians may be dying every year from what comes out of their taps.

Minister Kent's smooth assurances, meanwhile, might once have come in for sharp questioning from acclaimed reporter Peter Kent.

In the last decade, virtually every authoritative inquiry into the rules and practices protecting Canada's water has deplored the absence of anything like a "credible plan" to protect the nation's water, much less great evidence of a federal "commitment to developing, implementing and [most especially] enforcing world-class environmental standards." Less than six months after Kent's 2011 addresses in Toronto and Ottawa, his department eliminated 11 percent of its scientific staff—776 biologists, hydrologists, meteorologists, and others critical to the understanding of water resources—fuelling renewed skepticism about its commitment to scientific excellence.

In fact, the last time a Canadian government articulated a clear and comprehensive policy on water was more than a quarter-century ago. That 1987 effort is described in the next chapter. In 2006, the Senate Standing Committee on Energy, Water and Natural Resources complained that Ottawa's "continued lack of focus on water issues is lamentable. It is high time for the Government of Canada to provide leadership." The following year, ten leading water experts, brought together to address "Canada's escalating water crisis," expressed their concern about "[t]he erosion of the federal government's commitment to protecting Canada's water."[22] Updating its study of Canada's drinking water in 2010, Ecojustice (formerly Sierra Legal Defence) lamented that "little has changed in five years . . . We find that the federal government is failing in almost every aspect of water protection."[23]

At best, Canada has national *suggestions* for water quality: "guidelines" establish what federal and provincial scientists believe to be safe maximum limits for the presence of different kinds of known pollutants. But nowhere does Canada make these mandatory. Provinces and municipal utilities are free to ignore them—and frequently have.

The truth about Canada's stewardship of water, either in the tap or in the wild, is revealed in a damning accumulation of international comparisons. An illuminating series of report cards sponsored by the David Suzuki Foundation compared Canada's environmental performance with that of other members of the "rich countries club" of the Organisation for Economic Co-operation and Development (OECD) over a decade. Experts in environmental law at Simon Fraser University in Burnaby, B.C., assessed more than two dozen indicators in 2001, then updated their assessment in 2005 and again in 2010. Canada initially ranked twenty-eighth out of twenty-nine countries studied, failing in all but one category of environmental care. A decade later, Canada still ranked just above last place, twenty-fourth among twenty-five countries scored in 2010.

The same year, the C.D. Howe Institute, the oldest and most pin-striped of pro-business think tanks in Canada, published a commentary by Steve Hrudey, professor emeritus of medicine and environmental toxicology at the University of Alberta and a former advisor to the Walkerton Inquiry. Hrudey compared records of outbreaks of waterborne diseases among several developed industrialized countries. Canada, he found, had recorded *five times* as many case studies of disease outbreaks, on a population basis, as the United States. By contrast, the United Kingdom, with 60 percent more people than Canada, recorded a third fewer case studies.[24] The records, Hrudey concluded, demonstrated that "clear deficiencies" persist in the protection of municipal drinking water in Canada.

A no-less-mainstream research centre, the Conference Board of Canada, regularly compares this country's "quality of life" with that of our developed-nation peers. Its *Report Card on Canada* awarded the nation a barely passing D for overall environmental stewardship in 2011, ranking us fifteenth in a class of seventeen nations. "Canada's water quality is at risk from industrial effluent, agricultural runoff and municipal sewage," the Conference Board warned. "[E]utrophication is a serious water quality issue for the Prairie provinces, southern Ontario, and southern Quebec. The increase in toxic algal blooms in Canadian lakes and coastal water is also a risk to human health." Canadians received an additional failing D for their voracious consumption of this water—more than twice the average of the other nations studied.[25]

The World Economic Forum is often regarded as a cheerleader for global trade and multinational big business. Its high ranking of Canada's sustainable competitiveness is eye-catching. But a closer look at the index on which the WEF bases its judgement is less comforting. Researchers at the Yale Center for Environmental Law and Policy in Connecticut assessed 163 nations on 25 indicators "covering both environmental public health and ecosystem vitality"—factors that closely reflect (and, in the latter case, influence) the condition of water. Among countries scored, Canada came in forty-sixth, below such relatively poor nations as Portugal, El Salvador, Mexico, and Romania (though a full fifteen places ahead of the United States, which was pulled down by its low scores on climate change and ecosystem health).[26]

Our stewardship of most of the northern half of the continent is also under scrutiny by our partners in the North American Free Trade Agreement (NAFTA), through the Commission for Environmental Cooperation (CEC). Created as a side deal to the 1992 pact, the CEC was meant in large part to assuage concerns among activists in Canada and the United States that liberalized trade would pull those nations' environmental standards down to perceived levels in the third NAFTA country, Mexico. Instead, the Montreal-based agency has become a source of comparative research that sheds often unsettling light on those expectations.

In 2011, the CEC published a detailed study of pollutants reported under various laws as having been released into the water bodies of each NAFTA nation. Although the three countries have different reporting requirements, the available data revealed that public municipal sewage systems in Canada released almost as much toxic contamination into national waterways in 2006 as all of American industry that year.[27]

Earlier research compared pollution released by factories in the three nations in the 1990s. Although Canadian factories accounted for only 7.4 percent of the total number of NAFTA factories surveyed, they were responsible for more than a third of toxic discharges to surface water in the trading bloc. On average, Canadian factories released or sent away for disposal twice as much polluting waste as American ones. In fifteen of the twenty cases in which releases were directly comparable, Canadian sources released more pollution in absolute terms than corresponding sectors in the United States, despite its tenfold larger population.[28]

Again in 2010, a study by a consortium of environmental non-governmental organizations (ENGOs) compared Canadian and American pollution in the Great Lakes region. It examined emissions to the air, but these almost always fall back to earth, sometimes in drops of rain or flakes of snow, to enter surface and groundwater. "On a per-facility basis," the report concluded, "Canadian facilities emitted to the air, on average, almost three times more known carcinogens and more than twice the reproductive/developmental toxins than U.S. facilities."[29]

In 2008, researchers from the University of Calgary sampled populations of longnose dace, a silvery minnow, in Alberta's Oldman and Bow Rivers. The latter flows through downtown Calgary and supplies its drinking water.

To a casual gaze, a male dace is hard to tell from a female one, so it wasn't until the samples were dissected back at the lab that biologists noticed something very odd. Their random catch was overwhelmingly female. In some parts of the Oldman River, downstream from cattle feedlots and municipal waste treatment outflows, male dace had all but vanished from the population.[30] For Leland Jackson, the research leader who had directed the work, the alarm was personal. "The water I use to make my kids' orange juice is the same water those fish are living in," he told one of the authors in an interview.[31]

The Albertans were among a growing body of researchers to observe disturbing associations between waste-contaminated water sources and gender-bending effects among the organisms that live in or drink from those sources—including humans. The leading suspect is a broad range of potent chemicals that act on or mimic endocrine hormones—the chemicals that carry signals around the bodies of living creatures to trigger or turn off physiological activity.

These chemicals aren't limited to a few isolated "hot spots" downstream from cities or feedlots. Some 23,000 toxic compounds are estimated to be present in the Canadian living and working environment—with 1,000 new ones added every year. Another 7,000 pesticide formulations are registered with federal authorities; at least 60 of those are banned in most other industrialized nations.[32] What becomes of the molecular fragments of all these compounds when they mingle in the aquatic environment is unknown. Our lakes have become unsupervised laboratories conducting recombinant biochemistry in real time.

Although some provinces restrict the use of certain herbicides for purely aesthetic purposes, such as home landscaping, Canadian farmers increased their application of chemical pesticides by nearly 18 percent between 1990 and 2002.[33] More endocrine disrupting compounds may be reaching creeks, rivers, and eventually water-system intakes via the desiccated human waste that is spread across many farm fields as fertilizer and to dispose of the irreducible compost left over after sewage is fully treated. About half of all the processed waste from municipal waste treatment plants winds up on fields this way. And the acreage of farmland in Canada treated with either human waste or chemical fertilizers has tripled since 1970.[34]

Exotic chemicals may be concentrating in Canadians' bodies at an even faster rate. One such chemical group, polybrominated diphenyl ethers (PBDES), is used as flame retardant in furniture, cars, clothing, and consumer products. It's been found to accumulate in the bodies of such top-of-the-food-chain species as killer whales and grizzly bears—as well as in human breast milk. In fact, concentrations of PBDES in samples of breast milk collected in Vancouver over the decade ending in 2002 increased fifteenfold. Ground beef, salmon, and butter revealed PBDES at concentrations as much as one thousand times those detected in European counterparts.[35]

We do not know the full extent of the threat these compounds pose to Canadians, but we do know that many synthetic molecules slip unchecked through the most advanced water and waste treatment technologies, as well as past the placental barrier between mother and gestating child.

Canadians' confidence in the safety of their water is ill justified, by either international comparison or candid domestic assessment. The increasing presence of exotic, often powerfully bioreactive, synthetic molecules is one broad threat to the future security of our water. A second occurs on an even larger scale: a heat-driven redistribution of the world's water across the map, around the calendar, and even from one physical state to another.

Enough "new" water falls on Canada every year to nearly fill Lake Huron or sink the entire country under a puddle more than half a metre deep. That water income isn't recorded evenly, however, either across the country or through the year. In much of the nation, precipitation is heaviest in fall and late winter. Summers—when plants, wildlife, and human agriculture (including the domestic kind practised on suburban lawns) demand the most water—often deliver less moisture. Northern Canada gets more water than the south; southern Alberta and Saskatchewan get the least.

And that allotment is changing. A section of the 2011 Statistics Canada *Human Activity and the Environment* report examined water "yield" in Canada—roughly speaking, a given landscape's net water income. That is calculated by subtracting from the amount of water an area *receives* in precipitation (rain plus snow) over a period of time the amount that it *loses* over the same time through what scientists term "ET": not the movie extraterrestrial, but evapotranspiration—the volume of water that is transpired into the air through the leaves of plants and the breath of animals or that evaporates from open water surfaces.

With warmer temperatures, this natural clawback of precipitation has soared. Water yields in the southern parts of Canada, where more than 80 percent of us live, work, or farm, have "decreased on average by 3.5 km³ per year from 1971 to 2004, which is equivalent to *an overall loss of 8.5% of the water yield* over this time period." (Emphasis added.) Put another way, southern Canada has been losing enough annually from its water income to supply all of its households for a year.[36]

Some regions are harder hit than others. Alberta researchers have documented dramatic long-term declines in water flowing down major Prairie rivers in summer over the past century. Measured in August at Saskatoon, the South Saskatchewan River has dwindled to barely a sixth of its flow in the same month a hundred years ago.[37] The Athabasca—the stream that flows past Fort McMurray and its oil sands mines down to the Mackenzie—contains a third less water during most summers than it did forty years ago. Scientists attribute the decline to the combined effects of mountain glaciers having dwindled by half since 1980, increasing human withdrawals of water, and the amplification of ET as summer days get hotter.

A more muscular ET may also lie behind the rapid shrinking and outright disappearance of an uncertain number of the 1.3 million lakes that once were estimated to spatter the Canadian North with blue. Examining satellite records, a researcher in Maryland calculated that between 2000 and 2009 the region lost 6,700 square kilometres of lake surface—an area a third the size of Lake Ontario.

In other parts of the country, there is a documented increase in the wrenching violence of storms. Amped up by the additional heat and moisture that have entered the atmosphere in recent decades, weather systems are delivering extremes of wind and precipitation rarely recorded in the past.[38] Between 2003 and 2011, the greater Toronto area experienced three storms of the size supposed to strike only "once in a century" and five "once in fifty years" storms.[39] Plainly, old benchmarks are no longer meaningful.

These changes present multiple challenges to the present safety and future security of Canada's water. In the new normal weather, summers are longer, hotter, and drier in much of the country—just when nature and the economy are most demanding. That is a particular problem for parts of British Columbia and Alberta, where in some river basins existing water allocations already exceed available flows in some months. In central regions, and especially southern Ontario, summer dry spells may be broken by thunderstorms, but these now often drop more water at a time than formerly. Hyper-intense downpours overwhelm drainage systems and flush accumulated contaminants from roadways and fields into diminished rivers and lakes where less water is available to assimilate them.

For wildlife, less water, warmer water, and more contaminated water pose a triple threat. For utilities, the heightened unpredictability of water supply, and of receiving water available to dilute wastes, will test the limits of existing infrastructure, such as reservoirs and sewers, and challenge management. Even shorelines are likely to change, as the Great Lakes become a little less great over the decades ahead.

The water that supports Canada's wealth, in short, is neither safe today nor adequately protected for the future. Nonetheless, buried in the humbling record of our D-grade environmental stewardship are nuggets of hope.

Unlike, say, Singapore or the Netherlands, we do not have a large population crammed into a small space. Much of our national territory has been spared humanity's heaviest footprint. It remains within our power to preserve our land's ecological vitality and its related capacity to recirculate reliable flows of clean water. We have resources of knowledge, finance, and technology.

Our worst enemy is us. "Canada's poor record is not due to natural factors such as climate and geography," according to the researchers who compared our environmental performance to our Organisation for Economic Co-operation and Development peers. "[It] is due to poor... policies. *If Canadian environmental policies were comparable to the top three OECD countries, Canada's rank would move... to 1st in the OECD.*"[40] (Emphasis in the original.)

Our inadequacies are entirely of our own making. They are the result of specific choices. But like all human decisions, those choices are open to change.

And plainly Canadians care. From the grassroots of society to the experts' circle, our actual knowledge may be somewhat murky, but our passion is shared, bright, and clear. Nine out of ten Canadians say they want to lead the world in environmental stewardship.[41] An equal number say the consequences will be serious if we fail.[42]

THREE

The Road to Here

THE DATE we celebrate is July 1, 1867, when Queen Victoria's proclamation in London called Canada into existence. We forget that the real work of framing the institutional structure of the new Dominion took place later, through the long, gaslit afternoons and evenings of that autumn and the following winter as 181 men, representing those property-owning males among Canada's 3 million people who had been allowed to vote, debated the new Confederation's practical requirements.[1]

Members patriotically agreed on the desirability of expanding the Dominion west and north before "the Yanks" got there but skirmished over whether and how hard to pursue free trade with those same Yanks. They argued vigorously about the wisdom and route (especially the route, with its lucrative implications) of the new transcontinental railroad to which the Act of Union had committed Canada. A proposed fisheries ministry barely survived the sharp criticism that it would have nothing to do. Sitting opposite the government, Bluenose separatist Joseph Howe took every opportunity to denounce the entire enterprise.

Even so, in May of 1868 Prime Minister Sir John A. Macdonald presented Governor General Viscount Monck with a substantial body of legislation for royal assent. Included, despite those early misgivings, was an act for the regulation of fishing and protection of fisheries.[2] It was the first piece of Canadian legislation that might be said to have had an environmental objective.

The new act prohibited damage to spawning beds, set minimum sizes for some fishing nets, and authorized the creation of refuges for fish propagation. Several clauses directly addressed "Injuries to Fishing Grounds and Pollution of Rivers," prohibiting the release of "chemical substances or drugs, poisonous matter... or any other deleterious substance" into water "frequented by any of the kinds of fish mentioned" in the act, a list that included key species such as salmon and trout.

The clairvoyant or merely cynical might have read some significance into the caveat that immediately followed this last protection. The fish-bearing waters of Canada were not to be poisoned, section 14.2 of the new act read, "provided always that the Minister shall have the power to exempt from... [this protection] any stream or streams in which he considers that its enforcement is not requisite for the public interest."

That caveat was more in keeping with the view of nature that dominated the debates of the first Parliament, one that regarded wild landscapes mainly as vast storehouses of material wealth to be extracted and exploited by industrious humanity. Apart from a few references to concerns such as the destruction of fish-spawning grounds, most debate about the new fisheries act centred on how to enforce a "bounty" on American boats entering Canadian waters.

The word "water" appears far less often in the record of that winter's debates than either "fish" or "fisheries," and generally its use is figurative, in references to "watered stock" or keeping the aforesaid Yankee fishermen out of "our own waters." An illuminating exception is a brief inquiry late in November 1867 into the federal government's water leases at the Lachine Canal in Montreal.

The Lachine Canal endures today as a recreation corridor and ribbon of open water that runs for a little more than twelve kilometres from a turn of the St. Lawrence River at Lachine northeast to the Port of Montreal, near downtown. First dug in the 1820s to allow barges and small vessels to bypass rapids in the river below Lachine, its role had greatly expanded by 1867. The upstream end of the canal had recently been put to use as the intake for Montreal's first municipal waterworks—a response to a cholera epidemic that had killed more than a thousand people in 1854. It was the first node in an ever-expanding drinking water supply system whose failure a century and a half later would cause such commotion in Victor Schukov's neighbourhood, a little to the west.

Of much greater significance to the new Dominion's economy was the drop in water elevation between the canal's upstream end and its outflow: a hydraulic "head" of as much as six metres during summer that represented an enormous amount of kinetic energy. During this time before the electric motor, when steam engines were still large, expensive, and prone to exploding, the water wheel was the king of power sources, turning everything from the stones that ground wheat into flour to the stamping machines that turned sheet metal into nails.

Two decades earlier, in 1846, the government of Canada East—Quebec—had issued the first "hydraulic leases" on the water flowing into the Lachine Canal.[3] Since then, the banks of the canal had become lined with stone and brick factories drawing off water, using it to spin first water wheels and later a new generation of patent turbines, and returning it to the river or lower sections of the canal. Powered by the weight of water, the canal zone had become the silicon valley of colonial Canada, manufacturing everything from machine tools to pillows.[4]

So desirable had the Lachine's water power become, however, that by 1867 the number of weirs and races capturing it had far outstripped expectations. The use of so much water for industry had decreased the level of water in the canal for navigation and—the concern of members of Parliament—raised the important question of whether Canada's new government, under whose jurisdiction the canal now fell, was getting enough money for the water it had leased out. The issue would trigger one of the country's first Royal Commissions; it reported in 1887 that the national government was being shortchanged on the value of Lachine's water power and should raise its fees.[5] The advice would be ignored.

With the ink barely dry on their first constitutional document, Canadians were already arguing about whether there was enough water to go around, what it was worth to the commercial economy, and what Ottawa should do about it. For its part, the federal Crown was already choosing to do nothing at all.

Water's non-economic roles were hardly a concern. The idea that apparently clear water might breed illness was not widely known—or entirely believed. Louis Pasteur had demonstrated a decade earlier that air and water teemed with potentially pathogenic micro-organisms. But in Canada, outside of large settlements, deciding whether the water was safe to drink was mostly a matter of personal aesthetics and depended heavily on the other options (one reason for the era's heavy beer consumption; Ottawa boasted four breweries). Whether the huge Dominion's visibly abundant water was secure for the future was a question it would occur to no one to ask for decades to come.

Perhaps in consequence, in setting out the duties that would fall to the Crown in either its federal or provincial incarnations, Macdonald and his counterparts had thought water worth barely a mention. The word itself appears exactly once in the British North America Act (now Constitution Act, 1867), as part of an appendix assigning to the federal Crown certain public works, including "Canals, with Lands and Water Power connected therewith."[6] The federal government also received responsibility for fisheries, including those on landlocked inland lakes, and for navigation.[7]

Tucked on the list of federal Crown responsibilities, between "Copyrights" and "Naturalization of Aliens," was jurisdiction over "Indians, and Lands reserved for the Indians."[8] It would take a century and a half for Canada's shattered First Nations to regroup sufficiently to press their claims to economic justice before the Canadian state. When they did, it would provide a fulcrum for new readings of the country's founding ideals and perhaps even point a way out of the twenty-first-century economy's unsustainable avoidance of its ecological overdraft.

Other parts of the British North America Act, however, awarded powers to regulate "property and civil rights," natural resources, and "the management and sale of the public lands"—all activities central to managing water—exclusively to the Crown's provincial embodiment. In practice, the provinces would hand most of the responsibility for providing local services such as water supply and waste collection down to incorporated settlements and municipal governments—whose creation and oversight were another field of outright provincial power. Those powers would leave Canada's water security almost entirely up to the provinces for the next century and into the one to follow.

As a practical matter, most mid-nineteenth-century Canadians continued to get their water from a shallow private or public well or buckets dipped into the closest creek. For waste, there were outhouses. Mainly, this was true even for many among the minority of Canadians who lived in towns.

Running tap water had come to a few addresses in Toronto in the 1840s, flowing initially through pipes constructed of staves of wood held together with iron hoops, like continuous barrels. But household and industrial sewage continued to be directed into the nearest stream to be washed down to Lake Ontario. In the same decade, Toronto began to convert many of those reeking creeks into closed sewers by simply covering them over.

Much the same was occurring in cities along the length of the Great Lakes, from Chicago to Montreal, and across North America.[9] Whether open to the sunlight or bricked over, however, the repugnant flows still ended up in the nearest river, lake, or tidewater. As it happened, Toronto's first sewer (the repurposed Garrison Creek[10]) fed into Lake Ontario near where the new wooden water pipes sucked in the lake at Toronto Island. Soon subscribers to the new water system complained that what came from their taps was mere "drinkable sewage."[11]

Nor were piped water and sewer lines adopted instantly or universally when they become available. An early study of Montreal's working-class neighbourhoods, *The City Below the Hill*, reported that as late as 1897, only one family in four in poorer parts of that city enjoyed an indoor toilet connected to a sewer. For the rest, writes its author, Herbert Brown Ames, "[t]hat relic of rural conditions, that insanitary abomination, the out-of-door-pit-in-the-ground privy, is still to be found."[12]

Even so, offensive odours and a widening acceptance of the idea that pathogens carry disease prompted a growing number of towns and cities to bury their most noisome sewer streams underground. In 1873, Ontario passed its first Public Health Act. It enabled the creation of local health boards with the power to forcibly remove people from unsanitary homes and have the premises cleaned at public expense. The act also allowed any ten "inhabitant householders" of an area the lieutenant-governor identified as "threatened with any formidable, endemic or contagious disease" to compel local officials to call a public meeting and create a citizens' committee to contain the threat.[13]

In Quebec, Montreal turned the provision of sewers into a device for expanding its civic boundaries. The city grew nineteen times between 1883 and 1918 by providing sewer connections to suburbs that agreed to annexation.

Nonetheless, outbreaks of cholera and typhoid recurred into the first decade of the twentieth century. By then, most of Canada's major cities had developed more secure drinking water supply systems. In 1888, Vancouver began to bring water into the city from the same mountains that supply it today. In the years before World War I, some inland cities also began to recognize the health implications of dumping untreated sewage into the same freshwater bodies that filled their taps.

Toronto opened its first waste treatment plant in 1910, followed two years later by a new drinking water plant on Toronto Island that, in a then-novel technique, used chlorine to disinfect the raw lake water. Cholera infections dropped by half within twelve months.[14]

That same year, 1912, Ontario took responsibility for supervising water supplies and sewage treatment across the province. Its legislative lead prompted many cities and towns to build water treatment plants and at least rudimentary waste treatment systems.

Other provinces left the question entirely up to their municipalities. Many of those deemed it enough to keep water intakes and sewer outflows moderately well apart—even if they often drew from the same waterways they dumped into. As recently as the 1980s, Montreal's sewers, many still tracing the course of long-vanished forest creeks, continued to flush straight into the St. Lawrence River. Halifax used the vast, well-churned, and non-potable North Atlantic as its depository for municipal sewage until 2008. And as of this writing, Victoria still flushes its toilets and bathwater into the Pacific, though plans are under way to build the B.C. capital's first-ever sewage treatment plant by later in the decade.

While public sanitation was left largely to the Crown's expanding provincial incarnations, its federal manifestation also began to adopt the rudiments of environmental law. Much of it was incidental to other objectives involving water. The Navigable Waters Protection Act, proclaimed in 1882, was mainly designed to keep waterways clear for navigation. But it also provided legal grounds to prohibit or penalize the dumping of material into even potentially navigable streams or lakes. The Canada Shipping Act, made law in 1906, gave federal Crown agents the authority to board a vessel, inspect its cargo, and prevent the ship from discharging noxious material into Canadian waters. The National Harbours Board Act, passed in 1936, expanded federal authority to police pollution from ships loading or discharging cargo in Canadian ports.

In a spirit of laissez faire characteristic of the vapid political will that has often wielded these impressive powers, however, prosecutions under any of these acts were rare; significant penalties, rarer still.

What briefly threatened to escalate into a war for water in the first decade of the twentieth century produced an enduring advance for peaceful relations.

The dry foothills along the eastern slope of the Rocky Mountains are the only part of Canada whose first European settlers did not arrive here from either France or Britain. Rather, they were Euro-Americans of many generations' standing: ranchers and farmers, many of them Mormon. They had moved north from the Utah Territory and Montana as they became fully claimed. In 1905, those living north of the forty-ninth parallel became Albertans. By then, their can-do ambitions had brought them into tension with their figurative (and often literal) southern cousins.

The region is chronically arid. Spring sends a freshet of meltwater down from the mountains, but by midsummer many streams are reduced to trickles. For early Montanans, two of these were especially important: the St. Mary River begins high in the snowpack and flows well all year, but the Milk River flows from the foothills and exhausts its freshet quickly. The St. Mary also flows north into Canada; the less-reliable Milk does the same but then turns south again to re-enter Montana. In 1901, an enterprising bunch of Montanans conceived a solution to their late-summer water woes: a series of iron siphons and canals that would take water from the year-round St. Mary and deliver it forty-six kilometres away into the bed of the seasonally dry Milk. As the Montanans figured it, their water would then loop through Canada and come back to the eastern part of the state to irrigate thousands of hectares of dry-land prairie.

It didn't take long for word of the venture to reach the former Americans, soon to be Albertans, living north of the international border. Many of them had already tapped into the St. Mary River for their own farms or ranches; they were enraged at the prospect of having the water "stolen" by their American cousins. No strangers to enterprise themselves, they raised funds and began digging a canal of their own to intercept the enhanced flow of the Milk during its Canadian detour—in effect "stealing" the water back.

As feelings and expenses escalated on both sides of the border, the two national governments referred the matter to international negotiators. The outcome, secured in 1909, was the Boundary Waters Treaty. It allowed Montana to build its diversion, which still operates, but gave a greater share of the water at stake to Alberta. It also settled a separate disagreement about water in the Niagara River that had become increasingly valuable for its hydroelectric potential.

More famously, the treaty created the International Joint Commission (IJC), one of the earliest, most enduring, and most widely admired of such international organizations for resolving disputes.

The treaty also prohibited either country from allowing activity in its territory to pollute shared or transboundary waters to the detriment of the other party. Putting that admirable idea into effect proved difficult, however.

For some years, concern had been rising on both sides of the Great Lakes about the quality of the water they supplied. In 1912, the two governments asked the new IJC to investigate the extent and sources of lake pollution and recommend solutions

Its report, filed four years later, provides damning and prophetic testimony to how a mere quarter-century of industrialization had degraded the continent's largest bodies of fresh water. In what may have been the most extensive research of its kind conducted to that time in North America, the binational inquiry led by a sanitary engineer named Earle Phelps took more than nineteen thousand water samples over the length of the Great Lakes, testing them for the presence of *B. coli*, a human intestinal bacterium that indicates the presence of sewage.

The panel reported in 1916 that the water along more than three thousand kilometres[15] of the Great Lakes water boundary between Canada and the United States had become too dangerously polluted to drink. Its scrupulous methods showed that the world's longest freshwater frontier had been contaminated from Rainy River, "owing to the unrestricted discharge of sewage and other wastes," to the Thousand Islands, where pollution pileups made the St. Lawrence River "unsafe for local domestic consumption." The lower lakes' inshore waters, in addition to being "unsightly [and] malodorous," were in places "a serious danger to summer residents, bathers and others who frequent the localities."

The worst pollution by far was downstream from Detroit and Buffalo. The Detroit River received not only sewage from that city but also waste from its slaughterhouses and auto plants. By the second decade of the twentieth century, it had become so "grossly polluted and totally unfit" that Phelps's colleagues questioned whether any existing treatment method could clean it up.

The "Niagara River below the falls, from the whirlpool to Lake Ontario shows an intense pollution from shore to shore and from the surface to the bed of the stream," the report observed. A plume of contamination extended from the river's mouth into Lake Ontario at least twenty kilometres and sometimes farther. In 1892, the city of Oswego—two hundred kilometres away at the east end of Lake Ontario—blamed a typhoid outbreak on the Niagara River's toxic stream.

In addition, the lakes were busy with passenger vessels. These, the Phelps report said, "must be looked upon as moving sewer outlets... necessarily passing at times... in close proximity to waterworks intakes."[16] The pollution risk from shipping worked both ways, however: most vessels at the time also drew drinking water for passengers and crew from the lake around them. Among 750 people travelling on three lake vessels in the summer of 1913, officials recorded more than 300 cases of diarrhea, 52 of typhoid, and 7 deaths. Phelps noted "77 cases of typhoid fever" on a single ship, the result of "impure drinking water taken from the Detroit River."

The report provides a comprehensive inventory of how much the industrial economy had stained the continent's biggest pools of fresh surface water in just a few decades and before its era of great expansion was really under way. Strikingly, however, the investigators also reported that in the centre of the lakes, even in Lake Erie east of Point Pelee, the water remained "remarkably pure." From this fact, Phelps's sanitary engineers concluded that dilution was enough to neutralize pollution—so long as this capacity of natural water bodies was not overloaded.

The theory was right enough. Natural biological activity can neutralize ordinary organic waste. But the limits of a given water body's ability to metabolize the pollution it received had to be scrupulously respected. The IJC panel made a conscientious effort to give legislative traction to that all-important qualification in both Canada and the United States—but without success. In cities across North America, the precautionary warning was easily and often overlooked

The Phelps panel made a number of recommendations. Two were conspicuously prescient. First, there needed to be "a fixed standard [for water purity in the Great Lakes] either of sewage purification or of water purification."[17] Second, a binational body was needed to set and enforce those standards even-handedly in communities in both countries (the panel nominated the IJC for the role). No "untreated" municipal waste, it added, should be allowed to enter the lakes at all, though the "treatment" it advised entailed nothing more than running sewage through a quarter-inch mesh, allowing the heavy bits to settle out, and, if a place wanted to be really cautious, adding some chlorine before sending the effluent back out to nature.

Initially, the two governments appeared interested. In 1919, Ottawa and Washington asked the IJC to propose draft legislation that would enact the inquiry panel's main recommendations. The following year, Canada attempted to pursue the idea, but by then the United States had lost interest. The matter was shelved for half a century.

Phelps's rationale for dilution, stripped of its cautionary note about limited natural capacity, would encourage cities to continue dumping raw sewage into the environment for decades. (In Halifax and Victoria, into a new century.)

Around the Great Lakes, petrochemical plants put down roots near Sarnia, providing fuel for expanding fleets of cars and trucks. Cities from Port Arthur (now Thunder Bay) to Oswego added residents through the early twentieth century. Drainpipes, household sewers, and industrial waste continued to flow into the lakes, their linking rivers, and scores of tributary streams and smaller lakes.

Chicago and Toronto both instituted "primary" screen-and-settle waste treatment in the 1910s. But they were outliers. Neither Detroit nor Buffalo built primary sewage treatment plants for decades. Smaller towns and communities waited much longer. By the Roaring Twenties, one Buffalo historian notes, "heavy metals, phenols, oils and chemicals" had joined the human waste, animal offal, and other contaminants being flushed continuously into the Niagara just above its famous falls, the better to mix the resulting toxic broth on the rocks beneath them.[18]

It would take the Great Depression of the 1930s to spur many cities belatedly to clean up. When the economies of Canada and the United States failed to respond to an early dose of austerity, both federal governments launched job-creating public works programs. Buffalo received $6.75 million (equivalent to $108 million in 2011)[19] from the U.S. federal government toward the cost of the waste treatment plant it finally commissioned in 1938.[20] Similar "relief" spending in Canada brought primary waste treatment to Winnipeg, where pollution in the Red and Assiniboine Rivers had become "virtually intolerable."[21] The Greater Winnipeg Sanitary District was incorporated in 1935 and began providing screen-and-settle primary "treatment" for metropolitan communities a few years later.

Germany's invasion of Poland in September 1939, and Canada's declaration of war a few days later, pushed environmental concerns forcefully aside. Instead, the war effort justified further intervention in nature. In 1937, Ontario Hydro had redirected the Kenogami River north of Lake Superior from James Bay into the great lake. In 1943, the province approved another such inter-basin diversion. This time, Ontario Hydro reversed a second northern river that once emptied into James Bay, the Ogoki, flowing its water into Lake Nipigon and eventually Lake Superior—all to increase water available for power generation at Niagara Falls. In both cases, local First Nations protested unsuccessfully against the rerouting of the rivers. Both diversions continue to operate today.[22]

By the mid-twentieth century, peace had returned. The preoccupation of Canada's governments shifted to ensuring there were jobs to support the hundreds of thousands of new families being started by returning soldiers, sailors, and airmen. For another decade, urban expansion and industrial growth would continue to degrade the environment, particularly water, with little constraint and often with active encouragement from government.

For decades up to the Depression, a pulp mill had operated under various owners at Espanola on the Spanish River, about sixty-five kilometres west of Sudbury, Ontario. It became idle in 1930, and in the ensuing years the Spanish River flourished, becoming a magnet for fishermen and tourists. Then, in 1946, the mill reopened in the hands of the Kalamazoo Vegetable Parchment Company, which had a paper mill in Michigan. It almost immediately began releasing as much as four tonnes a day of waste wood fibre, soaked in powerful chemicals, into the river. Water along its forty-five-kilometre course soon began to emit a stench like rotting cabbage. Farm animals refused to drink it. Cottagers and homesteaders who drew water from the Spanish River found that even boiling did not render it fit for cooking or washing, let alone drinking. At times, odours rose from the river's plume as far as fifteen kilometres into Georgian Bay's breezy North Channel.[23] The pulp mill was clearly the source.

At least two deeply rooted tenets of common law were thus violated: the rights of riparian landowners and what is known as the tort of nuisance. The former holds that every property owner along the length of a river has a right to receive water from upstream that has not been degraded or reduced and is essentially in its natural state. The second says that my neighbours' activity on their land may not deprive me of the use and enjoyment of mine.

Half a dozen owners of land along the Spanish River went to court, arguing that the Espanola mill clearly flouted both protections. A trial judge agreed. High Court of Ontario Chief Justice James McRuer issued an injunction prohibiting the mill from altering the natural character of the Spanish River's water[24] and awarded the plaintiffs damages of $5,600 (equivalent to about $55,000 in 2011).[25] The injunction was challenged all the way to the Supreme Court of Canada, where it was upheld.

It was never enforced. To make sure it wasn't, Ontario's premier, Leslie Frost, used his majority in the provincial parliament to override centuries of common-law protection and quash the courts' injunction. As Frost's Attorney General boldly declared during debate on the manoeuvre: "We are just not interested in preserving the quality of the water in the river."[26] (Frost retired as premier in 1961 and accepted a position on the Kalamazoo company's board.)

Enthusiasm for replumbing nature on a grand scale persisted for another two decades.

British Columbia installed some of the largest hydroelectricity-generating dams in the world at the time on two of its biggest rivers, the Columbia and the Peace; it captured a third, the Nechako, to provide power for an aluminum smelter at Kitimat. Manitoba diverted water from its Churchill River to enhance the flow of the neighbouring Nelson, amping up output at generating stations along that river. New Brunswick dammed its biggest river, the Saint John, to produce power from a generating station at Mactaquac. Quebec reconfigured a northern watershed roughly the size of Florida to drive the eight power stations of its La Grande hydro facility, better known as the "James Bay project." The installation was completed in 1974.[27]

Still, the largely uninterrupted postwar economic expansion began to exact a price on Canada's landscapes and their services that could not be ignored.

In 1946, just a year after the war ended, Ontario had passed a visionary Conservation Authorities Act. It responded to a series of devastating floods by empowering local residents and municipalities to manage their regional landscapes to reduce the risk of high water and erosion.[28] On local request, the province would create and partly fund (with local communities) "Conservation Authorities" that had the power to regulate development in their river basin. Ontario's thirty-six Conservation Authorities now play a much larger role, managing water protection, biodiversity reserves, and recreation in watersheds that serve 11 million people—more than nine out of ten Ontarians.[29]

Even so, by the mid-'50s that province found it necessary to take additional steps. The Ontario Water Resources Commission, established in 1956, gave financial support to municipalities upgrading their waterworks and put pressure on (some) industries to treat effluent streams; it sponsored large-scale monitoring of the quality of water in Ontario's provincial waterways and, by the 1960s, in the Great Lakes.[30] New Brunswick created a Water Resources and Pollution Control Board in 1956 and in 1961 established a water authority, tasked to combat water pollution across the province but most urgently in the Saint John River.[31] Nova Scotia and Saskatchewan followed suit in 1963 and 1964 respectively, and similar agencies formed in Quebec and Prince Edward Island in 1965.

Canada's federal government became modestly more active as well. In 1961, it introduced a program through the Central Mortgage and Housing Corporation[32] to help municipalities pay for improved sewage treatment. Four years later, an adjustment to the Income Tax Act encouraged industries to invest in pollution-abatement equipment.

The Phelps board's far-seeing 1916 recommendations for the protection of the Great Lakes were never enacted. In 1948, the first automatic washing machines entered Canada. Inside each machine was a sample package of a cleaning product newly invented to work with the sought-after appliances: detergent. By 1960, beaches in the lower Great Lakes were routinely closed in summer. Algal blooms covered hundreds of square kilometres in Lakes Erie and Ontario.

In 1964, the Canadian and U.S. federal governments again turned to the IJC. The terms of the assignment were nearly word for word what had been asked of Phelps: to "investigate and report upon the extent, causes, locations and effects of pollution in the waters of Lake Erie, Lake Ontario and the International Section of the St. Lawrence River and to recommend the most practical remedial measures that might be considered necessary."[33] The commission extended the scope of its inquiry up the Detroit River as far as Lake St. Claire.

Its first report was blunt: "the situation, particularly in Lake Erie, is serious and deteriorating." Although passenger steamers and their sewage had long since disappeared from the lakes, the postwar introduction of laundry detergent and agricultural fertilizers had released a wave of phosphorus—a potent biological nutrient—into the

Great Lakes watershed. Some of it came through municipal sewers, untouched by either screen-and-settle primary treatment or chlorine disinfection. More flowed directly off fields. Concentrating in the lower lakes, the excess phosphorus was fuelling hyperactive algae growth, contributing to stinking, unsightly masses of floating organic goo. By September 1964, the fetid mess covered more than two thousand square kilometres of Lake Erie's surface, fouling seventy kilometres of shoreline there and in Lake Ontario.

"Algal growths," the IJC observed, "curtail commercial fishing and recreational activities, impart obnoxious odors, impair filtering operations of industrial and municipal water treatment plants, lower water front property values, interfere with the manufacture of certain industrial products, and generally threaten destruction of the lake as a valuable water resource."[34]

Such algal blooms also consume oxygen dissolved in lake water. In comparatively shallow Lake Erie, algal blooms and thermal stratification of the lake's water during summer left large areas of its depths—amounting in 1964 to a quarter of its volume—with less than two parts per million of dissolved oxygen. Fish need twice that to survive. When levels fall lower, they die.[35] The report also expressed concern about the concentration of chemicals that had been accumulating in bottom sediments since the IJC had last examined the lakes, a half century earlier.

As Canada prepared to celebrate its centennial by inviting the world to Expo 67 on an island in the St. Lawrence River, the decline of the country's most famous lakes became impossible to ignore. Easily overlooked in the excitement of the world's fair in Montreal was another example of the era's swelling national confidence: a federal research agency dedicated entirely to freshwater science, the Canada Centre for Inland Waters, also opened its doors that year.

Since the beginning of the decade, Canada's premiers had been meeting annually, nominally to coordinate policy in the national interest, more often to make a show of provincial solidarity in the face of their common rival, the federal Crown. By August 1969, water was prominent on their agenda. A concluding communiqué directed their respective resource ministers, constituted as the Canadian Council of Resource Ministers, to develop measures to speed up adoption of uniform national water quality standards and common approaches to pollution prevention.[36]

When the IJC delivered its final report on the Great Lakes in 1970, it perhaps resonated with Canada's new prime minister, the charismatic Pierre Trudeau. Shortly after receiving the IJC's report, his government entered negotiations with the United States to develop a joint response to the lakes' worsening contamination.

Trudeau's American counterpart, President Richard Nixon, privately considered Trudeau "an asshole."[37] Nonetheless, in April 1972, he travelled to Ottawa, and, beneath the newly refurbished chandeliers of Parliament's Confederation Room, the two men committed their respective nations to the terms of a Great Lakes Water Quality Agreement (GLWQA). This agreement and the IJC itself would come to form the twin pillars of Canada's formal relationship with the United States over water.

Initially, however, the agreement committed the two countries only to adhere to a common set of water quality objectives for the lakes and to introduce measures to reach those targets by reducing toxic and nutrient pollution, mainly from known municipal and industrial sources. Much of the attention was to go to reducing the flow of phosphorus into lake water. The '72 accord also instructed the IJC to step up its research and monitoring of water quality and to set the timer for an automatic review of its own effectiveness after five years.[38]

Later that same year, the U.S. Senate over-rode Nixon's presidential veto to enact legislation with the bureaucratic title of Federal Water Pollution Control Act Amendments of 1972 — better known as the Clean Water Act, a name it acquired formally in a subsequent repackaging. The act set national objectives for sharply reducing the release to or presence in American lakes and rivers of toxic compounds.[39] Two years later, Congress passed (and Nixon's post-Watergate Republican successor, President Gerald Ford, signed into law) the Safe Drinking Water Act. That landmark legislation set national safety standards for drinking water in the United States, made the contamination of groundwater illegal, and empowered the U.S. federal government to ensure that every municipal water provider in the country (though not the owners of private wells) complied with national drinking water standards.

Canada, too, inched forward unilaterally in this period. In 1970, Trudeau's government passed the Canada Water Act, giving the designated federal minister authority to work with provinces for the "conservation, development and utilization [of water resources] to ensure their optimum use for the benefit of all Canadians."

A government reorganization in 1971 created a new ministry—now known as Environment Canada—from units formerly housed in several federal departments, notably, the Departments of Fisheries and Forestry, and Energy, Mines and Resources. The initiative reflected advice the premiers had received a year earlier from the Canadian Council of Resource Ministers[40] to unify environmental responsibilities under single ministries. The government of the day also created the Environmental Protection Service within the newly consolidated federal ministry. Amendments to the Fisheries Act empowered the new service to regulate industry to "prevent the release of deleterious substances into waters frequented by fish."

For federal agencies of the day, however, phosphorus pollution was an urgent first priority. Research at the new Canada Centre for Inland Waters and elsewhere had confirmed the IJC's suspicion that phosphorus from detergent was largely to blame for the expanding algal blooms blighting Lake Erie and threatening Lake Ontario.

Through late 1969, then-federal natural resources minister Joseph Greene or his officials met repeatedly with representatives from the three biggest makers of detergent. They pressed Lever Brothers, Procter & Gamble, and Colgate-Palmolive to reduce the phosphate content that then constituted up to half the weight of their products. The industry refused to accept any connection between phosphates and lake pollution.[41] Rebuffed, Greene secured an amendment to the Canada Water Act, then making its way through

Parliament, authorizing the federal Crown to limit the concentration of any "prescribed nutrient" in laundry detergent. Regulation later set the cap at 20 percent, quickly reduced to 4 percent; in 2009, it was reset to less than 1.1 percent.[42] The federal government also supported municipal investment in upgraded waste treatment to remove more of the phosphorus being passed through to the environment in human sewage.

By the end of the decade, the threat from phosphorus was receding from the Great Lakes.

With Erie and Ontario recovering their sparkle, and municipalities across the country making fitful improvements to local water and waste treatment through the 1970s, Canada's top leaders had other preoccupations. A stalled economy, an Organization of the Oil Exporting Countries (OPEC) oil embargo, a hostage crisis in Iran, and a provincial government in Quebec even less enchanted with Canada than Joseph Howe (who had eventually come around on the subject)— all kept environmental issues in the shadow.

The capstone to Trudeau's long and accomplished political career was the 1982 Constitution Act, which "patriated" all remaining constitutional powers from Britain and added to Canada's foundational documents the Charter of Rights and Freedoms. The constitutional achievement was weakened by Quebec's refusal to endorse it, but the charter was a historic marker in the country's political evolution. It established for the first time in Canada that ordinary citizens possess independent and legally enforceable rights that are not gifts of the Crown's largesse, as most entitlements in Canada formally are, and so subject also to the Crown's arbitrary withdrawal. Quebec appearing (most of the time) to have agreed to disagree with the rest of the provinces about its constitutional place in the country, the charter has become a powerful influence in Canadian jurisprudence.

By the mid-1980s, however, several factors had combined to bring water's safety and security back into public focus.

One was the attention given to an erupting scandal at what became known as the Love Canal, in Niagara Falls, New York.

Named not for romance but for the nineteenth-century financier who dreamed it up, the canal was originally surveyed to flow from the upper Niagara River to Lake Ontario, generating power along the way. The venture failed, leaving a 1.5-kilometre-long unfinished trench leading away from the river. It became a receptacle first for municipal garbage and later for an estimated 19,000 tonnes of concentrated chemical process waste. In 1953, the last company to use the location covered it with dirt and sold it to the Niagara Falls school board for $1. Developers later acquired the thirty-six-block site and built a neighbourhood there.

By the late 1970s, a cluster of birth defects, miscarriages, strange smells, and black ooze invading basements and lawns attracted investigative reporters from a local paper to the area. Their stories exposed the abandoned toxic dump. U.S. president Jimmy Carter declared a health emergency, the first exercise of federal disaster powers in response to an environmental catastrophe. Authorities eventually relocated eight hundred families.[43]

A second factor pushing pollution back on the public's radar was the much-reported increasing acidity of lakes in the northeastern United States, Ontario, Quebec, and the Maritimes. Biologists reported that prevailing winds were transporting acidic chemical fallout—notably sulphur dioxide (so_2) and nitrogen oxide (no_x), dubbed "Nox 'n' Sox" by some—from coal-fired power plants in the U.S. Midwest to the continental northeast, where it mingled with moisture in the atmosphere to fall as acid rain. Many lakes, it was reported, had become so acidic they could no longer support game fish such as trout or even, in some cases, minnows.[44]

The third factor was political. Quebec businessman Brian Mulroney had put an end to nearly two decades of Liberal rule in Ottawa, winning a clear majority for his Progressive Conservatives in a general election in 1984. He set ambitious goals for his government. It would attempt nothing less than the realignment of Canada's two primary relationships: its internal one between Quebec and the other provinces, and the external one with the United States. He would fail in the first. But Mulroney's successful negotiation of a Canada–United States Free

Trade Agreement in 1987, and its potential threat to national sovereignty, became the focus of an election the following year.

Coincidentally, a consortium of Canadian promoters was advancing a hyperbolic scheme to export Canadian fresh water to the United States. The so-called GRAND (Great Recycling and Northern Development) scheme was led by a Newfoundland engineer named Thomas Kierans but had support from, among others, Quebec's then-premier Robert Bourassa. Kierans's blueprint would convert James Bay into a vast freshwater lake, from which water would flow through a chain of reversed rivers, canals, and eventually the Great Lakes to purchasers in the arid U.S. South. The scheme ignored fundamental challenges of physics, energy, and financing, but opponents of free trade saw in the proposed continental market an open door to such large-scale raids on Canadian water.

Thomas Michael McMillan had been an academic political scientist and advisor to Conservative candidates and leaders before winning a seat in the Commons for himself in 1979. In August 1985, already a minister of state for tourism and still two months shy of forty, the Charlottetown native received the much weightier portfolio of minister of environment. Under pressure to respond to acid rain, demands for more funding of urban water infrastructure, and fears for Canada's sovereignty over water, McMillan immersed himself in the economics and law of his new subject.

There was much to study. Several major independent reports landed on the new minister's desk within weeks of his appointment. Shortly after taking up his portfolio, McMillan shared a press conference podium with Peter Pearse. It had the potential to be an awkward moment. Pearse was a natural-resource economist on the faculty of the University of British Columbia, but the previous Liberal government had appointed him to lead an inquiry into "the balance of supply and demand, and the prospects for maintaining supplies of clean water" into the future.[45] Now that report was ready.

It contained a pivotal idea. Pearse proposed that Canadians stop receiving water for free or next to it and begin paying a price for it that fully reflected the cost of ensuring its safe supply today and secure sufficiency in the future. Pearse said the view was one he had heard from the majority of stakeholders and water experts who attended the inquiry's cross-country hearings.[46]

In November 1987, McMillan tabled the Conservative government's formal statement of its water policy in the House of Commons. The politically astute minister had prefaced its contents by making it clear that "the Government of Canada emphatically opposes large-scale exports of our water," winning the backing of Mulroney personally and of the Cabinet. But his policy suggested he had also listened closely to Pearse.

The forty-one-page water policy represented years of work by Environment Canada's senior scientific and policy staff, a comparatively deep and experienced resource at the time. It synthesized research and issue analysis across the full spectrum of activities and interests that impact water. It proposed specific actions on no fewer than twenty-five dimensions of water management, from climate change to heritage river preservation, tailored with a keen eye to the constitutional division of Crown powers. To support its aspirations, McMillan undertook to raise federal funding for water research, cooperate more closely with the provinces on water planning, review every major development project for its impact on water, and institute a program to control toxic chemicals "from production to disposal."

All these actions were organized in pursuit of two objectives.

The first was keeping Canada's water clean: "anticipating and preventing the contamination of all Canadian waters by harmful substances." The water policy proposed to do that by ensuring that polluters paid for using the environment as a dump. As the policy observed, "more stringent regulations and standards alone cannot protect our water resources *without the economic incentives (and penalties) to prevent their impairment.*"[47] (Emphasis added.) To the same end, the policy promised to "establish [federal] water quality standards and guidelines to better protect human health."

The second objective was more profound, nothing less than a fundamental shift in how Canadians regard water. "Canadians must start viewing water both as a key to environmental health and as a scarce commodity having real value," the policy stated. That required in turn, it argued, an end to treating water as free. Instead, it should be subject to "realistic pricing," based on more candour and accuracy about water's value. The goal addressed a recurring complaint of expert observers and picked up a central point of the Pearse inquiry's report: Canadians are profligate overusers of water and habitual under-investors in its protection or necessary infrastructure. In much of the country, rigid permitting systems designed for very different circumstances of use, demand, and climate raise barriers to the most productive allocation of water. Systematically, Canadians have under-budgeted water for the environment during periods of drought.

McMillan's policy acknowledged these shortcomings and sought to bring greater realism, flexibility, and ecological stewardship to decisions—with a sharp departure from centuries of Canadian practice.

Noting that the country's communities had hitherto "managed" water mainly by diverting more of it from nature, it observed that Canadians would increasingly need to make do within existing water budgets. This implied choosing among different uses for the limited available resource—something impossible to do without a clear idea of what value to expect in return for different uses in different circumstances.

The key to efficient resource allocation, the policy observed, is pricing, both in the literal sense of realistic charges for water services, and in the general sense of taking the resource's many values into account. Putting that insight into effect, the federal government would encourage water "pricing and other strategies such as the beneficiary/polluter-pays concept, to encourage efficient water use."[48]

McMillan's quarter-century-old document remains Canada's national policy of record on water. It was the last time the federal Crown tried, in an informed and comprehensive way, to come to grips with the many facets of water in nature and our economy. Subsequent policy statements have addressed aspects of the complex challenges raised by water's ubiquity; none has considered them so fully. From the perspective of time, and the scores of expert diagnoses of water mismanagement that have emerged since, the 1987 document remains remarkable for its scope, its readiness to confront the disconnect at the heart of Canadian attitudes toward water, and the far-reaching remedies it envisages.[49]

As the twentieth century ended, a new threat claimed the concern of the environmentally conscious. Heat accumulating in the atmosphere seemed to dwarf fears for Canada's apparently ample and generally no longer grossly polluted water (overlooking the impact that heat was having on the distribution and condition of that water). If no one any longer expected to take a drink from a Great Lake, or even from a creek chuckling across the countryside of populated Canada, an ever-responsive marketplace had provided a solution in the form of bottled water, now available at every convenience store.

Over many decades, Canada's federal Crown has expanded the remit of its environmental responsibilities. It has put money into the bricks and piping of municipal waste and water treatment facilities. It has come to the defence of the Great Lakes—both their waters' purity and their protection from removal. It has undertaken to track and contain any harmful chemicals entering our water supply. It has required proponents of disruptive industrial developments to anticipate and mitigate their injury to the environment. It has sternly warned those who pollute that they will pay. At every turn it has promised the fullest of cooperation with its provincial counterparts and the best of scientific research to support their decisions.

Canadians might guilelessly conclude that the water underwriting their wealth is at least as safe and secure as it would be in the world's other rich, educated places. We've already seen some reasons to withhold that conclusion. We'll put the evidence to closer scrutiny again in Chapters 7 and 8.

FOUR

~~~~~~~~~~

What Others Did

Now the Lord can make you tumble
And the Lord can make you turn
And the Lord can make you overflow
But the Lord can't make you burn.[1]

"Burn On" by RANDY NEWMAN

THE 1969 fire that inspired American songwriter Randy Newman's sardonic verse brought the Cuyahoga River at Cleveland,
Ohio, instant fame for all the wrong reasons—a river so filthy it
was a fire hazard. In fact, one reason the oily scum of debris burning
at a bend of the Cuyahoga that summer day was extinguished in less
than thirty minutes was that by then Cleveland's fire department had
had plenty of practice putting out its river.

The Cuyahoga begins east of Cleveland, fewer than twenty kilometres from the Lake Erie shoreline. But like a riverine "Wrong Way"
Corrigan, the Cuyahoga sets off to the south and runs for about eighty
kilometres in that direction before executing a hairpin bend at Akron
and heading back north. Its estuary on Lake Erie attracted the pio-
neers whose settlement there became Cleveland.

As that city developed its steel foundries and other industries in the first half of the twentieth century, the river served both as an extended harbour, bringing lake freighters right alongside the mills, and a free sewer for the discharge of their waste and that of the growing communities around them. By the mid-1950s, the last nine kilometres of the Cuyahoga, which meander through Cleveland at the same level as the lake, were a stagnant, fetid mass of floating garbage and semi-congealed hydrocarbons, whose thickness on the water could sometimes be measured in inches.[2] By then, river fires were almost commonplace. The first of more than a dozen recorded river fires on the Cuyahoga occurred in 1868. Others made the 1969 blaze seem minor: one in 1912 killed a dozen people; another raged for five days in 1936. Yet again in 1952 the river caught fire and burned for days, leaving behind $1.5 million worth of damage to waterfront buildings ($13 million in 2011 dollars[3]). The city had a fireboat standing by for precisely such events.[4]

The 1969 fire created a political spark, however, one that would be fanned by the media and the public mood and ultimately reach the feet of the U.S. Congress. *Time* magazine splashed the Cuyahoga fire across its pages (illustrated with a photo of the more dramatic blaze in '52[5]). Newman and others memorialized the "river that caught fire" in song. Within three years, under a staunchly conservative Republican president, the United States would pass some of the most significant anti-pollution legislation the world had yet seen.

The United States and Canada are in some ways doppelgängers; each country is the twin that took the road the other renounced. But both countries' laws are based on British law as it stood in the late eighteenth and mid-nineteenth centuries.

Likewise, the framers of the American Constitution and the delegates who drew up Canada's Confederation were caught up in similar social and historical imperatives. Mainly, they aimed to seize a continent from its indigenous residents and reorganize its administration along lines that were familiar and, they believed, conducive to liberty and wealth (for its new tenants if not those being evicted). The constitutions they designed further reflected the limits of their day's technology. America's Declaration of Independence was drawn up by the light of candles and whale-oil lamps at a time when the stagecoach represented elite high-speed travel.

In both Canada and the United States, most of the practical work of daily public administration was left to the jurisdiction of the provinces and states. In part, this reflected the formerly separate colonies' insistence on retaining as much as possible of their established autonomy. In part, it acknowledged the simple reality that they were closer to the ground than the federal authority, both figuratively and physically. Under both constitutions, these junior jurisdictions became sovereign (expressed in Canada as the "Crown in right of..." the particular province) in matters such as providing education, determining the rules of commerce and business, managing towns and cities, bringing criminals to trial, adjudicating disputes between citizens, and protecting public health. In both countries, unless rights of navigation or federal public land were at stake, the environment was regarded as an arena for state authority and no place for central government meddling.

Consequently, America's states, like Canada's provinces, were left largely to themselves into the early twentieth century to deal with whatever noxious spillover their expanding iron and steel mills, their foundries, canneries, slaughterhouses, refineries, and chemical plants—to say nothing of the daily waste from growing populations— left in rivers, lakes, and groundwater. Although most U.S. cities had covered sewers by 1910, all but a handful passed the human and industrial waste they collected directly to local waterways without any form of treatment.[6] On the discovery that chlorine could be used to disinfect contaminated water for drinking, most cities concluded that treating outbound sewage as well was redundant.[7]

The 1916 Phelps report to the International Joint Commission, recalled in the previous chapter, revealed how that worked out. Episodes of typhoid and cholera recurred well into the first decades of the new century. "[I]ntolerable" gross pollution drove residents away from Great Lake shorelines.

Notwithstanding the worsening pollution visible or evident by its stench in waterways from Baltimore to Chicago, little changed in the treatment of America's waters for more than two decades. Washington deferred to the states. Most of these had established some sort of public health agency, but water supply and security were left largely up to their cities, with occasional bouts of financial assistance to those installing water or sewage treatment facilities. Even so, it was increasingly evident that some water issues couldn't be resolved by individual states on their own.

The most significant of these was competition for water in the arid southwest. More specifically: how to divvy up the Colorado River.

That 2,330-kilometre river crosses seven U.S. states before entering Mexico for the last 100 kilometres or so of its course. By the first decade of the twentieth century, it was already being tapped and transported west, setting southern California on its way to becoming the engineered paradise it is today. A 130-kilometre canal, opened in 1902, drew water from the Colorado just before it slipped into Mexico and conveyed it to a searing depression in the earth once known to Spanish explorers as the *Valle de los Muertos*—valley of the dead. Watered, the desert bloomed into some of the most productive farmland in America and was renamed (aptly enough) the Imperial Valley.[8] Scores of other large and small diversions followed up and down the Colorado's length, from Wyoming to the California-Arizona border.

The region was still thinly populated, however, and those withdrawals made little impact on one of the continent's greatest rivers. What finally forced the issue, uncharacteristically, was an act of initiative from the centre. In 1921, then-U.S. commerce secretary Herbert Hoover decided to dam the Colorado for its hydroelectricity. States and local business interests suddenly had a reason to focus on who owned the water and by extension was entitled to share in the profit from the sale of the power it produced. The agreement that Hoover reached with state representatives after nearly a year of negotiation gave each U.S. state along the Colorado a defined volume of its water (a small amount was later set aside for Mexico, which had not been invited into the bargaining). An act of Congress cemented the agreement as a "compact" among the Colorado River states—essentially a domestic treaty that may be adjudicated before the Supreme Court of the United States.

Hoover's dam was finally built on the Colorado a decade later. The frantic optimism of the 1920s had by then collapsed into the long, grey decade of the Great Depression. The Colorado hydroelectricity project was one of numerous federal investments in infrastructure made under the New Deal's public works programs to counteract unemployment. Another was Buffalo's first sewage plant. So many U.S. cities installed waste treatment between 1933 and 1939 that the portion of American household sewage receiving at least rudimentary treatment (still typically of the screen-and-settle sort) more than doubled. Even so, it was not until the end of that decade that most of America's municipal sewage was given at least primary treatment before being released into the nearest river, lake, or ocean.[9]

Even during the extended economic crisis, however, political leaders were feeling voters' concern about the degradation of the environment. The Congress elected in 1936, for example, passed an act instructing the U.S. Public Health Service to create a Division of Water Pollution Control. Then-president Franklin D. Roosevelt declined to sign the legislation, not because he disagreed with its intent, but because of its impact on presidential budgeting authority.[10]

By then, Roosevelt himself had already dragooned one of his uncles, railroad financier Frederic Adrian Delano (the *D* in FDR), into leading a high-level review of U.S. "National Resources." His committee included Cabinet secretaries of war, commerce, labor, and agriculture, along with the administrator of public works.[11] Among other research, the National Resources Committee commissioned several reports on the state of America's waters.

"Water pollution is a national problem," the committee reported to Congress in February 1939. "The present situation is serious."[12]

Surveying the forty-five most important American river basins from the Hudson to the coast of southern California, the researchers found that every eastern watershed they studied, from Delaware to the Great Lakes, was seriously polluted. The upper Mississippi basin, Chesapeake Bay, and upper Great Lakes exhibited serious contamination in half their watersheds. The other half were only somewhat less seriously polluted.[13]

This, the high-ranking committee noted, was despite the fact that "[a]ll states have laws for the abatement of water pollution." Many of those states, however, did not give their agencies effective power to "determine [the presence of] pollution and to compel the action necessary for its abatement." Many set no standards for water purity at all, effectively legalizing any amount of contamination; exempted big polluters from what requirements did exist; or failed to prosecute known infractions.[14] Of the forty-eight states it examined, the study found shortcomings in the laws of thirty-three.[15]

A cautionary note in the Depression-era National Resources Committee's final report carries a disturbingly contemporary ring. "Failure to conserve the natural wealth of the Nation, wealth embodied in land, waters, forests, mineral deposits will inevitably result in a drop in the standard of living," it warned, seven decades ago.[16]

Within months, however, Europe was at war. The committee was disbanded, and Roosevelt's energies went to preparing the United States for a conflict that it could no longer avoid after Japan attacked Pearl Harbor in December 1941. War, and thereafter the reconstruction of Europe and Japan, and the new global challenge of the Cold War, would again eclipse polluted rivers and lakes as national issues.[17]

In a handful of cases during this period, water shared by several states became so badly polluted that their citizens demanded a response. The most elaborate of these took the form of compacts, the same device used to settle the allocation of the Colorado River. An early example committed New Jersey, Connecticut, and New York State to upgrade the treatment of sewage flowing into New York Harbor.

Inger Weibust, an expert on international relations at Ottawa's Carleton University, examined these compacts in detail in a book comparing the effectiveness of different federal states' pollution policies. She notes that only three of thirteen U.S. state compacts signed over time relating to water pollution proved at all effective. Most created toothless agencies with no ability to enforce their decisions or directives. In any event, those states that joined compacts typically also reserved the right to veto any mandate they might impose. "On the whole," Weibust observes of the postwar period, "the efforts of the states, individually or collectively in compacts, were unable to prevent the continuing deterioration in water quality."[18]

That goes a long way toward explaining how, as late as the summer of 1969, the Cuyahoga River could be a stagnant sump of waste hydrocarbons and flammable municipal trash, just waiting for a spark to set it ablaze.

By then, the social ferment of the decade had already brought several landmark initiatives from an activist Congress and White House.

The 1963 Clean Air Act dangled generous federal subsidies before states willing to enter into compacts to control smog. When the Clean Air Act failed to bring states together by the end of that decade, Congress passed new amendments mandating the establishment of enforceable national air quality standards in the United States. President Nixon signed the tighter terms into law in 1970.

Even more significant advances were to come. The Federal Water Pollution Control Act had been in force since 1948, empowering the United States Surgeon General to develop plans with the states and other agencies to reduce pollution in interstate waters. But the federal act's focus on interstate waters did little for streams entirely within a single state.

Because the states had failed to deal with air pollution—even when it affected their own populations—Congress accepted that the same states were not likely to act on water. Instead, an extraordinary four-year period of legislative initiative laid the foundation for a new and assertive federal role in protecting American water.

Reform started in 1970. The agency in charge of administering the old Water Pollution Control Act was rolled together with those responsible for the new Clean Air Act and other legislation into the new Environmental Protection Agency (EPA), with its role baked into its name. In 1972, Congress retired the 1948 act, rolling some of its terms and additional powers into the renamed Clean Water Act. The new act's remit was to establish and enforce binding regulations to limit discharges of pollutants into surface waters in the United States.

Two years later, Congress passed the Safe Drinking Water Act. For the first time, it required and empowered the federal government to set maximum permissible limits for contaminants dangerous to human health in drinking water and ensure that those drinking water standards were met. The act also prohibited the injection of potentially dangerous substances into groundwater. President Gerald Ford, like Nixon a Republican, signed the last of the three landmark pieces of legislation into law in December 1974.

This trio of acts—the Clean Air, Clean Water, and Safe Drinking Water Acts—was strategic in range. It tackled the causes of water pollution (contaminant releases, whether directly to water or via emissions into the air that settle out into surface water later); pollution's extent in nature (through enforceable surface water quality standards); and implications for public health (by protecting drinking water through enforceable standards).

The acts' passage, supported by a dedicated agency with the explicit task of enforcing their terms, set the United States on a course that would see the air in its major cities once again become breathable, its tap water drinkable, and its waterways at least habitable by wildlife, if not entirely pristine. In 1969, Cleveland's fire-hazard Cuyahoga River had been lethal even to worms in the bottom ooze of its most toxic lower reaches. After numerous EPA interventions[19] and remediation of known sources of pollution along its length, those same parts of the river now support dozens of aquatic species.[20]

The three acts and their central agency have been modified over the four decades of their existence, both extending and in some cases restraining their scope. Amendments in 1986—the same period that saw Canada's government articulate its first, last, and only fully formed water policy—extended the Safe Drinking Water Act's coverage and amplified the EPA's enforcement powers.[21] Lead was regulated for the first time as a contaminant in drinking water. Later amendments, however, reflected changing political winds. Republican vice-president Richard Cheney, who before joining his party's ticket had been CEO of the world's largest company conducting hydraulic fracturing—the practice of injecting large volumes of water and chemicals into the ground to stimulate production of oil and gas—secured an exemption from the Clean Water Act for the activity.

In the present decade, the EPA continues to come under attack, ironically from the same Grand Old Party, or GOP, that established it. Voicing the GOP's increasing belligerence toward any non-military government initiative on behalf of the public interest, and echoing falsehoods advanced by well-funded campaigns[22] to cast doubt on the science documenting environmental threats, several candidates for the GOP's 2012 presidential nomination demanded the Environmental Protection Agency be disbanded. In the wake of their party's decisive loss in the subsequent election, however, the EPA and its three key acts setting out what constitutes clean air, healthy wild water, and safe drinking water continue to anchor America's defence of its natural security.

Additional legislative instruments have meanwhile joined these three in the arsenal of the U.S. federal government. In 1980, Congress passed the Comprehensive Environmental Response, Compensation, and Liability Act (CERCLA), better known as the Superfund.

The legislation extended federal responsibility, mandating the EPA to identify and secure the cleanup of toxic hot spots—or prevent the occurrence of others—anywhere in the United States. It empowered the agency to recover its costs from those responsible for the contamination wherever possible (giving meaningful teeth to the principle of "polluter pays"), but it also set aside money to clean up orphan sites even when the cost could not be recovered—the eponymous Superfund. President Jimmy Carter, a Democrat, signed CERCLA into law a month before leaving office. In 1985, Congress raised the Superfund to $8.5 billion (equivalent to $18 billion in 2011). The following year, it assigned the EPA the additional responsibility of tracking the movement of toxic chemicals in commercial quantities through the economy and their release into the environment.[23]

But CERCLA also acknowledged that past pollution had often done enormous injury to ecological assets and services. Recognizing that state, federal, and tribal governments acted as "trustees" of the public's interest in "the economic value of lost services provided by the injured resources, including both public use and nonuse values such as existence and bequest values," CERCLA gave those governments as well the right to seek compensation from polluters for such losses on the public's behalf.[24]

In this, CERCLA called upon an idea with roots in Roman law; expressions in several legal traditions, including our own; and a growing relevance to the existential tests of the twenty-first century. In essence, the so-called public trust doctrine holds that certain natural assets such as large bodies of water are the common property of all citizens and are managed by the sovereign "in trust" for the benefit of the public. In the United States, it has been used to overturn the sale of a public harbour to private interests and to revive a landlocked lake being drained by the thirst of a distant city. As we wrote this book, the same doctrine was being used in an effort to oblige U.S. legislators to take climate change more seriously.

Although the idea of public trust is less developed in Canada than in the United States, it has deep roots in Canadian law and echoes in our own jurisprudence, as we'll see when we return to the subject in Chapter 10.

Europe's experience is also instructive. The most important river in the western half of the continent is the Rhine. It begins as an ice-cold alpine stream in eastern Switzerland and flows through Germany, France, Liechtenstein, and Austria on its 1,200-kilometre route to the ocean. The Netherlands occupies its delta, where it enters the North Sea as several broad streams. Antwerp, Rotterdam, and Amsterdam, among Europe's busiest ports, sit astride a few of its outlets to the sea.

The river's main stem carries 90 million tonnes of cargo every year.[25] Since the onset of western Europe's industrialization, the Rhine has also served as its biggest sewer. In addition to the outflow of major cities along its banks, such as Cologne and Düsseldorf, the Rhine receives that of scores of tributaries large and small. Passing Germany, it drains the Ruhr region, home to Germany's steel, chemical, and armaments industries through two world wars.

Those conflicts bedevilled, to put it mildly, cooperation among the European states as factories multiplied and cities along the Rhine expanded early in the last century. Sewers were of long standing in Europe (Paris got its first in the fourteenth century), but as in early Canada and the United States, they mainly emptied directly into the nearest waterway.[26] Through the late nineteenth and early twentieth centuries, European cities improved water treatment in step with North America but similarly neglected liquid wastes. Public health improved as the river's declined.

Notwithstanding the wars that shattered the region's economies and capital stock twice between 1914 and 1945, cooperation has a long history on the Rhine. In 1816, the Rhine states created the Central Commission for the Navigation of the Rhine to unify rules for river shipping. With a scope later expanded to tackle other problems, such as the discharge of noxious material from vessels, the commission is the world's oldest such international agency.

By the mid-twentieth century, the Rhine's visible decline prompted an acceleration of efforts to organize a common response. In 1963, France, (then-West) Germany, Switzerland, and the Netherlands created the International Commission for the Protection of the Rhine against Pollution; its role, however, was purely to research and advise. In 1968, the Council of Europe (a predecessor to the European Union) proclaimed the Water Charter, articulating a dozen "principles" for protecting watercourses like the Rhine. The council's efforts to translate those principles into a more binding convention faltered, however: a draft was completed by 1974 but then languished.[27]

Meanwhile, most of those within the Rhine's watershed continued to dispose of their liquid wastes into it or its tributary waterways. By the early 1970s, the Rhine's water was thick with heavy metal contamination; it was estimated that it carried 47 tonnes of mercury, nearly ten times that much arsenic, and no less than 1,600 tonnes of lead every year as it crossed (sluggishly, one can only imagine) into the Netherlands.[28] "[T]he romantic Rhine, home of Lorelei, was being transformed into an open sewer," lamented Alexandre Kiss in a 1985 analysis of efforts to clean up the river.[29]

Yet another effort at collective action was made in 1976. The ten-member European Economic Community (EEC)—another pre-EU formation, which included all the Rhine riparian states—issued a directive to its members setting a common goal of identifying and eliminating the worst toxins then being released into their environments. It followed up with the Drinking Water Directive in 1980, which mandated clear standards for safe tap water in EEC member states. As of 1985, however, those states had managed to reach agreement on safe amounts of only 2 of 1,500 contaminants on the directive's original "black list."[30]

Then, in late 1986, the Rhine had its Cuyahoga moment. In this case, the fire broke out ashore, at an agrochemical warehouse owned by the giant Sandoz chemical company near Basel, Switzerland. But in containing the flames, firefighters hosed an estimated twenty-seven tonnes of unburnt pesticides, solvents, and toxic precursor ingredients into drains that led directly into the Rhine River.[31] The building had also stored a fluorescent dye, which stained the water a deeply symbolic red and lingered on the world's television screens for ten days as the poisonous pulse made its way the length of the Rhine to the sea, devastating eel, salmon, and trout populations as it went.[32]

In 1988, the EEC set about stiffening standards for pollution from agricultural runoff and urban waste water (the route by which water and chemicals sheeting away from the Sandoz fire reached the Rhine). Directives followed in 1991, issuing standards for maximum permissible pollution levels downstream from city outfalls and intensively worked farmland.[33]

In 1986, the Single European Act[34] set an agenda for the creation of a regional free-trade area and the development of new European political institutions. It came into force the following July 1—

Canada's 120th birthday. The impulse for continental integration reached a tipping point two years later with the fall of the Berlin Wall and Germany's subsequent reunification. In 1992, delegates from countries meeting in Maastricht, the Netherlands, signed a treaty that would culminate in the creation of the European Union and the establishment of its new currency, the euro.[35]

This new institution would raise European policy in many fields to a new level of transnational integration—with particular ramifications for water.

If the Rhine is an iconic stream to western Europeans, the River Thames may hold the same evocative place in the imagination of the anglosphere. The Industrial Revolution led to an explosion in urban poverty and unchecked pollution in England. Both left their mark on the Thames.

London had enclosed its open street drains at the end of the eighteenth century, but they still emptied directly into the river. Through the first half of the nineteenth century, the introduction of "water closets" allowed Londoners to move their business indoors from privies and do away with bedpans. But they drained into cesspools that eventually filled to overflowing. Soon a growing number were being connected to drains that formerly had carried away mainly rainwater. But cesspools that had not yet been provided with drains became an olfactory nuisance to neighbours, and the city passed a law in 1847 to require that all household wcs drain directly into sewers. Over the following six years, the contents of (and ongoing contributions to) some thirty thousand cesspools were evacuated into the Thames. To this was added the offal and waste from the city's slaughterhouses and tanneries; all kinds of oils, dyes, and chemicals from the new industrial factories; and the extremely toxic by-products of converting coal into gas for the metropolis's new lighting system.[36]

By midcentury, the river outside the windows of Britain's Parliament had become anything but an amenity. According to one contemporary account, work in committee rooms "was only rendered barely tolerable by the suspension before every window of blinds saturated with chloride of lime and by the lavish use of this and other disinfectants."[37]

In 1856, the city's Metropolitan Board of Works began the eighteen-year task of capturing the waste from all the existing outfalls on each bank of the river in two main trunk sewers. These conveyed their Stygian flows a few kilometres downriver, collected them in large and unimaginably foul reservoirs, and released them into the Thames on the falling tide. When reeking banks of sewage sludge then developed farther down the estuary, London became one of the first cities in the world to treat liquid waste with "precipitation and chemical clarification," beginning in 1891. (It still barged the residual sludge out to the North Sea to be dumped).[38]

By then, Imperial London's golden age of growth had already overwhelmed those early facilities. As the city's population quadrupled between 1850 and 1930, scores of subsidiary sewage plants and outlets were installed to serve new neighbourhoods. Measurements of the oxygen dissolved in the Thames's water—a critical limit for aquatic life—plummeted. So did fish populations. The river's estuary had supported a thriving commercial fishery at the opening of the nineteenth century. By 1843, the year that up-and-coming young writer Charles Dickens published his *A Christmas Carol*, the Thames had lost its most valuable fish, such as migratory salmon. By 1920, every other kind of fish in the lower reaches of the river was also gone. None would be spotted for the next forty years. By the 1950s, the Thames was effectively devoid of oxygen.[39]

The low point led, however, to the same infusion of new energy into remediation that North America and continental Europe also began to experience. Investments in improved sewage treatment and new facilities begun in the 1950s were expanded in the following decade. The Royal Commission on Environmental Pollution, created in 1970, issued a report on estuary and coastal waters two years later that prompted new restrictions on industrial waste emissions to the Thames.[40]

By then, the fabled river was already showing a remarkable resilience. In 1964, biologists found fish in the Thames as far upstream as Kew, above London, for the first time in four decades. As oxygen returned to the river's water over the following years, so did fish. By 1980, more than ninety varieties were again making the Thames home. In the new century, not only did salmon return to its waters; so did trout, estuary shellfish, and even otter.

The Thames today is recognized around the globe as one of the great success stories of river revival. In 2010, the world's richest environmental honour, the AU$350,000 Thiess International River*prize*, was awarded to the U.K. Environment Agency for the Thames's restoration. Yet recovery remains tentative: accepting the Thiess prize on behalf of his agency, U.K. Environment's national conservation manager, Alastair Driver, warned that the Thames was still "fragile, and under increasing pressure from a growing population, ageing infrastructure and climate change."[41]

The truth of that was underscored in June 2011. Heavy rain, of the kind forecast to become more frequent with climate change, overwhelmed many of the Victorian-era "combined" (storm and sanitary) sewers still serving London. Nearly half a million tonnes of raw industrial and domestic sewage gushed into the river, killing tens of thousands of fish. In a desperate effort to limit the devastation, authorities injected oxygen and hydrogen peroxide directly into the water to neutralize the contamination. The incident was notable only for its size, however: lesser overflows occur on average once a week in the lower Thames.[42]

The Thames and the Rhine have been pulled back from the brink. Both rivers remain at risk—a status that could be said to include every major river in the middle latitudes of the planet. But with Europe's achievement of union, its disparate states at last acquired a rough correlate to the central government power that was constituted into federations such as Canada and the United States from the outset.

Integrated Europe's new government confronts challenges of jurisdiction in dealing with water that are similar to our own. Individual states hoard their remaining autonomy. Water is irrepressibly mobile, forever crossing political boundaries. And it is intimately involved in every other aspect of the economy. That last fact, along with water's enduring cultural resonances, ensures that multiple stakeholders will always compete in any decision respecting its management.

The EU's response to those challenges stands as the newest—as well as perhaps the most ambitious, comprehensive, and broadly considered—strategy yet to come to grips with the fluid nature of water pollution within a democratic legal framework. If there is a "state of the art" in water policy, then the EU's Water Framework Directive (WFD)[43] may be it.

Enacted in 2000 after a decade of development, the WFD set out unprecedented goals on a number of fronts. In keeping with other European "legislation," the directive does not directly bind Europe's citizens. Rather, it requires member states to incorporate its principles and goals, which are often detailed and stringent, in their own national legislation.

Enforcing that obligation is an international instrument little known outside Europe but central to its efforts at integration. The 1993 Treaty of Amsterdam is what gives the European Union its traction, imposing fines—which may be substantial—on member states that fail to adhere to EU policy.[44] The WFD is subject to its provisions.

Ambitiously, the WFD set a specific target for all of Europe's surface water to be restored to "good" condition by 2015. The directive's definition of "good"—meeting *both* "chemical" and "ecological" standards of high quality—was no less innovative. The former is based on meeting defined maximum concentrations of named pollutants. The latter requires exceeding minimum scores on indices of organic health, such as biodiversity. Some variation is allowed to account for varying natural conditions. Lakes fed by mineral hot springs, for example, might "fail" both criteria and still be pristinely natural.[45]

Europe's stewardship plan explicitly embraced water in all its manifestations. The WFD sets objectives not only for surface and subsurface water but also for water in "transition" zones (estuaries) and near-shore marine water within 1 nautical mile, or 1.8 kilometres, of the coast. Equally significantly, the WFD mandates that Europe manage its water by watershed—even where hydrographic frontiers clash with political ones. Cooperative bodies already existed to oversee some of Europe's international rivers, the Rhine among them; these had their authority extended. Where they were lacking, the WFD instructed that they be created.

To facilitate this enforced fraternization, the WFD also instituted a variety of implementation measures. The directive set out requirements for public consultation on watershed plans. And to help smaller or poorer countries with less technical capacity, or those facing more legislative catch-up, it established expert working groups with membership from across the EU to develop non-binding "best practice" documents, which coordinated policies and avoided time wasted in the reinvention of existing knowledge. More subtly, the exercise helped create pick-up-the-phone relationships among officials and bureaucrats responsible for managing related water bodies in different countries, further expediting transnational cooperation.[46]

There were procedural innovations as well. Before the directive, Europe's countries employed two approaches to regulating pollution. Emission limit values (ELVs) capped permissible pollutant releases. Environmental quality standards (EQSS) limited the concentration of those contaminants in the water receiving them. The WFD employed both. ELVs would be set for polluters that were calculated to accomplish targeted contaminant concentrations (EQSS) in waterways. If those targets were not met, emission limits would be lowered until they were.[47]

In parts of Europe, as in much of the world, water had been removed from nature, whether from surface bodies or groundwater, without regard for its replenishment by natural inflows. The WFD required basin plans to limit withdrawals to less than the natural recharge of aquifers and the constraints needed to maintain "good" ecological quality in waterways.

"Sunlight," U.S. Supreme Court Justice Louis Brandeis famously and sagely observed, "is the best disinfectant." In that spirit, the directive mandated that member states both conduct regular monitoring of their water's quality and quantity and make those findings public to their citizens.

A last innovation was candour about water's economic value and the costs of providing it. The WFD instructed the various agencies developing watershed plans to examine how water was used in their basins. Where pollution was impairing any of those economic uses, it mandated that polluters pay to mitigate the damage. And once the real cost of securing water's safety and future supply in any particular basin was determined, including the cost of whatever additional drinking or waste water treatment might be needed, the WFD required that those costs be passed on to water users. (To prevent poor citizens from having to bear the full weight of this rule, the directive was softened to require that prices only "reflect" the full cost of water supply.)[48]

Ambition's reach often exceeds reality's grasp, of course. A decade after the directive was adopted, challenges in implementing virtually all of its innovations cast doubt on its goal of restoring all of Europe's surface water to "good" quality by 2015.

Of more than a hundred river management plans mandated by the directive, only a dozen or so had been submitted by a March 2010 deadline. Of those, many drew criticism from environmentalists. In Britain, where submitted plans set the timid goal of a 5 percent improvement in the two-thirds of British rivers that failed the WFD's "good" status test, the World Wildlife Fund and the Angling Trust filed suit, asking the courts to order the government to review the plans and set more ambitious goals.[49]

The directive's effort to impose the disciplines of "user-pay" and "polluter-pay" on water consumers had also met resistance. Cyprus balked when its Water Development Department calculated that charging the full cost of supplying water to residents would more than double their water bills. And a decade after the WFD's inauguration, water for agriculture continued to flow for free or next to it.[50]

The continental union's financial crisis in 2011 raised an even greater challenge to the Water Framework Directive when several eastern European members admitted the "looming impossibility" of meeting their WFD commitments.

Among European water professionals, support for the directive remained strong, despite setbacks and the scale of its task. "The wfd has lost none of its visionary power, and still provides inspiration for those who support a wide-ranging, all-encompassing approach to water issues," the industry observer *Global Water Intelligence* editorialized shortly after the directive's tenth anniversary. "And yet... its goal of achieving sustainable water use in an ecologically safe environment remains as elusive as it ever was."[51]

In Europe and elsewhere, other programs less far-reaching than the directive are nonetheless worth noting.

Europe's Registration, Evaluation, Authorisation and Restriction of Chemicals (reach) regulation, established in 2007 along with a new central eu agency, the European Chemicals Agency (echa), requires any company within the twenty-seven eu countries that manufactures or imports more than one metric tonne of a chemical to register it with the agency, along with details about its properties, uses, and safe-handling practices. If the compound is suspected of posing a potential risk to human or environmental health, echa may require additional testing. If the material is determined to pose serious and irreversible risk, it cannot be used without official authorization.[52] Before an industry receives authorization, however, it must "analyze the availability of alternatives and consider... the technical and economic feasibility of substitution."[53]

American lawmakers have been urged to take Europe's reach as a model in reforming the '70s-era Toxic Substances Control Act.[54] Sweden, an eu member, has set 2015 as its target for a sweeping purge of *all* products containing—or processes using or releasing—any of the heavy metals lead, cadmium, and mercury, or compounds identified as carcinogens, mutagens, or reproductive and endocrine disrupters.[55]

Recently, more than forty nations, mostly in Europe and central Asia, have activated a treaty that doesn't bear directly on water but does give their citizens a powerful new tool to ensure that governments fulfill their responsibility to protect water's safety and security.

The Convention on Access to Information, Public Participation in Decision-making and Access to Justice in Environmental Matters— better known as the Aarhus Convention, from the name of the Danish city where it was signed in 1998—mandates governments to gather enough information about their environment to establish its health status. The convention obliges signatories to make that data available on request to any petitioner, whether a citizen of the country or not.

More audaciously still, Aarhus allows any citizen or organization with a complaint that a signatory is failing in its commitments under the convention to initiate an investigation by an international panel of legal experts. Their verdict and recommendations are not binding, but petitioners may ask national courts to compel compliance.

Perfection remains elusive in water policy as in every other human endeavour.

The European Union launched a review of its Water Framework Directive in 2012 to address the shortcomings that have emerged in its implementation and to expand the directive's scope to deal with anticipated climate change and mounting threat of both drought and floods.[56]

An audit by the U.S. Environmental Protection Agency's Office of the Inspector General in 2011, meanwhile, found that it was failing to ensure that states fully enforced its clean water standards, leading to inconsistent levels of protection. "State enforcement programs frequently do not meet national goals and states do not always take necessary enforcement actions," the office reported. "State enforcement programs are underperforming: EPA data indicate that noncompliance is high and the level of enforcement is low."[57]

In neither Europe nor the United States, however, was there any doubt where the responsibility for ensuring the current safety and future security of the public's water lies. In both jurisdictions, Canada's peers in scale of geography, development, wealth, and democracy, water evokes a duty of care acknowledged at the highest level of governing authority. That has continued. In 2010, U.S. president Barack

Obama released the United States' first comprehensive ocean policy and established an inter-agency council to implement it.[58]

Signatories to the Aarhus Convention, a group that includes the European Economic Community,[59] have explicitly recognized that states owe their citizens not only a secure and healthy environment but also credible and enforceable means to determine whether their governments are fulfilling that duty.

FIVE

Leaving It to Junior

IN 2009, Ontario regulators issued a long-pending approval to build a landfill over one of the province's most pristine aquifers, in the delightfully named Township of Tiny, 130 kilometres north of Toronto. The Alliston aquifer, between Ontario's Lake Simcoe and Georgian Bay, contains some of the purest groundwater ever tested.[1] It feeds scores of artesian wells in the area and, ultimately, flows north into the surface water of Lake Huron. It's also an "open" aquifer, meaning it is replenished by precipitation. That desirable quality carries an offsetting vulnerability: the aquifer is also open to contaminants that water may transport down from the surface. That threat aroused fierce local opposition to the landfill project. Bright blue-and-white placards appeared in windows and affixed to trees, fence posts, and the backs of tractors, rallying passersby to "protect our water!"[2]

Our water. Most Canadians believe that water in nature is a public resource, that it belongs to all of us.

Common law and much legislation confirm this view. Water is the quintessential public good. In legal and constitutional terms in Canada, it is the property of the public's institutional embodiment: the

Crown. Water's safety and security are exposed daily to the decisions of dozens of public bodies, from the federal cabinet to local officials. As a matter of law, principle, and practicality, then, it is up to the public through its agents in government to protect our water.

In Canada, these agents come in two constitutional ranks: the "senior" Crown, in right of Canada, and the family of "junior" Crowns, in right of provinces and the emancipated territories of Yukon and Nunavut (soon to be joined by the Northwest Territories). Our politicians exist in Parliament's case to advise and in that of Cabinet to serve (the root meaning of "minister") the Crown—the figurative public interest.

Canada's citizens have repeatedly told those elected to represent them, in surveys, polls, and submissions to public hearings, that an effective defence of our country's natural security is a priority. More than 80 percent of Canadians polled in 2011 voiced their concern about future water supply and wanted leaders to make environmental protection their "top priority." Nearly nine in ten feared for the *quality* of Canada's water: its safety from the kind of contamination that threatened Tiny Township. Four out of five surveyed Canadians wanted "stricter rules and standards" to protect water, more discipline over industrial water use, and the requirement that government decisions about water be based on science.[3]

With financial jitters haunting much of the globe, Canadians continued to rank the environment as the world's top problem. A majority (56 percent) expressed a willingness to pay more for goods, services, and taxes if it would slow down the damaging ecological effects of climate change.[4]

Our representatives know what we want. Briefing notes provided to acquaint the current minister of environment, Peter Kent, with his portfolio warned him that "Canadians generally feel that their governments do not go far enough in enforcing environmental laws."[5] Kent seemed to receive the message: in an appearance before the Senate Standing Committee on Energy, the Environment and Natural Resources in October 2011, he testified that Canadians considered clean water "a top priority."

We saw previously that even as the American and European unions suffered crises of confidence in the new century, their leaders accepted their duty to defend their citizens' water and the ecological assets that secure it as existential strategic interests. U.S. president Barack Obama pressed ahead with a national evaluation of the vulnerability of America's groundwater to contamination from hydraulic fracturing for oil and gas. The EU expanded its Water Framework Directive to plan for changing weather patterns.

Canada has taken another path.

The water policy articulated a quarter-century ago, in 1987, remains Canada's position of record on the subject. In it, then-environment minister McMillan announced "broad courses of action" under "federal leadership" to keep Canada's water safe and secure.

The document's remaining pages, however, were cushioned with soft diplomacy. "The federal government intends to work with the provinces and territories to encourage the provision of safe and sufficient water supplies," it read. A little later, it concedes that the federal Crown "counts on a continuing high degree of co-operation" from provinces to meet its goals. Ottawa would promote research, encourage provinces to create watershed plans, and establish "water quality standards and guidelines to better protect human health and the diversity of species and ecosystems."[6] The rest would be up to the junior Crowns.

Prime Minister Jean Chrétien's ministry, which succeeded McMillan's Conservatives in 1993, had other priorities. Even so, David Anderson, a former diplomat who served as its environment minister for five years, saw the ecological challenges confronting Canada clearly. "Problems... are very real," Anderson told a gathering of mayors in 2001. He cited the example of glaciers, which "provide an incredible water resource for western Canada. But rising levels of greenhouse gases will melt the snow, threaten migrating fish, end the ski areas and damage water supplies for cities and towns. This is already happening in the Himalayas."[7]

Anderson's notion of his role was as limited as his predecessor's, however. "The provinces and territories are the principal managers of freshwater resources," Anderson told his audience. "The federal government respects this provincial jurisdiction. We will continue our role in identifying and regulating toxic substances, promoting pollution prevention, and conducting water quality research."

Current minister Kent, speaking to the Senate, observed that economic storms were creating anxious times for business and government. "What has not changed," he assured his listeners, "is the Government's commitment to proactively address a wide range of environmental issues."[8]

"Address" is an ambiguous verb. It helpfully conflates three very different ideas: acknowledging that a problem exists, making a plan to fix it, and then doing whatever it takes to fix the problem in reality. Kent's report to Parliament's upper chamber did not reach for the third meaning. Rather, it put its stress on "taking the time to consult extensively," not rushing to regulate and avoiding any measures that might endanger "an economic environment that's every bit as sensitive as our natural environment."[9]

Canada has taken a road that the two jurisdictions most like us— places with large geographies, regional rivalries, market economies, and democratic institutions—turned away from after finding it led to suspect drinking water and dying waterways. Europe and the United States independently determined that individual states make poor defenders of environmental quality. Both elevated that job to their highest federal authorities—who then acted.

Canada's national leaders, down decades and across party divides, have instead opted to shrug. The federal Crown offers intelligence, some objectives, a little coaching, but leaves any actual on-field contact to its constitutional juniors.

Locating a big landfill in Tiny Township would put at risk one of the purest pools of groundwater in Canada's most populous province, an aquifer that flows into Georgian Bay—a fish-bearing, navigable, and, through its connection to Lake Huron, international water body. Nonetheless, in the decade and a half that developers had been planning the landfill, neither the senior nor the junior Crown in a position to halt the proposal and protect the Alliston aquifer did so. In the end, it was the humblest government of all—the local Simcoe County Council—that, under intense public pressure, suspended the land-fill's construction permit. Eight months later, the province of Ontario belatedly also rescinded its approval.

Was such buck-passing of responsibility for a valuable water resource, leaving its defence ultimately to an unusually plucky but legally puny county council, out of the ordinary? Or was it per-haps representative? In this chapter we'll explore how the Canadian approach to water protection has worked out, both on and under the ground.

In passing the 1970 Canada Water Act, Parliament declared that "pollution of the water resources of Canada ... has become a matter of urgent national concern." [10]

That language seemed to invite the federal Crown to invoke its full constitutional powers to act for the general good of the country. Indeed, the legislation empowered it to act unilaterally if necessary to establish water quality management agencies to restore distressed watersheds. It allowed these agencies to fund their work by charging discharge fees to liquid waste emitters for their use of natural ecosystems as pollution treatment facilities.

Alarmed by the perception of intrusion into their jurisdictions, Canada's provinces strongly resisted that part of the Water Act. As public concern about the environment receded over the next few years, however, and inflation and unemployment brought voters' attention back to the economy, it became clear that Ottawa was not going to force its environmental goals on the provinces. As water safety slipped out of public focus, most provinces did eventually take up the federal Crown's offer to help pay for water-related planning and research.

Dozens of bilateral agreements signed under the act over the following decade supported research into particular problems or developed solutions for them. Some purchased management plans for the important Saskatchewan, Mackenzie, and Saint John River basins, among others. Other federal-provincial projects developed remediation plans for the Peace-Athabasca river system (sorely damaged by hydro development in British Columbia decades before the large-scale expansion of bitumen mines in Alberta) and mercury pollution in the Churchill River system. A flood damage reduction program mapped areas prone to flooding so that local authorities could limit development there.

Information does not make decisions, however. And although dozens of these exercises expanded specialists' understanding of river systems and the stresses on particular water resources, the data and analysis they produced often did not result in much change to the human activities imperilling water's safety and future security.

An agreement with New Brunswick, for example, was intended to improve its ability to manage the Saint John River—an historic artery that runs the length of the province and provides water to its capital and its biggest city. The agreement paid for a master plan and no fewer than thirty reports on narrower issues involving the river. But the insights they contained "may be the most valuable remnants" of the effort, a 1996 academic study concluded, "as the implementation of recommendations was problematic."[11]

A few of that era's initiatives have endured into the present century. The Prairie Provinces Water Board continues to bring Alberta, Saskatchewan, and Manitoba to the table to agree on how to share the water that runs off the Rockies and reaches the eastern two provinces through the Saskatchewan River system. Likewise, the federal Crown has at times reduced, but never entirely eliminated, support for agreements it maintains with every province to share the job of monitoring the quantity and quality of surface water across the country.[12] But federal funding to support initiatives under the Canada Water Act, fairly robust during its early years at about $20 million annually (equivalent to nearly $90 million a year in 2011), was long ago reduced to trivial amounts that barely keep the correspondence flowing among bureaucrats.

The most far-reaching of the powers the Canada Water Act conveyed, the ones that give our national leaders muscular powers to protect high-priority watersheds, remain on the books, law of the land. They have never been put to use.

McMillan's 1987 water policy attempted to revive federal activism on several fronts. It proposed to promote research, encourage provinces to create watershed plans, and establish "water quality standards and guidelines to better protect human health and the diversity of species and ecosystems."[13] But again, it relied mainly on federal-provincial agreements to put its ambitions into effect.

By 1999, seven provinces had reached agreements with Ottawa, ostensibly to reduce overlap and duplication in enforcement of federal and provincial water pollution regulations. The federal Auditor General advised Parliament the same year, however, that several provinces were not providing the enforcement they had agreed to. The federal Crown had no plan to resume its own activity to ensure that federal legislation was being enforced.

The ambitious Green Plan unveiled at the end of 1990 initially set aside $3 billion (equivalent to $4.5 billion in 2011) to be spent over the following five years to overhaul how the federal Crown defended Canada's environmental security. Senior figures in the environment ministry hoped to see recurring reviews of the state of Canada's natural security, equivalent to the economic assessments that inform government's financial budget making. Few of their hopes survived political review.

In a study of the Green Plan for Germany's Parliament, policy analyst Robert Gale observed that "coercive instruments that would change behaviour to protect the environment, such as taxes and regulations, were avoided" in the version that eventually emerged. "Priorities were geared to 'soft' policy areas such as research and public education."[14]

In any event, Gale noted, within three years Prime Minister Chrétien's incoming Liberals scrapped most of the remaining Green Plan projects altogether.

The federal two-step of bold statement and craven follow-through persists. In 2009, the Harper government passed an impressively named Environmental Enforcement Act. It allowed for fines of as much as $6 million for environmental offences, imprisonment of individuals found responsible for pollution, and additional penalties equivalent to whatever profit resulted from the polluter's illegality.[15] The act was proclaimed and, according to Environment Canada's website, "came into force" in December 2010.

A year later, that force remained purely symbolic: the detailed regulations needed to give the act's impressive armoury of sanctions traction in the field—including penalties to be levied against specific environmental offences—had yet to be written or distributed.[16]

But perhaps our skepticism is misplaced. Could it be that, in taking an approach that Europe and America found ineffective, Canada has tapped into some ineffable national uniqueness? Canada's provinces may possess a different quality, a particular virtue that enables them to deliver more robust protection for water than counterpart junior jurisdictions in other federations.

All the provinces and territories have certainly enacted a range of legislation intended to protect the safety and security of water within their borders.

The acknowledged leader is Ontario. The province that brought in the country's first nineteenth-century public health act was also the first to manage water resources along the natural contours of river basins instead of the arbitrary geography of counties and towns. Ontario's Conservation Authorities date to the late 1940s but long ago eclipsed their initial mission to protect residents from floods. Ninety percent of Ontarians now live in river basins where thirty-six such authorities, independent agencies with representation from local municipalities, oversee a range of services from managing recreation and wildlife areas to reviewing development proposals for their impact on flooding and water quality.[17] Some have large budgets: the $100 million that the Toronto Conservation Authority spends annually is twice what the province of Nova Scotia dedicates to its entire Ministry of Environment.[18]

Uniquely among the provinces, Ontario has even enacted an Environmental Bill of Rights. Proclaimed in 1993, it acknowledges that Ontarians "have a right to a healthful environment" and to "the means to ensure that it is achieved."[19]

The deaths of at least seven people who drank contaminated water from the town of Walkerton in 2000 jarred the province into a decade of reform. In 2002, it passed the Safe Drinking Water Act, which tightened oversight of municipal utilities, mandated water testing and reporting to provincial authorities, and penalized failure to meet provincial standards.[20] The Clean Water Act followed four years later. It empowered Conservation Authorities to work with local stakeholders to assess available water supplies and reduce pollution risk to water sources. Both of those, along with other existing legislation, such as the Ontario Water Resources Act (which permits and regulates municipal sewage discharge, among other tasks), received further updates in a suite of related amendments in 2009.

In 2010, the Water Opportunities and Water Conservation Act authorized a variety of measures, including mandatory community plans for water sustainability, intended to raise the efficiency of water use in the province. One motivation was to allow some of the country's most densely populated cities to add more residents without overtaxing a diminishing natural water supply.[21] Another, the government argued,[22] was to equip Ontario businesses to seize a larger share of the $1.5 trillion estimated to be spent globally every year on water-related goods and services and water-dependent farm products.[23] And in June 2012, the same government tabled the ambitious Great Lakes Protection Act and Strategy aimed at protecting tributaries and near-shore areas.

Other provinces have taken similar steps. Watershed-based councils (in Alberta and Saskatchewan) or districts (in Manitoba) have been created, with varied mandates to manage and protect water within their basins. Quebec's 2002 *Politique nationale de l'eau* (National Water Policy) undertook a comprehensive overhaul of water management in that province; it directed a score of existing watershed-based advisory agencies to develop management plans for thirty major river basins.[24]

In the decade after Walkerton, in fact, every other province enacted new legislation, made major amendments to existing law, or launched major reviews of its water policy—frequently all of those.[25]

Many of the changes were directed at better protecting public water systems from being contaminated by adjoining land uses—the source of Walkerton's woes—or stepped up the frequency and stringency of water testing for safety. The criteria used to determine that margin of safety continued to be a province-by-province hodgepodge, however.

But perhaps the variable standards across the country are insignificant. It may not matter if every province follows the same exacting protocol for ensuring the safety of drinking water or adheres to the same standards for effluent released back to nature. Perhaps the job is getting done adequately in all provinces.

But this cannot be confidently supported, in part because the federal Crown's withdrawal from the defence of Canada's water has left a fractured and inconsistent data record.

"A major consequence of the decentralized nature of Canadian environmental policy is a critical lack of information," Weibust wrote in her 2009 comparison of federal-state pollution regimes. "It has been very difficult to obtain and compare information on environmental quality and environmental regulations in Canada. Interprovincial and international comparisons have been very difficult, if not impossible, to make."[26]

Where individual provinces have been put under scrutiny, however, the results suggest our water is not receiving the protection we expect. Consider the Ontario environment commissioner's annual report, delivered to the Ontario legislature in November 2011.

"I have 30 years of environmental experience," Commissioner Gord Miller reminded reporters after releasing his findings, "and I'm nervous." He pointed to a "culture of inaction and procrastination" in defence of water-productive ecosystems, marked by a demonstrable decline in resources dedicated to protecting Ontario's overtaxed landscape. With 150,000 regulated "systems, facilities and activities" to police, its Ministry of the Environment (MOE) had lost nearly half (-45 percent) of its budget since 1992–93, a period in which overall provincial spending soared by 72 percent (in constant dollars). The Ministry of Natural Resources lost more than a fifth (-22 percent) of its budget during the same time. Overall, the province was spending less than a penny of every tax dollar to defend its natural security.[27]

The Ministry of the Environment's vanishing budget had coincided with another trend Miller found disturbing: trusting without verifying. The environmental commissioner said he was "troubled... that MOE relies on voluntary compliance" rather than enforcement. "MOE only inspects about 5 percent of all regulated facilities (not even including those facilities operating without approvals) each year," Miller noted, "meaning that regulated facilities can go, on average, twenty years between inspections."[28]

Miller wasn't the first to draw attention to Ontario's light environmental oversight. An academic study in 2001 pointed out that the MOE then had the capacity to investigate only 1,200 of 6,000 suspected violations it was aware of that year.[29] And in 2007, the Sierra Legal Defence Fund (now Ecojustice) called attention to "continued chronic non-compliance with Ontario's water pollution laws by industry," more than two years after Walkerton.[30]

Roughly one Canadian in three lives in southern Ontario's portion of the Great Lakes watershed. The safety of their drinking water today and its security tomorrow are intimately bound up with the health of the region's ecosystems and hydrology, both above ground and below.

An expert panel convened to examine Great Lakes basin groundwater on behalf of the International Joint Commission Boundary Waters Treaty reported the following:

· One-third of Ontario wells exceed guidelines for the presence of harmful bacteria, such as the *E. coli* present in human feces.

· Tests for such bacteria do not cover another class of pathogen, viruses from human waste; these "are common in groundwater due to malfunctioning septic and seepage systems and leaking sanitary sewers."

· Ontarians are installing 25,000 new "on-site human-waste treatment systems" (mainly septic tanks with drainage beds) a year; an estimated 5,000 of those "fail to treat waste adequately."

· Between 500 and 3,500 underground storage tanks in Ontario are leaking toxic fuels, solvents, or other chemicals (the low end of that range is cause for alarm on its own).

· And, more than twenty years after the Love Canal was exposed, releases of toxic industrial contaminants into the Niagara River and Lake Ontario "do not appear to be decreasing."[31]

Three and a half decades after the signing of the original Great Lakes Water Quality Agreement, another review lamented that "historic victories, such as the restoration of Lake Erie, are eroding. The oxygen depleted 'dead zone' is back." The 2007 report, from the Canadian Law Association, cited Environment Canada records documenting "various species of fish [that] now suffer from tumors and lesions" and noted that "their reproductive capacities are decreasing."[32] The water the fish inhabit eventually fills Montreal's faucets.

Another province that deserves close attention is Alberta.

The wild rose province is often painted in villainous terms by environmentalists, who deplore the development of its oil sands on multiple grounds. But Alberta's singular role in the way Canadians employ and manage water includes much to admire. Chapter 3 recalled how early Albertans' spirited defence of their water created the diplomatic tension that brought forth the International Joint Commission, an early exemplar of international cooperation. Through skilled engineering, Alberta has built irrigation systems that have turned its semi-arid southwest into rich farmland and a source of profitable agricultural exports (half the country's irrigated acreage lies in Alberta).

The province was the first in Canada to "hit the wall" of available water in some river systems. In response, it began overhauling its water legislation in 1999—before the Walkerton and North Battleford scandals prompted other provinces to act—and later instituted watershed councils with mandates to work with land-use planners to integrate water security into development plans for their basins. The province funds leading centres of water-related research.

Alberta has consistently been an early adopter of Ottawa's various generations of federal-provincial agreements meant to align provincial actions with national water objectives. It is one of the few provinces that require their drinking water facilities to match or exceed the Guidelines for Canadian Drinking Water Quality established by federal and provincial health ministries. The province was also one of the first to sign, and last to abandon, its Trudeau-era accord with the federal Crown under the Canada Water Act. When the Mulroney government offered it, Alberta was quick to take over enforcement of Canadian Environmental Protection Act (CEPA) regulations as well as its own under an equivalency agreement. And Alberta has much deeper pockets than most other provinces from which to fund whatever protection it wishes for its water resources in the wild or at the tap.

In short, if charging provincial authorities with our natural defence is going to demonstrate its value anywhere, it ought to be here.

By 2010, Alberta's northeastern oil sands region had become the United States' largest single source of crude oil. Its production was anticipated to double by 2020. Alberta was also the Canadian beachhead of a global rush to exploit so-called tight gas, distributed in tiny pockets throughout a rock layer rather than in compact reservoirs, as conventional deposits are. Economic commentators hailed this resource for introducing a vast new supply of what they often described as inexpensive and relatively "low-carbon" (compared with coal or oil) fossil fuel, revolutionizing the global energy marketplace.[33]

Both fossil fuel streams rely on almost unimaginably vast volumes of water. Despite decades of research, production of a barrel of crude oil from the Alberta oil sands continues to require the effectively irrecoverable pollution or sequestration below ground of between one and three or four barrels of fresh water, depending on the technology used.[34] Each injection to "hydrologically fracture" rock and release its gas (a process repeated dozens of times on each of the hundreds of wells drilled annually in Alberta) can require between 250,000 and 3.7 million litres of water—roughly the contents of an Olympic swimming pool per pop. The used water recovered after the process must be treated in the same way as toxic waste. The technique has been linked as well with the contamination of groundwater by hydrocarbons and production chemicals through a variety of channels.[35]

Prime Minister Stephen Harper has made plain his government's view that both products, oil sands crude and unconventional gas, are strategic economic assets. After securing a long-sought parliamentary majority in 2011, the prime minister focussed on the construction of an oil pipeline to deliver more of Alberta's synthetic crude to coastal refineries in Texas, from where their refined products could be sold on to European buyers, and on similar links for gas and oil to the British Columbia coast so that both commodities could reach new customers in Asia.

However strategic these fossil fuels may be for Canada's economy (and that can be debated), the impact, scale, and accelerating pace of their production raise no-less-significant risks for Canada's natural security. We'll leave to another forum a discussion of how the hydrocarbon industry contributes to climate disruption. Our concern here is our water's safety today and security tomorrow.

From headwaters in the Rocky Mountains, rivers that cross the southern third of Alberta, passing much of its gas industry and all of its irrigated farmland, flow on to supply southern Saskatchewan and its large Lake Diefenbaker reservoir with most of their water. Farther downstream still, in northern Manitoba, much of the Rockies' remaining water, by then flowing through the Nelson River, helps drive hydroelectric turbines.

After Alberta's northeastern Athabasca River runs its gauntlet of oil sands developments, it mingles its water with the Peace and Slave Rivers. Their combined flows feed the Mackenzie, whose role in weather systems downwind in central Canada and in the health of the Beaufort Sea downriver is far from fully understood.[36]

Alberta, in sum, holds the water and wider environment of much of Canada in its hands. How is it caring for that trust?

Again, the answer is partly obscured by an absence of information. After taking over much of the responsibility for meeting federal pollution standards in the 1980s, Alberta—a relatively small province in population at the time, with a strong pro-business culture—initially contracted much of the necessary monitoring to private consultants. When a drop in oil prices cut into provincial revenues, the monitors' activity was cut back.[37] In 1997, the province handed the task of monitoring how oil sands development was affecting water in the lower Athabasca River to an arm's-length agency. The Regional Aquatics Monitoring Program (RAMP) received its money from oil sands companies but reported to a stakeholders' board that included First Nations and environmental groups, alongside representatives from industry and government. In 2000, the province created a separate agency, on the same model, to conduct research on the cumulative effects of oil sands development.

Over the decade after RAMP's establishment, the environmental NGOS and most First Nations abandoned its board, saying their concerns were not being addressed.[38] In 2004, a legislated review of the industry-funded monitoring program found it guilty of "inappropriate statistical analysis and unsupported conclusions," among other shortcomings. "[T]here was a serious problem related to scientific leadership, no overall plan, clear questions were not addressed in the monitoring and there were significant shortfalls with respect to statistical design of the individual components," reviewers found.[39] By 2010, the RAMP board was dominated by a dozen industry representatives and eight members from Alberta's development-friendly government, as well as one aboriginal group and someone associated with a gravel-mining company.[40]

That year, the program received an even more scathing scientific review than five years earlier. The expert panel found RAMP was delivering fully on only one of its nine mandated missions: to review its own performance. On the performance of its substantive mission, the experts found the program was uniformly failing.

About RAMP's highest priority, monitoring Alberta's aquatic environment to detect cumulative and regional impacts from oil sands development, the 2010 review was blunt: "The program is currently incapable of detecting regional trends and cumulative effects." After thirteen years of existence, RAMP had failed even to collect enough consistent observations to construct a credible baseline to detect future environmental impacts. Moreover, because RAMP tracked different indicators from those used by oil companies to make environmental commitments, "it cannot be determined" whether oil companies were living up to monitoring requirements they had assumed as conditions of their operating licences.[41]

The federal government finally ordered its own review of Alberta's program for monitoring its most important northern river. Late in 2010, it concluded, just as others had, that Alberta's oversight agencies could provide no reliable insight into the sustainability of regional aquifers, their susceptibility to contamination, or the "cumulative impacts of multiple environmental stressors on aquatic ecosystem health and integrity."[42]

Despite the deficiencies in credible data documenting the impact of two decades of hydrocarbon development on Alberta's water, what we do know is disturbing.

Trace amounts of some hydrocarbons are believed to have entered the Athabasca's water current for centuries, as its meandering course eroded the oily sand first on one bank, then the other. But several studies conducted since the middle of the last decade, mainly by researchers working without government funding or approval, have established that the concentration of those chemicals rises sharply downstream from the oil sands mining region.

Independent ecologists Kevin Timoney and Peter Lee installed water-sampling devices on an Athabasca tributary both up- and downstream from a major oil sands development in the summer of 2006. Their sampling revealed that more than two dozen polyaromatic hydrocarbons (PAHs, naturally occurring chemicals that can be carcinogenic for fish) roughly doubled in concentration in water that had passed by an oil sands mine waste tailings pond. The downstream concentrations of some individual chemicals (including PBTS

- 93 -

dibenzothiophene and anthracenes) were as much as fifteen times greater than those naturally present in water above the oil sand development.[43]

Further evidence that toxic compounds were building up quickly in the river system downstream of the oil sands region came in 2010. University of Alberta limnologist David Schindler led an eight-member team that tested water and winter snowpack at more than thirty locations across the region, both in areas with high concentrations of undisturbed bitumen and in those being actively mined. They found more than half a dozen toxic compounds, including heavy metal PBTs lead and mercury, that had increased in the river as a result of oil sands development. "The pollutants form a bull's-eye in the water around oil sands facilities," Schindler later commented.[44]

Many pollutants came from the strip mines that in some places are separated from the river by only the width of a dike. Heavy metals such as arsenic, mercury, and lead turned up in snow as much as fifty kilometres downwind of "upgraders," the heavy-duty refineries that turn raw bitumen separated from sand into synthetic crude oil acceptable to markets (RAMP's monitoring, the study noted, had not included either toxic fallout on snow or its later concentrated release during spring melt).[45]

Additional unsanctioned research dug into the sediment being carried down the Athabasca and deposited in its great interior delta. By testing the chemical content in layers of silt laid down over decades, scientists determined that the concentration of PAHs in the river's mud—and by inference its water—was increasing with time. With each year, more carcinogenic chemicals had lodged in the delta's muck, a food source for many bottom-dwellers figuratively as well as literally at the foundation of the aquatic food chain.[46]

Environment Canada's own personnel reported that releases from open-pit oil sand mines of powerful toxic compounds into the air or deposited into tailing ponds were growing in volume. Over just the four years between 2006 and 2010, the mines' emissions of arsenic, lead, and other toxins had jumped by 26 percent. In 2009 alone, more than 70,000 tonnes of volatile organic compounds (a broad family of hydrocarbon molecules, many carcinogenic or highly toxic) floated into the air from mining and upgrading operations, along with more than 110,000 tonnes of sulphur dioxide, which produces acid rain.[47]

Yet more confirmation that those emissions were building up in the environment came early in 2013. Researchers—this time funded by the federal government—determined that sediments deposited recently in lakes as far away as 90 kilometres from oil sands operations contained concentrations of PAHs 2.5 to 23 times higher than sediments laid down in the 1960s. As the study's lead author, Queen's University biologist John Smol, put it: "Now we have the smoking gun."[48]

In the 1970s, neither First Nations anglers nor western scientists pulling fish from the Athabasca River and Lake Athabasca reported deformities in the animals they caught.

As late as 1987, the Athabasca's fish, at least, seemed to have suffered no great impact. Alberta Environment researchers tagged seventeen thousand fish in the river and lake that year and noted no deformities, lesions, or other external physical evidence of chemical stress.[49] Over the following decade, however, commercial and subsistence fishermen living in Fort Chipewyan, a mainly Metis and First Nations community on Lake Athabasca downstream from the oil mining region, began to see those symptoms in a growing number of fish. When fish not too deformed to eat were cooked, people found their meat was not firm and flaky as in the past but soft and mealy.[50]

With decades of personal observation (and in the oral record, centuries) of Athabasca wildlife to draw on, the lake's aboriginal fishermen became alarmed enough by 1995 to alert Crown scientists to the defects they were seeing. Neither provincial nor federal agencies showed interest. At least one attempt to provide samples for testing was frustrated when Alberta Environment failed to collect two hundred kilograms of deformed pickerel sent for examination, allowing the fish to rot beyond use. As late as 2010, Environment Canada continued to insist that the rate of deformities and tumours in Athabasca fish was "stable."[51]

In September that year, ten days after releasing damning evidence that northeastern Alberta was becoming drenched in chemical by-products from oil sands activity, Schindler joined several Fort Chipewyan fishermen at a news conference to draw attention to the effects those toxins might be causing.

The men presented photographs and actual carcasses of fish caught in the river and lake system over the previous three years, allowing reporters to view first-hand the lesions, back tumours, and oddly shaped bodies the animals displayed.[52] The show-and-tell exercise gave the Canadian public powerful new images to illustrate the gross failure of environmental stewardship beyond the moonscape of the oil sands mines themselves.

In December 2010, the *Globe and Mail* reported that RAMP itself had found hundreds of deformed fish in rivers under its mandate but had not mentioned them to either government or local communities.[53]

The conclusion that oil sands operations were polluting the Athabasca and Mackenzie river systems had, despite the absence of "smoking gun" science, become settled wisdom.

"Recent studies suggest elevated levels of pollutants near mining sites, including hydrocarbons and heavy metals," senior advisors warned federal minister Kent in candid briefing papers in 2011. "Contamination of the Athabasca River is a high-profile concern [and] raises questions about possible effects on health of wildlife and downstream communities."[54]

Prodded at last into action, the federal and Alberta Crowns undertook jointly to develop a new and improved, "world class monitoring program" in the region.[55] Unveiled early the following year, it promised to expand the chain of water- and air-monitoring stations, integrate and rationalize "the current constellation of monitoring arrangements," and target research into concerns such as wildlife health and the condition of aquatic and terrestrial ecosystems. Information gathered would be made public "in a timely, standardized, coordinated manner... freely accessible." Late in 2012, the Alberta government announced that it was creating a new environmental management agency to undertake integrated monitoring of development impacts on the province's air, land, water, and biodiversity. The new agency would operate where the province determined it was "required" (starting with the lower Athabasca region) and be operational by 2015.

The program was estimated to cost $50 million per year, but the two Crowns proposed no new public money for the effort. Rather, industry would pay the scientific piper, as it had under the discredited RAMP program—much of whose spending would simply be transferred from the old scheme to the new.

Meanwhile, Alberta was whittling away its environmental protection for the rest of the province as well. In 2008, the budget of Alberta Environment was cut by 30 percent and fell further in the next two years.[56] By the end of the century's first decade, the "absence of sufficient scientific information and understanding of the state of the Lower Athabasca River... applies equally well to the majority of rivers in Alberta," wrote Bill Donahue, a staff scientist with the Alberta non-profit Water Matters.[57]

In November 2011, Alberta's newest environment minister, Diana McQueen, assured the public that she would "advocate strongly" for the restoration of funds to her department in order to provide "world class" monitoring of the province's water and air. A quarter-century after being entrusted with the headwaters of some of the nation's most important river systems, Canada's richest province asked the rest of the country to be patient while it made a plan and perhaps found a little money to pay for it.

Alberta's dereliction in defence of its water's safety and security is unique only in scale.

Reviewing provincial budgets over the 1990s, we find repeated cuts to funding for environmental science, monitoring, and enforcement. Adjusted for inflation, the cuts imply that provincial capacity in those fields shrank by more than a quarter during those years—and by twice that much in Ontario. In some provinces and the northern territories, comparable reductions in capacity were prevented only because there was so little to cut (Alberta's reductions in spending were more than some Maritime provinces' entire environment budget).[58]

Two comprehensive studies over the last decade reached similar conclusions about the water protection provided when the federal Crown relies on provinces and territories to accomplish its rhetorical ambitions.

"Canadian water legislation is a patchwork of provincial and federal laws," an ad-hoc panel of water experts assembled by the Walter and Duncan Gordon Foundation concluded in 2007. "Rather than selective harmonization and subsidiarity, we have fragmentation and an ill-coordinated downshifting of responsibilities." Such "passing the buck," the experts added, had generated "significant inconsistencies and gaps in responsibility and oversight."[59]

A subsequent examination confirmed those conclusions. Created in 1988 to find consensus among business, public administration, labour, and NGOs on how to reconcile habitat with prosperity, the National Round Table on the Environment and the Economy (NRTEE) found that Canada's water management suffered from "complicated and fragmented statutes and policies across the country; limited knowledge of actual water use and availability; and a general lack of capacity and expertise."[60] Its verdict described water regulations in place across the nation in 2010 as "burdensome and complex, due to the jurisdictional division of powers between the federal and provincial governments and the fact that provinces also delegate some of their authority to municipalities."

Meanwhile, Canada's water continued to degrade—sometimes visibly.

Manitoba became the first province to establish a ministry with exclusive responsibility for water. Notwithstanding that symbolic gesture, the water in Lake Winnipeg continued to suffocate under recurring blooms of green algae. By 2011, gooey masses covered as much as fifteen thousand square kilometres of lake—an area larger by more than one half than the record "dead zone" in the Gulf of Mexico.

"We have created the largest inland freshwater dead zone in the world," lamented Bob Sandford, the chairman of the Canadian Partnership Initiative in support of the United Nations Water for Life Decade and a leading international advisor on water policy.[61]

Winnipeg's Depression-era treatment plant meanwhile continued to release three-quarters of the city's liquid waste into the lake's main tributary still loaded with nearly 250 tonnes a year of phosphorus— prime algae food. A standoff between Winnipeg and the provincial government over which contaminants to target for removal had, as of the end of 2011, stalled plans to upgrade the facility at all.[62]

Canada's leave-it-to-the-provinces approach has not entirely pre- vented national-scale projects to protect water at the tap or in the lake.

The provinces have, on their own initiative, often acted together, at first through the annual meetings of their premiers begun in 1960, since 2003 as the Council of the Federation. This purely political cre- ation is unmentioned in the Canadian Constitution. Nonetheless, it has acquired a secretariat housed in Ottawa and anchors a brood of satellite bodies bringing together provincial (and sometimes federal) ministers holding similar portfolios. One, the Canadian Council of Ministers of the Environment (ccme), a body that includes the fed- eral minister, has had its own office in Winnipeg since 1988.

An idea of the effectiveness of these institutions can be drawn from their decades-long pursuit of consistent, enforceable standards to ensure that every Canadian is equally protected from degradation of the water in their environment and in their taps.

Health Canada issued its first Guidelines for Canadian Drink- ing Water Quality in 1968. The following year's conference of nine provincial premiers (Newfoundland's Joey Smallwood stayed away) directed the Canadian Council of Resource Ministers, a forerunner of the ccme, to accelerate the adoption of minimum national water pol- lution standards.

"It is significant," political historian Kathryn Harrison has written of the time, "that all provinces stressed the need for minimum national standards. Provincial politicians were acutely aware of the dilemma of trying to satisfy public demands for environmental protection with- out placing local industries at a competitive disadvantage. The Alberta minister was particularly candid in acknowledging the difficulty of clamping down on industry if other provinces did not do the same."[63]

Two decades later, in 1987, the Pearse inquiry into the security of Canada's water reported, after listening to scores of Canadians in hearings across the country, that "there were frequent calls for federal legislation that would specify and enforce maximum contaminant levels in drinking water."[64]

Another quarter-century has passed since then. Policy analysts and public health and other interest groups continue to urge the adoption of enforceable nationwide standards to ensure that all Canadian citizens can be equally confident that the water in their taps is safe and the water in their environment secure.

Such standards remain elusive.

Safe drinking water and pollution in waterways are different; they require different approaches to measure and limit contamination.

In the case of drinking water, toxins and pathogens that could make us sick must be eliminated, and so standards typically set maximum limits for the presence of these. Water in the wild must not be overloaded with pollutants; as a result, standards limit the volume and toxicity of effluent releases.

These standards are necessary for the same reason that speed limits are: it's impossible to hold a polluter to account for contaminating water without a legally established standard (a "speed limit") the polluter can be shown to have violated. Similarly, the people running the expensive processes meant to disinfect the water in our taps need clear metrics to confirm they're meeting that critical objective.

This is not as simple as it might seem. Very little water outside a laboratory is perfectly pure. Natural minerals are present in most groundwater (traces of arsenic occur in an astonishing number of Canadian wells). Dip a cup into even the most pristine alpine stream and your drink will teem with microscopic life. Modern equipment is capable of detecting molecules in mind-bogglingly dilute presences. And not everything in the water will necessarily hurt us in any event. Many Canadians actually pay a little extra for the fizz they get from a glass of water "contaminated" with carbon dioxide.

For all these reasons, safeguards are designed to ensure that water is safe to drink rather than completely clean or pure (the state of distilled water). The presence of other compounds is accepted. The challenge lies in determining precisely how much of which compounds can be present in a given quantity of water without hurting you.

Although we're all much alike beneath the skin, determining what adulterants are safe at what levels requires at the very least making a list of candidate contaminants and establishing tolerable limits for the presence of each. This may be relatively easy for the familiar pathogens behind outbreaks of gastrointestinal illnesses. But for other substances—naturally present metals such as arsenic, for example, let alone more exotic manufactured chemicals—the answer is not immediately obvious.

And although all Canadians are more or less vulnerable to the same contaminants, the waterways that receive their wastes vary widely. A lake as vast and untaxed as Great Bear will have no difficulty digesting raw sewage from a village. The diminished summer trickle of the South Saskatchewan River, steeped in the treated waste of cities upstream, might have more trouble. Similarly, although human waste varies little from town to town, industrial waste differs dramatically among businesses. Different circumstances require different standards to cover specific industries—mining, say, or pulp and paper manufacturing—and settings, such as a certain waterway or ecosystem.

Over the decades, as more contaminants have aroused public concern, additions have been made to Canada's 1968 Guidelines for Canadian Drinking Water Quality. The current version covers the basics of primary sanitation in a set of "parameters" for microbiological contaminants, the category to which those feared *E. coli* and other fecal bacteria belong. A second set of parameters covers chemical and radioactive contaminants (low levels of radioactivity occur naturally in some places) and is occasionally expanded to include new pollution threats. A third set provides metrics for water qualities that are not directly related to its lethality but that affect its aesthetic quality. These set guidelines for acceptable colour, odour, and taste.[65]

But these are guidelines only. Suggestions. The federal Crown makes no effort to ensure that water utilities implement them. Most utilities belong to local governments, created by provincial Crowns. Federal leaders argue, therefore, that only provinces have the constitutional authority to mandate that those utilities meet any national standard. Jealous of its autonomy, every province continues to regulate drinking water to its own parameters, testing protocols, and reporting requirements. As of 2006, only Alberta, Ontario, and Nova Scotia had adopted the meticulously established Guidelines for Canadian Drinking Water Quality as standards.[66]

As an aside, Minister McMillan's 1987 water policy had proposed to "consider" whether to provide enforceable drinking water safety standards for federal lands and the northern territories, including First Nations reserves. In 2010, after a series of scandals exposed appalling lapses in water quality on several reserves, the Harper government belatedly introduced a bill to keep at least part of McMillan's commitment, sort of. Its proposed Safe Drinking Water for First Nations Act would have established enforceable standards on reserves. But these would still not be consistent everywhere. Instead, each reserve would adopt whatever standards were in force, or not, in the province or territory where the reserve was located.

In any case, an election intervened and the bill died on the order paper.[67]

The pursuit of consistent and enforceable standards to prevent the pollution of waterways receiving liquid waste has gone on almost as long—with no more to show.

Just a year after the Canada Water Act, the Trudeau ministry created the Canadian Environmental Protection Service, giving it the task of establishing national, sector-specific regulations to limit water pollution under the Fisheries Act. In 1975, the same government signed Accords for the Protection and Enhancement of Environmental Quality with every province except Quebec, British Columbia, and Newfoundland. A central objective of these, in the eyes of Ottawa, at least, was to secure provincial adoption of a consistent set of regulated pollution limits from sea to sea.

After five years, only Alberta and Ontario renewed their accords. By 1985, even those had fizzled out, their standard-setting goals unmet.

The Mulroney ministry's Canadian Environmental Protection Act (CEPA), created in 1989, demonstrated the same weakness yet again. Its legislation empowered the federal Crown to relinquish enforcement of regulations under the act to any province willing to confirm in writing that its pollution rules would meet or beat the feds'. This got even less uptake than the Trudeau-era accords. As of 2008, nearly two decades after the offer went out, only one such "equivalency" agreement had been signed—with Alberta. (Revisions to the CEPA in 1999 did little to address enforcement.)

In 1993, the Canadian Council of Ministers of the Environment (CCME) stepped into the vacuum. It made closer alignment of provincial pollution policies its top priority. The Canada-wide Accord on Environmental Harmonization, signed in 1998, purported to bring the country closer to consistent, enforceable, Canada-wide standards for safe limits to water pollution. Revisions in 2001 clarified federal, provincial, and municipal roles and identified how to delegate authority down to the last. But neither the original nor the revised versions of the accord required any province to enact or enforce regulations to put its envisioned standards into legal effect. (Quebec, in any event, never signed on to the accord).

In 2009, the CCME again took up the unfinished task of many decades. This time it established the Canada-wide Strategy for Managing Municipal Wastewater Effluent. The strategy set a number of unambitious goals, including limiting sewage released from combined sewer-storm drains to no more than its then-current volume (while establishing several acceptable reasons for failing to meet that goal). It offered to "consider" the Canadian Environmental Protection Act's determination of chemicals so dangerous and difficult to remove from common sewage that their release should not be permitted at all, but it accepted no obligation to respond.

In the strategy's most significant advance, the provinces signing on (Quebec, Newfoundland and Labrador, and Nunavut did not) undertook to accept Canada-wide standards the federal government would develop for determining whether effluent released to the environment was adequately treated.

Federal environment minister Kent duly announced these in mid-2012. His claim that they had been "implemented" was a stretch, however—as was the boast that they would produce "safe and reliable waste water."[68] In fact, the standards required only that liquid waste released to nature not be "acutely lethal" and meet upper concentration limits of only four key indicators: "biochemical oxygen demand," suspended solids, residual chlorine (left over from disinfecting sewage), and un-ionized ammonia.[69] Although all of these are important and valid parameters for determining the polluting impact of liquid waste, they do not address thousands of other contaminants of emerging concern that we will get to know better in Chapter 8.

The federal Crown also planned, once again, to leave the task of ensuring that these standards were met to its provincial counterparts. This was to be accomplished under another generation of federal-provincial "administrative agreements."

On the date Minister Kent announced the "implementation" of the federal standards, no such agreement had yet been signed. Not that there was any evident reason to hurry: the earliest deadline to bring the most "urgent" streams of waste into accord with the new standards was 2020. Lesser remediation was put off until 2030 or even as late as 2040.

The long and fruitless effort across nearly half a century to establish enforceable national standards for either safe drinking water or tolerable limits to water pollution sadly reflects a recurring manoeuvre in our Crowns' defence of Canada's natural security—a federal retreat in three acts.

Whenever public concern about pollution rises to a threshold of political heat, the federal Crown appears to respond. It proposes initiatives with sweeping goals. Sometimes it even enacts new laws and announces accompanying regulations. In Act II, however, these initiatives meet resistance from one or more provinces jealous of jurisdiction over their resources and fearful of incurring economic disadvantage by too-scrupulous protection of the environment. As public alarm subsides on the appearance of action, the provinces parry Ottawa's initiatives over subsequent political cycles, often enacting competing legislation. Act III finds the federal Crown negotiating its own retreat, routinely sealed with the latest round (and nomenclature) of toothless federal-provincial accord.

This pattern has been followed so often that historian Harrison titled her study of environmental policy under the Canadian Constitution *Passing the Buck*.

Canadians still cannot refer to consistent and enforceable standards to hold providers accountable when their drinking water is suspect. And despite the recent flurry of apparent activism by the CCME and federal Crown, many of the nearly nine hundred waste treatment facilities (about a quarter of all those in Canada) now releasing effluent unsafe to human and wild life will continue doing so for decades.[70]

SIX

A Negligent Crown

▼

I T S H O U L D be no surprise that our provinces have not stepped up in full and equal measure to the defence of Canada's water, any more than the states of Europe or America have stepped up to defend the water of those larger entities.

First, these junior Crowns have very different capacities. The entire population of Prince Edward Island (145,000 people in 2011[1]) could find room to spare in the city of Sherbrooke, Quebec (147,000[2]). Second is the fear, routinely and predictably stoked by self-interested businesses, that more stringent controls on pollution in one province will drive investment, along with jobs and tax receipts, to other jurisdictions. We saw in the previous chapter that Alberta's government expressed this concern explicitly in the late 1960s and pleaded for national water safety standards that would trump competitive provincial rules. We'll question the basis for that fear in the next chapter.

Here, we continue to assess how Canada's "cooperative federalism," as it has sometimes been described, protects our water and the natural life-support systems that water travels through and sustains.

We have just seen how four decades of counting on provincial authorities has left Canadians subject to a patchwork of protections from coast to coast to coast—some capable, others not, but all degraded in the last decade by budget cuts in even the richest provinces. The disinclination of Canada's junior Crowns to accept a common interest in meeting a national level of protection for drinking or waste water, or to take seriously their own commitments to enforce regulations entrusted to them, doesn't have to be the legal last word, however. That is largely up to the senior Crown.

Legislation currently in force and Confederation's founding documents empower Canada's federal Crown to take robust action to defend water, waterways, and the life that inhabits them. The Constitution gives the federal Crown exclusive jurisdiction over fisheries, both inland and marine. Those powers extend across jurisdictional boundaries and beyond the shores of rivers and lakes to the landscapes that impact their ecological health. Navigation and the water supporting it are other areas of exclusive federal authority.[3]

Legislation such as the Canada Water Act and the Canadian Environmental Protection Act rests on these constitutional foundations. Certainly the Athabasca—the river that flows through Alberta's oil lands into the Mackenzie, impacting the Northwest Territories— qualifies as an example on all counts: crossing jurisdictional borders, it supports both fish and commercial navigation.

Beyond that, the federal Crown has nearly limitless power as the ultimate civil authority for Canada when no other authority is capable of responding. In constitutional language, this is expressed as its residual power to legislate for the "peace, order, and good government" of the country and to undertake any activity on Canadian soil it deems of general advantage to the country.[4]

Any of these constitutional authorities could be invoked to authorize the protection of any Canadian waterway or its sustaining watershed.

The federal Crown's undiminished authority is most apparent in the case of regulations issued under various pieces of enacted federal legislation, even where the enforcement of these has been ceded to provinces. The equivocal success of generations of federal-provincial agreements notwithstanding, the authority provided by Parliament under the Fisheries Act, Water Act, CEPA, and other legislation to enforce their requirements remains active (despite some recent whittling away by the current Harper ministry). Likewise, federal agencies tasked with accomplishing various of their objectives also endure: an example is the venerable and too-little-known Canadian Wildlife Service, the successor to a force created almost a century ago to protect migratory waterfowl.

Plainly, where provinces have failed to step up to defend Canadians' natural security, our federal Crown *could* act on its own legislated authority to do so.

Has it?

Now and again, here and there, yes.

After residents reported dead fish floating in Alberta's Battle River in June 2009, Environment Canada charged the town of Ponoka under the federal Fisheries Act with releasing toxic levels of municipal sewage into the river. The town pled guilty to a single charge and was fined $3,750 and ordered to pay an additional $66,250 into a fund to restore habitat in the river.[5]

On another occasion, the federal agency determined that Charlottetown had been polluting its harbour by allowing waste to overflow from its sewage treatment plant. In November 2011, Environment Canada gave the PEI capital six weeks to develop a plan to prevent further overflows—and demanded it send the agency a note every sixty days thereafter to let it know how the plan was coming along. It did not issue any penalty.[6]

The federal agency has, on rare occasions, even been known to imprison offenders—sort of. A month before it scolded Charlottetown, Environment Canada finally brought to a successful conclusion its six-year pursuit of a British Columbia farmer who had ignored recurring fines and orders to keep his cattle from damaging Robin Creek—a fish-bearing stream in the province's interior. A B.C. court sentenced John Boonstra to three days in jail—one day for each violation of the Fisheries Act—and ordered him to pay $17,000 to a habitat-restoration fund.[7]

Two smallish cities and a rural farmer seem modest targets for an agency possessing the full weight of the federal Crown, but they are fairly representative. By contrast, prosecutions of large industrial corporations whose activities have the potential to impact entire watersheds have been rare.

In 1984, the Law Reform Commission of Canada, a non-partisan legal research body, assessed how well the first Trudeau-era round of delegations of environmental duty from the federal to provincial Crowns had gone. Its verdict: "The federal delegation of enforcement authority amounts to a virtual abdication of responsibility... and has promoted discrepancies in the nature of enforcement responses across Canada."[8]

Four years after that judgement, the Mulroney government enacted the Canadian Environmental Protection Act. CEPA established timelines and targets for preventing the release to the environment of harmful chemical toxins. In the first year or two of its existence, Environment Canada conducted some two thousand inspections a year of facilities handling or releasing pollutants to ensure that they were meeting its objectives. But the effort flagged over the following decade. In 1998, a parliamentary committee warned that inadequate funding was impairing its enforcement.[9] By the turn of the millennium, inspections under CEPA had fallen by two-thirds from its early years, even while Canadian industry and its pharmacopoeia of potent new chemicals had both expanded.

The broad goals established in the CEPA legislation had been given traction in detailed regulations covering thirty eight aspects of environmental management. Each affected thousands of municipalities and businesses. Remarkably, in the nine years between 1998 and 2007, violations of these resulted in only thirty-four convictions.[10]

In late 2001, federal environment commissioner Johanne Gélinas reported to Parliament that budget cuts and executive lassitude had left the federal Crown's ability to defend Canada's water adrift. "Declining and unstable funding to federal departments has significantly impaired their ability to achieve environmental objectives and meet Canada's international commitments," Gélinas wrote. "Some of the government's stated priorities and policies... exist only on paper."[11]

Nearly a decade later, a successor commissioner again reviewed Environment Canada's performance. In a damning indictment of feckless inactivity, Scott Vaughan described a department that by 2009 had abandoned many of its own rules entirely, had no idea how to go about meeting even its core constitutional obligations, and was incapable of determining whether its efforts were effective in any case.

Although legislation and numerous sets of industry-specific regulations give Environment Canada wide power, Vaughan discovered that it had effectively raised a white flag over all but two of these; it continued to enforce its rules only on pulp and paper making and metal mining. With respect to its duty under the 141-year-old Fisheries Act to prevent the release of "substances harmful to fish in waters they frequent" (a description that cannot help but evoke the plight of the deformed creatures swimming in the Athabasca), Vaughan reported, "Environment Canada has not clearly identified what it has to do to fulfill its responsibility."[12]

The agency had stopped reviewing the natural security implications of many "low-risk" industrial projects entirely, Vaughan added, "relying instead on project proponents to voluntarily comply with habitat protection measures and conditions." But while it trusted, Environment Canada had no ability to verify that compliance followed—and seldom tried. "Moreover, the Department reduced enforcement activity by half and at the time of our audit," Vaughan reported, "had not yet hired habitat monitors to offset this reduction."

Two years later, Commissioner Vaughan put Environment Canada under scrutiny again. His report to Parliament in December 2011 found that "key challenges [in enforcement] have not been addressed."[13] The agency lacked adequate intelligence on potential violators. Enforcement officers were undertrained for their jobs.

Even more disturbing failures were found embedded in the very wording of the rules those officers were expected to apply. Nearly half of CEPA's regulations (41 percent) were so poorly written that they were probably unenforceable. One of these supposedly controlled the disposal of tetrachloroethylene, a solvent used in dry cleaning that has been linked to Parkinson's disease and is a suspected carcinogen.[14] Omissions in the regulation text, Vaughan found, meant that "officers do not have any enforcement measure at their disposal to stop or prevent a dry cleaner from disposing of tetrachloroethylene down a drain or in the garbage or allowing the release of this toxic substance from a leaking dry-cleaning machine."

Environment Canada, Vaughan concluded, could not determine whether "its enforcement activities are improving compliance or minimizing environmental damage and threats to Canadians."

Put that another way: as of 2011, the federal Crown agency on the front line of Canada's natural security defence *has no idea whether it's doing its job.*

That year, the environmental NGO Ecojustice (formerly Sierra Legal Defence) conducted its own review of federal environmental enforcement. It found that even though Environment Canada had added personnel since 2003, "the number of CEPA inspections, prosecutions and convictions has declined steadily." The same was true for the Fisheries Act. Moreover, convictions under CEPA in the three years preceding the report had carried an average penalty of just $10,524, "an amount," Ecojustice observed, "unlikely to deter large industrial actors from committing violations." In fact, in more than twenty years of CEPA enforcement, Environment Canada had collected a total of $2.4 million in penalties from violators—less than the Toronto Public Library collected from delinquent borrowers in 2009 alone.[15]

The North American Free Trade Agreement (NAFTA) often comes in for criticism from environmentalists. But a provision in the pact allows private citizens to petition the NAFTA Commission for Environmental Cooperation for an investigation if a signatory nation fails to enforce its own pollution laws.

In April 2010, Environmental Defence Canada, U.S.-based Natural Resources Defense Council, and three individuals invoked that

NAFTA provision to accuse Canada of failing to enforce its Fisheries Act or sanction oil sands companies for letting toxic compounds leak from tailing ponds into adjacent groundwater and the Athabasca River. Shortly afterward, Fraser Riverkeeper and the David Suzuki Foundation laid similar charges that Ottawa had failed to enforce the same act against a sewage plant releasing waste into the Fraser River at Vancouver.

Both complaints remain under investigation at this writing.

"We're out of options when it comes to trying to get the government to enforce its own laws," said Environmental Defence policy director Matt Price of the tactic. "This is one avenue where we can, at the very least, embarrass the government."

The Constitution and federal law notwithstanding, for more than four decades Canada's national leaders have shrunk from playing anything more than a supporting role on the environment, leaving the muscular work of defending the nation's water to others. A central aspect of that supporting role, however, and one that Ottawa has long embraced, has been research.

Water is a familiar mystery. It constitutes most of our physical being. We use it constantly. It transports oxygen through our veins and grain to our foreign customers. It is essential to industry and a participant in every biological process. Its safety today and security in the future hang heavily on our ability to anticipate how our decisions about water will resonate through the rest of our experience, from the intimate exchange of molecules within our bodies to the movements of weather systems across the continent and the resilience of our planetary life-support system. Some of these are well understood; others, not so much.

Underwriting science that sheds new light on such critical relationships is one of the most valuable public services the federal government can provide. Through a variety of channels, it supplies the lion's share of public support for science generally in Canada.[16]

Federal spending on water science took a practical turn in the 1970s. Several watershed agreements signed under the Canada Water

Act produced extensive bodies of research. Even now, Environment Canada continues to acknowledge an obligation to provide Canadians with information about water. The Canadian Environmental Protection Act "requires the government to maintain a system for monitoring environmental quality in Canada," an Environment Canada guide to the act states.[17]

Whether that information is sufficient for Canadians to know with confidence that our water is being defended and kept safe for our families and future is another matter entirely. The budget provided for Environment Canada to meet those objectives was cut by about 20 percent over the 1990s. Between 1992 and 2007, Environment Canada shed a quarter of its scientific and technical personnel. The Department of Fisheries and Oceans Canada (DFO), where much of the federal government's water science is located, lost a fifth of its research personnel.

Various federal Crown agencies once monitored water flows at 4,000 sites across the country. They now watch only 2,500.[18] In December 2010, environment commissioner Scott Vaughan revealed in testimony to Parliament that the federal government maintained precisely one water quality monitoring station downstream from Alberta's oil sands—and it was looking for pollution from pulp and paper mills.[19]

For nearly two decades, the documented decline in resources has corroded the federal Crown's ability to understand what is happening to the water and landscapes under its trust.[20]

An example is the hazard posed by oil spills. Daily occurrences in small volumes at gas docks and ship terminals in every province, spills of fuel gasoline and diesel oil, oil carried as cargo, or hydrocarbons from production sites are perhaps the leading cause of marine and aquatic environmental mega-disasters. The likelihood of such spills is a central factor in opposition to the expansion of pipelines to carry oil and gas from Alberta to British Columbia for sea shipment to Asia.

Yet the federal leaders beating the drum hardest to expand such shipments have almost no way of knowing what a spill would do to

Canada's Pacific coastline—or even whether one occurred. After decades of neglect, the federal Crown's coastal surveillance is so patchy that it "cannot accurately determine the actual size of spills, how many spills required onsite responses, how many spills required the use of Coast Guard equipment, and the results of the cleanup efforts," environment commissioner Vaughan revealed in 2010.[21] A year later, the DFO withdrew the field officers it had previously maintained along the B.C. coast to monitor fish habitat.

Advisors to Minister Kent warned him in 2011 that shortcomings in his department's research and data-gathering capabilities had left an "absence of scientific evidence" to support his forceful and frequent public assertions that Canada's oil sands were being responsibly developed.[22] But fossil fuel development is far from the only threat hanging over Canada's water. Changing climate has altered the timing and volume of rain and snowfall. Decades of development and the scouring of river currents have resculpted stream beds. Both alter areas likely to be at risk of flooding. The federal program that once mapped those risks no longer exists, however. Funding for it was dropped in the 1990s.

At the other end of the wild-weather spectrum, climate change is producing deeper, longer, and hotter droughts. The last of these, in 2001–02, cost the Canadian economy $5.8 billion. Federal support for research into droughts was cut off in 2010.[23]

Expanding populations in already settled regions such as southern Ontario, along with the rollout of hydraulic fracturing for gas recovery, have intensified pressure on groundwater while multiplying threats to its purity. Once contaminated, buried aquifers are effectively impossible to "clean." The pollution they contain may migrate and spread for years or decades.

That should underscore the urgency of knowing the water under our feet: its extent, its limits, and the unseen currents flowing between hidden underground pools. The Council of Canadian Academies pointed out in 2009 that the last—and fragmentary—effort to map Canada's groundwater had been made in 1967. Surveying continued, it noted, but at a glacial pace that would not see Canada's thirty most significant aquifers outlined for another two decades.[24]

The increase in deformed and cancerous fish in the lower Great Lakes and Athabasca River is suspected to be linked to chemical contaminants in their water—pollutants also suspected to lie behind similarly rising counts of birth and gender defects in humans and wildlife.

The 1999 CEPA mandated Environment Canada to review thousands of industrial chemicals then in use for their danger to humans and the environment. It took the agency until 2006 to choose an initial 200 high-priority substances for detailed review. Work on those was almost complete by the end of 2011. At the rate of progress to date, however, another 4,300 substances awaiting review would not be examined until 2020. By then, it must be guessed, industry will have introduced hundreds if not thousands of additional molecules into the environment.

The World Health Organization (WHO) held negotiations that led, in 2004, to the Bonn Charter. It sets out a best-practices "framework of institutional, managerial and operational requirements for assuring safe drinking water."[25] Organizations and water agencies from Australia, the United States, Britain, and other countries helped craft the charter.

"Notably," University of Alberta emeritus professor Steve Hrudey observed in a commentary on Canadian water policy, "no organization from Canada participated in this initiative."[26]

Refusing to defend Canada's water, failing to account for its present safety or expose threats to its future security, inflating rhetoric while deflating critical budgets, conflating "commitment" with accomplishment—indeed, every pusillanimous trend of the last few decades accelerated under the Harper Conservatives.

Brushing aside a decade of warnings that Canada's natural security was being left vulnerable, the Harper ministry stripped Environment Canada's diminished capacity further still. In August

2011, the agency decimated its remaining work force, giving notice to 776 physical scientists, biologists, chemists, and computer scientists that their positions could be cut within 90 days.[27] Fisheries and Oceans warned 275 of its professional and support staff to be ready to be tossed overboard.[28]

Lower-profile decisions shut down, defunded, or shackled advisory groups that had served as conduits for knowledge from the worlds of science and practical experience to government. In 2010, Transport Canada advised six regional advisory panels on oil spills—created under the Canada Shipping Act after the *Exxon Valdez* disaster in 1989—that their views on proposals to change marine safety rules were not required; it also revoked the panelists' authority to meet on their own initiative.[29]

The following year, Environment Canada ended support for the Canadian Environmental Network and the Canadian Foundation for Climate and Atmospheric Sciences. The former had linked generations of policy-makers to some six hundred organizations across a wide spectrum of environmental interests.[30] The foundation for climate sciences had co-funded critical water research with Canadian universities, flowing their discoveries back to Ottawa.[31] The theme of its final meeting held a particular irony: it discussed the critical role of science in ensuring Canadian water security.[32] A third consultative network, the Canadian Water Network, had its funding renewed after a review.[33]

The extent of the Harper ministry's apparent antipathy to scientific knowledge reached nearly comic depths when it revealed that it would not tolerate certain inquiries *even when they cost the taxpayer nothing.*

In early 2012, natural resources minister Joe Oliver learned that his department was examining the trade-off between environmental security and economic development on Canada's Pacific coast. Its study area north of Vancouver Island was one where tankers would be required to negotiate narrow coastal channels to pick up Alberta oil and gas, delivered there by a proposed pipeline, for shipment to Asia. While ministry personnel from Fisheries and Oceans were conducting the project, its costs were being covered by a private philanthropic environmental trust, the Gordon and Betty Moore Foundation.

As it happened, the U.S.-based foundation's $8.3 million contribution had also passed through the hands of a Canadian charity—the Tides Foundation—that Oliver had previously targeted for criticism as a conduit for foreign interference in Canada's energy politics. After pipeline promoter Enbridge Inc. complained to fisheries officials about the U.S.-funded research work, Oliver ended it.[34]

While cutting itself off from outside expertise and bleeding national agencies of the capacity to monitor Canada's natural security, the Harper government also seemed determined to keep whatever knowledge its remaining scientists might generate out of the hands of the public, which paid their salaries.

In 2007, Environment Canada instructed its researchers that they were no longer permitted to share their observations or analyses with the public through the media. Every interview request from a reporter was to be referred to the ministry's politically sensitive media office.[35]

The most overt suppression of knowledge purchased with Canadians' tax contributions occurred right under the roof of Parliament. In mid-July 2010, the government-dominated Standing Committee on Environment and Sustainable Development called an abrupt halt to eighteen months of taxpayer-funded hearings into pollution threats facing the Athabasca River. Copies of a draft report were destroyed.[36] Sixteen months later, the same committee again dropped its axe, this time on unfinished hearings into changes proposed to the Canadian Environmental Assessment Act.[37]

The reforms were among several the government undertook with the apparent intent of reducing the possibility that foreseen environmental damage would derail any business project. One such change removed responsibility for reviewing large energy projects—the majority of high-risk developments, from oil sand mines to gas pipelines—from the Canadian Environmental Assessment Agency entirely, giving the task to the National Energy Board, an agency more attuned by culture, history, and mandate to assisting industry.[38] The Harper government also moved to raise the threshold of project size requiring environmental assessments to reduce the number of projects reviewed annually from six thousand to a few hundred.[39] The change would drain the CEAA of a third of its staff and nearly half of its budget, the agency's director objected.[40]

Natural resources minister Oliver fired back, in a statement as striking for its logical contradiction as for its frankness. "We respect the integrity of the regulatory process," Oliver claimed, *but we do need to get these projects approved.*"[41] (Emphasis added.)

At times under Prime Minister Harper, the federal Crown simply redefined geography to help industry bypass environmental review. Invoking authority that had been created by an earlier Liberal government but seldom used, Conservative ministers took to approving requests from mining companies to redesignate living lakes as "tailings impoundment areas." The change allowed applicants to use the lakes as waste dumps without the expense or embarrassment of cataloguing the consequences in an environmental assessment process.

Science and national standard-setting are two roles in defence of water that the federal Crown accepts—even if it does not always fulfill them. A third is its constitutional responsibility to conduct Canada's relations with foreign governments.

With respect to water, this has in practice, until quite recently, meant managing our relationship with the United States. The melting of the Arctic has begun to expose potential frictions with both Denmark and Russia over underwater and marine resources there. But it is in more than 100 shared watersheds along 6,416 kilometres of the southern boundary and 2,475 kilometres of the western one between Canada and the United States that binational interests are most likely to lock horns—or find opportunities to work together.

Of these the most significant, economically, politically, and ecologically, is the vast eastern basin occupied by the five Great Lakes.

The Great Lakes Water Quality Agreement (GLWQA) originally signed nearly four decades ago by U.S. president Richard Nixon and

Prime Minister Pierre Trudeau has been renewed and expanded several times since. An update in 1978 added an array of persistent toxins to biological pollutants, such as phosphorus, that were targeted for reduction or elimination from lake water. Other updates in the 1980s identified numerous specific "areas of concern" in the lakes (including Hamilton Harbour), and the two signatory nations started cleaning them up. A fourth review, begun in 2006, was directed at adding three new annexes to the original agreement, covering habitat protection, response to climate change, and invasive species.

These negotiations appeared to conclude with the signing of a protocol to extend the venerable agreement in September 2012, this time at Canada's embassy in Washington. The renewed GLWQA did indeed contain commitments to research the impact of climate change, invasives, and ecosystem needs. But it had abandoned the specific commitments to action on the part of both nations, clear target dates for their accomplishment, and measurable indicators of their success that had distinguished the pacts of earlier decades. These critical substantive elements were still to be determined in further negotiations over the next half decade.[42]

The real measure of Canada's present commitment to the decades-long effort to restore the Great Lakes, however, can be read in its parsimony with resources. While the U.S. federal government has set aside $475 million in recent years to implement its Great Lake commitments, Canada's federal Crown scraped together just $8 million for its share of the cleanup.[43]

Most of what we need from government is done best by the government closest at hand. We ask municipalities to put water in the tap and take away the trash, and locally elected boards to oversee our schools. This subsidiarity principle has strong instinctive appeal, though it contains the seeds of disturbing unintended consequences. There is really not a lot we need in the way of public services that *only* Canada's federal Crown can provide.

There is, however, an irreducible minimum that comes, quite literally, with the territory. To be recognized by other powers, any authority claiming to wield national sovereignty must, for example, be capable of defending its state's borders—hence federal primacy in national defence, a role the Stephen Harper government embraced with enthusiasm on taking office in 2006. The maintenance of a stable currency is another essential national public good that not even the most radical libertarian disputes. But if defending the political integrity of the state and its coinage are inalienable functions of the Crown, so surely is sustaining its biological integrity, adequately supplied with clean water.

Many Canadians were caught by surprise when environment minister Kent, safely returned from a climate summit in South Africa in 2011, announced that Canada was withdrawing from the Kyoto accord on greenhouse gas reductions. Others perhaps were not. One of the first things advisors told Kent when he moved into his portfolio was that "Canadians generally feel that their governments do not go far enough in enforcing environmental laws."[44]

Canadians are not stupid. They are quite right about their governments. At neither provincial nor federal level have governments stood on guard for Canada's water.

Our most senior leaders, those acting for the Crown in right of Canada, for all of Canada's people, do not lack legal means to defend this country's water. What they have lacked is interest. The truth is that they have *chosen*, again and again, to expose Canada's natural security to attack, to attrition, to contamination, and to waste. Our water as a result is not as clean, as safe, or as secure as it could be.

SEVEN

Are We Rich Yet?

T HE QUESTION is loaded. What do we mean by "rich"? To say
that interpretations differ is an understatement.

"Wealth" has been interpreted in many ways: by acreage of
landholding, by number of slaves, by the ability to pay for lavish public entertainments. In parts of North Africa it is measured to this day
by the number of cattle owned. In North America it is on display in
trophy homes and the trappings of expensive pursuits: yachts or rare
cars. We are more inclined to count warm connections of family, or
the satisfactions of meaningful work, as reliable constituents of that
experience of "well-being" from which the word is derived. Nevertheless, in the last century the part of the world that participates in the
global economy has, for almost all public purposes, accepted a single
reductionist measure of this elusive quality.

This has been accompanied by the conversion of the wealthier parts
of the world to a new, secular, and remarkably catholic creed. Scarred
repeatedly by conflicts rooted in blood or faith, with spasms of geno-
cide in Europe, Asia, and Africa, liberal democracies in the last century
became skeptical of religion or ethnicity as the basis of civil order. Most
prohibited commercial or workplace discrimination on such grounds.

Outside the United States, religion lost influence as a guide to behaviour. Into the vacated space a new faith stepped forward, ecumenically free of deities. It offered a higher power that all could understand: greed. This faith was economics.

For most people, wealth is a subjective experience. To economists, it became a number: the gross national or domestic product of a province or a country. As secular wealth supplanted more traditional values, economic rationales trumped all others in political appeals to voters. With exceptions (typically in Canada around language and Quebec's place in the country), GDP became the accepted yardstick of political performance, its growth a form of shorthand for responsible management of the public interest.

There is much this measure overlooks—almost everything, as Robert Kennedy observed, "which makes life worthwhile"—and much it mischaracterizes. But let us accept it for the moment and ask our question in its narrow terms: does putting our water at risk, as we saw in the previous chapter that we have done, pay off in a bigger GDP?

Or to put the question another way: is it true, as generations of our leaders have told us and our present government insists, that to see our GDP climb, we must sacrifice our water's safety and security, along with the ecological life-support systems that it sustains?

To a point, the transformation of pre-colonial landscapes for a variety of purposes has incontestably inflated Canada's GDP. From breaking tall-grass prairie for grain farming to chewing up the boreal forest for bitumen, the conversion and extraction of natural resources directly transferred new value to the commercial books of the economy, without noting the corresponding debit from our natural-wealth account.

The "Bank of Nature," it's been joked, does not offer deficit financing, however. Biophysical transactions of energy and material are settled in real time. And as our resource demands have pushed the planet's countless interwoven budgets ever further out of equilibrium over the past quarter-century, the adjustments required to balance nature's accounts have begun to show up on humanity's.

Heat waves that incubated roaring fires in the forests around Moscow in 2010 also shrivelled Russia's wheat crops—sending grain prices soaring. A drought that began in Texas that year lasted into the one following, sending beef prices in the region into a U-shaped plunge and rebound, as ranchers slaughtered cattle they could no longer feed—flooding the market with carcasses—and subsequently were left with few head to offer. The drenched spring of 2011 prevented many Canadian Prairie farmers from sowing a crop. Fields that were planted later baked under drought.

A Swiss-based insurance research institute judged 2011 to be an *annus horribilus* for that industry all around, thanks to a record volume of claims arising from natural disasters. More than 90 percent of the year's 820 major disasters, roughly double the number typical of the 1970s, were weather related. "The number of natural catastrophes has been rising almost continuously since the 1980s," the report observed.[1]

Recognizing that we appear to be moving from the immemorial era of nature surplus that nurtured the emergence of our species to one of unprecedented natural scarcity, a few economists have begun to re-examine their conventional wisdom.

Michael Porter, a Harvard professor, was among the first to question whether protecting the environment must come at a cost to companies. Pollution, Porter reasoned, represents wasted resources—inefficiencies, in economic terms. Reducing those inefficiencies should, therefore, improve productivity. Many advisors on economic policy agree with that. But Porter argued more: that stringent but well-designed environmental regulation, especially a regime open to market dynamics or presenting incentives for performance, might trigger innovations that more than paid for the initial cost of a company's compliance.

That thesis was contentious in 1991, when Porter first presented it. Two decades later, a symposium of experts met at Montreal's McGill University to assess whether the experience of the years supported it. A review of economic literature prepared for the event buttressed at least one of Porter's theses: that strong environmental innovation could enhance, rather than impede, business productivity.

In one study, oil refineries in the Los Angeles area demonstrated substantially higher productivity than competitors in low-oversight states such as Texas, despite operating under much stricter regulations for air emissions. Other researchers examined Mexico's food-processing industry and found that the pressure of increasing regulation (not the "race to the bottom" that NAFTA's opponents had predicted) was improving productivity there as well. After a sweeping survey of data from more than four thousand companies in seven OECD countries, Montreal economist and business professor Paul Lanoie reported in 2010 a "positive and significant link between the perceived severity of environmental regulations" and business performance.[2]

Productivity is not profit, however. And Lanoie's study seemed to confirm the sentiment that regulations to protect the environment come at a cost to business profits. "The positive effect of innovations" in process or technology, his research team found, "does not outweigh the negative effect of the regulation itself. On balance, regulation appears to be costly."[3]

That judgement may have been premature, however—or at any rate, drawn from evidence collected too soon after regulations took effect. Lanoie and his associates also examined the impacts of tighter environmental regulation on businesses in seventeen Quebec manufacturing sectors. In these businesses, productivity dipped in the year after regulations took effect but recovered in the second year. Subsequent productivity gains more than offset the initial losses by the end of year four—especially among companies facing competition from beyond Quebec.[4]

Another study, conducted at the Massachusetts Institute of Technology in the mid-1990s, compared the economic performance of strongly regulated U.S. states (like California) against that of lightly regulated, "pollution haven" states (like Texas). It found "a very weak positive relationship—albeit one that is statistically insignificant—

between state environmentalism and economic performance." In other words, if strict environmental regulation of industry had any economic effect, it was probably slightly to the good. It certainly did no harm.

Inger Weibust also examined the question at length. She found much anecdotal evidence to confirm that political leaders, especially in federated provinces or states, are "hypersensitive to the possibility of impact on competitiveness whenever environmental regulations are contemplated."[5] Examples go back to the nineteenth century, when first-generation industrialists opposed controls on the coal smoke plaguing London and other British cities on the grounds that they would put them at a disadvantage to factories in Germany and the United States. True races to the bottom are rare, it turns out, but not unknown. Countries willing to provide "flags of convenience" to ships, imposing minimal safety requirements and letting risks play out on the high seas far from their shores, boast some of the world's largest merchant fleets.

"The paradox," Weibust writes, "is that governments appear to compete on environmental regulations and yet gain no economic or employment benefit from doing so."

The number of plant shutdowns that can be traced to the imposition of additional environmental requirements, compared with other causes—such as technological change, global reallocations of production, or corporate reorganizations—she reports, "are simply tiny." There is little evidence that environmental regulations either deter investment or encourage disinvestment (capital flight). Rather, some research indicates that where plants are at risk of closing under stricter rules, enforcement agents systematically relax their scrutiny to ensure they continue to operate. One study, Weibust reports, done for the OECD in 1997, concluded that "jobs are more likely to be at risk where environmental standards are low and no innovation . . . is taking place."

"Estimates of regulatory costs and job losses caused by environmental protection," Weibust was forced to conclude, "are poorly substantiated and politically motivated."

Those seeking to scrap regulations seldom acknowledge the *benefits* those may also bring to the economy. More and more research is focusing on that missing value, and it can be large.

An official of China's State Council—roughly, its national cabinet—conceded in 2006 that pollution effectively nullified all the gains posted by that country's blazing 10 percent annual growth in GDP. Poisoned rivers, advancing deserts, and polluted air were imposing additional costs every year in health care and lost productivity that offset every yuan of nominal financial gain.[6]

Britain, a small country with a large population in the crosshairs of climate change, conducted one of world's first thorough inventories of the value it receives from its ecosystems—in essence, the annual cash value to the U.K. of its habitat. Completed in 2011, it calculated that one single ecotype alone—coastal wetlands and inland marshes, bogs and fens, and the communities of plants, insects, birds, worms, amphibians, and mammals whose collective "invisible hand" (or wing) maintains their equilibrium—provided Britain's economy with an average of $2.4 billion worth of water purification, water supply, and coastal protection each year. Wetlands provided inland flood protection worth an additional $577 million.[7]

A related finding suggests that Canadian municipalities may have been investing unwisely in heavily engineered "big pipe" drainage systems for storm water. A comparison of the cost and return of alternative strategies for handling storm water in three U.S. cities with high rainfall (Portland, Oregon; Seattle; and Portland, Maine) revealed that investing in watershed improvements that allowed natural features and ecosystems to absorb and buffer storm flows was between 7.5 and 200 times *cheaper* than building more catch basins, storm sewers, and engineered outfalls.[8]

In 2011, the city of Philadelphia opted not to spend $6 to $8 billion to expand its system of storm sewers and catchment tanks. Instead, it invested $2 billion to replace hard paved surfaces that sheet storm water into drains with green spaces and absorptive surfaces that will allow heavy rainfall to soak into the ground, replenish aquifers, and relieve pressure on local waterways.[9]

Canada's own Council of Ministers of the Environment (CCME) commissioned a study of the costs and benefits of upgrading every municipal sewage treatment plant in Newfoundland and New Brunswick. It found that the investment would yield a net positive return to the economies of the two provinces of $204 million and $450 million, respectively, over the twenty-five-year lifespan of the upgraded infrastructure. Those returns would come from better health (and correspondingly lower medical costs), marketable benefits from increased tourism to a more attractive region, and increased property values as result of the same boost in local amenity values.

Were the same return established on a national scale, it would imply a potential net benefit to Canada's GDP of $500 million to $1 billion a year. To put it another way, by *not* improving waste treatment, we may actually end up $500 million to $1 billion a year *poorer.*

In 2010, an Ottawa consulting firm conducted a cost-benefit analysis for Ontario's Ministry of the Environment of potential investments to protect and restore degraded wetland and aquatic habitat around the Great Lakes. IFC Marbek resource consultants weighed the return on a five-year ecological rehabilitation program from a basket of direct and indirect ecoservices over the quarter-century after the investments ended. These ranged from flood control and recreation to better water quality and contained greenhouse gasses and might reasonably have been expected to continue indefinitely as long as the restored ecosystems flourished. Calculated nonetheless over twenty-five years, with a social "discount rate" of 3.5 percent, Marbek's calculations forecast benefits that outweighed costs everywhere, in many places by huge multiples.[10]

At the low end, restoring streams in the Toronto area would deliver benefits estimated to be nearly double their cost. Doing the same around Prince Edward Bay in eastern Lake Ontario would give back benefits eight times the invested cost. Wetland is more productive than stream margins. Its restoration and protection would return even higher ratios of benefits to cost, from 13:1 in Prince Edward Bay to a high of *35.2:1* in the Toronto region.

Research is exposing other economic costs that polluters fail to pay. In an ironic nod to the GDP, environmental economists at Vermont's Middlebury College and Yale University in Connecticut have created a grimly illuminating measure of industry's "gross external damages," or GED. The novel measure attempts to capture social cost, the damage an industry causes that is not reflected on its balance sheet or in economic data. Examining only one environmental hazard—air pollution—in a single year (2002), the investigators calculated various industries' GED and set it against the value each was known to add to America's GDP.[11]

For seven industries—coal and oil-fired power plants (studied separately), stone quarrying, sewage treatment, solid waste incineration, petroleum and coal derivative processing, and, oddly, marinas—the ratio of GED to GDP was greater than one. Those industries' emissions to the air (not counting any other pollution or negative social cost they caused) incurred identifiable losses to the U.S. economy that were greater than their positive contribution that year. The worst case was that of liquid petroleum used to generate electricity: its full cost to America's economy outweighed its contribution by more than *five to one*.

Public health researchers are also drawing links between landscapes altered for economic ends—such as forest cleared for agriculture—and epidemics with the potential to be both tragic and costly. Increasing deforestation in the Amazon by just 4 percent, one study found, generated a jump there of 40 percent in malaria cases.[12]

Farming enjoys a default image in the urban imagination of fresh air and green fields. The childhood impression created by colourful play sets and counting books featuring Farmer Mary's cows and chickens, however, is far from the reality of industrial food production. Dairy farming has been a source of manure pollution in eastern Canada's rivers. Manitoba grain and canola fields release sediment and fertilizer into Lake Winnipeg, feeding its annihilating algal blooms. Several of the places where male dace minnows have vanished from Alberta's Oldman River are immediately downstream from intensive livestock operations—feedlots—where hundreds or thousands of animals are concentrated in a few hectares of manure-soaked paddock.

The impairment of ecological services incurred by some of these practices, and the damage to the economy that results, are under mounting scrutiny. In Manitoba, for instance, research suggests that each hectare of land a farmer ploughs and harrows before seeding, instead of managing by no-till methods, costs him and his fellow citizens $143—the price of cleaning silt from water infrastructure downstream and lost services and income from Lake Winnipeg.[13] That annual charge to the public is close to half the $310 that a typical hectare of Manitoba farmland planted in barley earned its owner in 2009 and an appreciable percentage even of the $840 the year's most valuable crop, canola, might have brought in.[14]

British investigators found that municipalities and utilities in Britain were bearing $357 million in costs annually to repair damage done by farm runoff to water infrastructure and to remove agricultural contaminants from tap water.[15] In the United States, others worked out that excess nitrogen and phosphorus washed off heartland farms was causing American waterways to eutrophy, lowering their biological and economic productivity by $2.2 billion a year.

Far from impeding prosperity, stricter environmental regulation may, just as Michael Porter predicted, enhance it.

Early in 2012, the Chesapeake Bay Foundation, a non-profit entity focussed on preserving the storied estuary, reported that U.S. federal mandates to improve the water flowing into it would create 230,000 new jobs—more than *ten times* the number forecast to be created by an oil pipeline proposed to be built from Alberta to the Texas refinery belt along the Gulf coast.[16]

By 2020, the U.S. Environmental Protection Agency estimated, its regulations to curtail pollution in the air Americans breathe will prevent nearly a quarter of a million deaths a year and save 17 million days of work lost to sickness, for a total annual economic value of $2 trillion; complying with the regulations will cost industry about $65 billion that year.[17]

Researchers for the World Bank reached a similar conclusion about Europe's plan to sharply restrict the use and release of toxic and exotic chemicals. As noted in Chapter 4, the European Union's Registration, Evaluation, Authorisation and Restriction of Chemicals (REACH) regulation, instituted in 2007, obliges any company that imports or manufactures more than a metric tonne of a material to register it with a central database in Helsinki, along with information about its effects on human health and the environment.[18] Over time, REACH requires manufacturers to replace extremely toxic compounds with more benign alternatives.

A review by the World Bank forecast that the system will take fifteen years to fully institute, costing governments and businesses $3.5 to $6.5 billion. But it will also save Europe's health care system, along with all the public and private parties that pay into it, $60 billion over the same time: a *more than ten to one* return on investment.[19]

If Porter is right and pollution represents wasted resources and inefficient production, Canadian industry is underperforming compared with its continental competitors.

According to information collected from each of the three NAFTA nations by the Commission for Environmental Cooperation, Canadian factories were worse polluters than their American counterparts in 15 of 20 matched industrial categories. On average, Canadian facilities released or shipped off-site for treatment *twice as much pollution* as U.S. factories. Even though Canadian facilities accounted for only 7.4 of the total number surveyed, they released 35.8 percent of the pollution streamed into local waterways. In some categories of effluent, Canadian plants released more pollution in absolute volume than all the factories in the United States, which has 10 times our population.[20]

Additional analysis of the data by Canadian researchers revealed that Canadian factories are also significantly less efficient than American equivalents. Factories here created one and a half times as much pollution and toxic waste for each dollar of produced value, and for each job created, as their U.S. competitors did.[21]

Nor does Canadian industry appear to be improving its performance much. Researchers found that while U.S. facilities reduced emissions to the air by 45 percent between 1995 and 2003—and by implication improved their materials efficiency by a comparable figure—Canadian industry achieved barely a 2 percent improvement.[22] A 2011 update of the Commission for Environmental Cooperation's earlier cross-NAFTA comparison of pollutant releases found that *Canadian facilities continued to release slightly more waste to surface water bodies, in total absolute terms, than U.S. counterparts* (115 million kilograms versus 113 million kilograms).[23]

Some of the surprising equivalency may result from different reporting requirements in the two countries (most of the reporting Canadian polluters were municipalities; most of the American ones, industry). Nonetheless, it seems apparent that Canadian facilities possess the same technical means as their U.S. counterparts to reduce polluting releases but have often chosen not to implement them.

If other research surveyed here is valid, Canadians are paying the price for that failure in unnecessarily high health costs, foregone productivity, neglected innovation, and lost wealth, both financial and intangible. That should cause us to question our leaders' insistence that we can become wealthier while our environment deteriorates. The opposite is the case: the emerging recognition that pollution amounts to economic waste simply underscores the folly of abandoning Canada's natural security in the belief it will advance the economy.

Failure to account for the cost to citizens of polluted streams, lakes scummed in algae, or other environmental injuries distorts public decision making.

A relevant example is the federal government's devotion to the misnamed notion of "smart" regulation. Introduced in the mid-2000s, that doctrine demands that any regulation of industrial activity proposed in the public interest—limits on its use of fresh water, for example—not only be scrutinized for direct and indirect costs to government and industry but also demonstrate effects that would produce GDP-visible economic gains. In thus shifting the onus of regulation from protection of the public to inflating economic throughput, "smart" choices proceed from the assumption that whatever problem initiated the need for regulation—closed beaches, deformed fish, dying citizens—it is secondary to raw economic growth. In this light, no environmental damage may be too great if it improves the GDP. A focus on immediate costs to business ignores the evidence that fully accounting for nature's scarcity through its effective protection will ignite innovation, inspire more efficient use of materials, and promote greater productivity, sustainability, and ultimately profits for enterprise. Instead, "smart" regulation's "economic impact" test requires proponents of new protection for water or any other public interest to anticipate the unknowable: how creative businesses may innovate in response to environmental constraints.

Confronting such challenges, public officials considering whether to respond to an emerging public concern, such as the presence of exotic chemicals in Canadian drinking water, might well conclude that their political masters were categorically opposed to *any* regulation—and suggest nothing. One of us witnessed just such a chilling effect on the problem-solving initiative of senior advisors to a succession of Canadian ministers of the environment through the late 1980s and into the 1990s.

If so-called smart regulation amounted to dumb disregard for real problems and costs, Canada's federal government has been even more obtuse about other linkages between environment and economy.

Numerous authorities, including the National Round Table on the Environment and the Economy (NRTEE), the Organisation for Economic Co-operation and Development (OECD), and even the International Energy Agency (IEA), which tracks world petroleum flows, among other duties, have pointed out the incoherence of subsidizing activities such as fossil fuel extraction and use, which degrade natural wealth, while taxing others that may be non-polluting or even environment enhancing, such as the purchase of weatherstripping.

In a comparison of environmentally positive taxes as a percentage of GDP, Canada ranks in twenty-fourth place among the twenty-five

OECD countries surveyed. Moreover, between 1995 and 2005, the ratio of Canadian environmental taxes to GDP slipped from 1.7 to 1.2 percent. Denmark, by contrast, levied "green" taxes equivalent to 4.8 percent of its GDP—and enjoyed the best environmental ranking within the OECD.[24]

For a nation whose prosperity has been built on nature's bounty, Canadian policy has been strangely resistant to acknowledging the connection between economic and ecological wealth. Instead, we pretend that our extractive economy can endlessly appropriate value from the physical environment without recording the debit to our natural wealth, taking no account of consequential costs to our health and other aspects of our material prosperity and without acknowledging mounting ecological liabilities such as the rising incidence of floods, droughts, seasonal water contamination, and harvest failures.

In short, we have systematically failed to put an adequate price on the ecological risk attending our economic activity.

This has had a predictable effect, one more familiar in discussions of financial lending but equally true here. In the financial world, people who borrow money without any sanction for failing to pay it back are said to be in *moral jeopardy*. When the recent collapse in house prices in the United States left many homebuyers owing more on their mortgage than their property was worth, conservative commentators repeatedly raised the incitement to moral jeopardy as an argument against public measures to reduce their debts (an argument not applied to large financial houses facing giant losses). Ignoring our looming environmental liabilities, however, places our entire modern economy under a thickening cloud of moral jeopardy with consequences far more onerous to contemplate than an underwater mortgage.

Some of these are becoming apparent, even in the most conventional of commodity marketplaces. In mid-2011, according to documents revealed by a media inquiry, senior officials warned environment minister Peter Kent that the government's inability to present "credible scientific information" that Canada's unconventional oil resources were being developed in an environmentally safe manner "represents a growing threat to the economic future of the industry... affecting the industry's ability to raise capital from and sell into foreign market(s)."[25]

Other frictions loom. Several treaties between Canada and the United States specify the volume of water that each country must allow to flow into the other where various streams cross the international border. Canada's government was warned a decade ago that alterations in rain and snowfall as a result of climate change would make it impossible for either country to meet these commitments in some seasons. Until now, those warnings have prompted neither serious national efforts to stem climate change nor diplomatic initiatives to bring Canada's international commitments into line with environmental reality.

Several important transnational rivers—the Milk and Souris, which have water apportionment agreements, and the Red, which doesn't but ought to—are in what Canadians call the Prairies and Americans refer to as the Midwest. The last of these, the Red River, flows north from the upper tier of Midwest U.S. states into Lake Winnipeg, draining eventually into Hudson Bay, creating the potential to spark particularly sharp conflict.

Climate change is bringing new threats to upstream communities in North Dakota: too little water in some seasons, too much in others. To both problems, local residents propose engineered responses. Some of these would transfer water from the Missouri River basin to the south (which drains into the Mississippi and Gulf of Mexico) into tributaries of the Red. The proposed transfers might relieve periodic water shortages in North Dakota, but they raise concerns for Canadians downstream. Proponents of the transfers argue that without them, the only water left to flow across the border during dry spells will be North Dakota's treated sewage. Critics worry the water may carry unwanted organisms alien to the northern river system.[26]

Several North Dakota cities, including the capital of Bismarck, have been threatened repeatedly as the Red has flooded each spring since 1992.[27] In response, some officials propose digging a variety of diversion channels (similar to one that protects Winnipeg) to divert high water around the affected cities.[28] Other Dakotans, living around the ominously named Devils Lake, complain that it is growing as a result of rising precipitation, inundating property. They also want to drain the extra water into a tributary of the Red.[29]

Any of these projects would have impacts for Manitobans downstream. An absence of clear and mandatory Canadian national water standards, however, weakens our standing in any future negotiations to mitigate those effects. Inadequate and inconsistent monitoring of waterways for volume and quality puts into question whether Canadian diplomats would even be equipped with a clear picture of the hydrology at risk. Lacking sufficient "credible scientific information" to establish the present state of southern Manitoba's most important river, they would be poorly positioned to protect its future security.

Identical handicaps stand in the way of equitable solutions to similar tensions elsewhere. Mines proposed in northern British Columbia could pollute rivers that flow into Alaska. The developments alarm scientists, environmentalists, and profitable fishing and tourism industries that rely on the ecoservices sustained by clean water.[30]

The rivers that flow east from the Rocky Mountains, watering Canada's most intensive belt of irrigated agriculture, in southern Alberta, before flowing on to fill the taps of communities across Saskatchewan and Manitoba, have been managed since 1969 under a three-province agreement on apportionment.[31] It divides the rivers' flow among the three Prairie provinces, setting annual allocations that are measured at their respective boundaries.

Few regions have seen such unequivocal impacts from climate change and rising human demand for water. Temperatures around Lethbridge, in the heart of Alberta's $7.6 billion[32] agribusiness corridor, were 2 °C warmer in the first decade of this century than in the second decade of the last (when records commenced). But rain and snowfall were down by more than 18 percent over that time.[33] An even more dramatic change was invisible but alarmed the few who took note. By early in the new century, researchers estimated that rising evapotranspiration (ET) around Lethbridge would soon be clawing back nearly half again as much of the region's water income as it had in the 1900s.

Dwindling mountain glaciers, more water pulled from streams to irrigate timothy grass and table vegetables, and amped-up evaporation during hotter, drier summer days have left little water in riverbeds to flow east. By mid-August, barely one-tenth as much water as in the twentieth century flows past Saskatoon in the key main stem of the South Saskatchewan River.[34] That not only means less water available to that city but water that is dirtier, warmer, and more expensive to clean up to potable standards, and that has less capacity to dilute liquid waste from sewage plants. The water that any community downstream must treat for drinking and bathing will have that much more concentrated sewage content to neutralize or remove.

Echoing events from a century earlier, when sewage from Buffalo ignited typhoid outbreaks at the eastern end of Lake Ontario, declining water quality in Prairie rivers may place downstream cities such as Saskatoon at the mercy of upstream industry in Alberta. The alternatives are inescapable: beefed-up water treatment and conservation downstream or beefier waste treatment and containment upstream.

Technology exists for either, but it may not come from Canada.

Worsening degradation and acute shortages of water in less-favoured parts of the world have cultivated a flowering of invention. Much of it has occurred in Israel, one of the world's most water-challenged countries, now a leader in technology for water efficiency and desalination. With more water per citizen than any other country on Earth, Canada barely makes a ripple in the $500 billion annual global marketplace for water-related services and technologies.

To a degree, that is a matter of categorization. Canada is among the top five exporters of farm and "agri-food" products, and food, of course, is largely water. But water is used to make every other product as well. And in global trade of this so-called virtual water—the water embedded in other products or commodities—Canada looms large indeed. Although Canadians import virtual water as well, incorporated in everything from California lettuce to iPads from China, we are the world's second-largest net exporter of it.

Much of our virtual water leaves in the form of grains and other agricultural exports. Our exports of oil extracted from bitumen represent the virtual daily departure of three to four large *Exxon Valdez*–size tanker loads of water as well (that much having been rendered unfit for further use during the processing of the crude).[35] Collectively, Canadian product exports are estimated to ship abroad about sixty cubic kilometres of water[36]—roughly half a year's flow of British Columbia's Fraser River—annually. The natural account of some countries receiving these exports would be bankrupt without them. Egypt, for example, relies on virtual water imported as food for the equivalent of a quarter of its actual supply.[37]

Such markets are expected to expand greatly in the decades ahead. The world's human population, now estimated at 7 billion,[38] is forecast to add another 2 billion mouths within forty years—if they can all be fed. Many will expect more meat and varied diets than their grandparents ate. To satisfy them, the Food and Agriculture Organization of the United Nations (FAO) estimates that the world's farmland will need to produce 70 percent more food in 2050 than it does now—notwithstanding its dwindling extent and degrading soils.[39] Canada is among relatively few countries in the world with the potential to increase food production and export enough to bite off a significant part of that goal.

Together with the world's demand for minerals, fossil fuels, and other natural resource commodities, its appetite for food is likely to be a major contributor to Canada's prosperity in the century of nature scarcity. But all these industries are voracious consumers of water.

By the draw of geography, Alberta hosts two of Canada's most water-intensive clusters: irrigated agriculture in the south and water-intensive energy extraction in the north. It is also the country's driest province, in some regions getting even drier. In much of its south, Alberta no longer gives out new licences to take water from its rivers. Increasingly, it will face hard choices as competing economic users demand opportunities. Similar choices confront other regions where population centres and economic activity tax available water sources—among them, southern Ontario and British Columbia's Okanagan Valley.

As decision makers better understand the water requirements of living ecosystems, and the essential services they provide, their choices should reserve more water for nature than was often the case in the past. But water must and will be extracted from nature for the human economy to function. Clearly, it should be a priority to make the best use possible of every litre of that water. And although the GDP-visible, dollar-denominated return on a litre of water ought not to be the only consideration in how it is allocated once municipal services and ecological needs are satisfied, it is nevertheless germane to ask which of several competing commercial uses of water will return the greatest value to the economy.

Public bodies facing these kinds of choices do not know where to direct water to secure its greatest economic return. Private interests seeking return on investment are equally in the dark about where water is available in the supply and quality their plans require, or for how long. These uncertainties handicap Canadian enterprise and frustrate its beneficial public management.

"We simply don't have the information we need... to understand which activities provide the most economic benefit per volume of water used," venture capitalist Nicholas Parker wrote in the introduction to a 2011 study of water's contribution to the Canadian economy.[40]

Despite well-stoked fears, international trade in large volumes of water itself has not yet materialized and may not for some time yet. Water is heavy and expensive to move. In most, if not all, potential markets for "bulk" water sales, treating or protecting local supplies are much cheaper choices.

What is recorded in global accounts as trade in water-related goods and services, therefore, refers to equipment (sensors, pumps, laboratories), materials (treatment or testing chemicals), and human services (engineering waterworks, consulting on environmental impacts, project management). Sales in that market sector were forecast to more than double by 2020, to $1 trillion a year.[41] Only in hydraulic engineering could Canadian companies claim a significant presence.

If necessity begets creativity, Canadians have rarely been forced to be inventive about water. But as the report Nicholas Parker introduced noted, "inability to distinguish higher- from lower-value water uses...handicaps efforts" to expand this country's share of more than $500 billion dollars the rest of the world is already spending every year on services and technology to make better use of its own water.

By every measure, Canada's relative abundance of clean, fresh water ought to be an asset whose value can only rise in a crowded, thirsty, and warming world. Yet our failure to collect and release detailed information about our water's location, volume, temperature, contaminants, and flow, or the vitality of its associated water-bearing ecosystems, means that decision makers must resort to guesswork and the public is vulnerable to unsupported claims, threats, or assurances.

The question we asked at the outset of this chapter was "Are we getting richer by endangering the safety of our water today and its future security?" The answer turns out to be, as most are, more complicated than a simple yes or no.

The "development" of Canada's lakes, forests, minerals, and prairies has enriched many Canadians and made the country one of the wealthiest by economic measure of any on Earth. But the metric used to make that judgement is deeply flawed and fails to account for the decline of natural assets converted into financial ones. On top of that, our leaders' failure to closely monitor the stock and flows of our natural wealth beyond its one-time extractive value leaves us unable to say what our economic wealth has cost us in injuries to our health, overpayment for water services that nature might deliver less expensively, and the opportunity cost of other foregone ecoservices.

The value of our remaining ecoservices can only rise. In the new and unprecedented experience of nature scarcity, much of what was up is down, and what was down is up. But not all things. The law of supply and demand is as reliable as ever. Scarcity drives value.

Biological and ecological services that both depend upon and produce water will constitute the coming century's overarching scarcity and its highest source of value.

The year 2011 experienced a staggering assortment of strange turns in weather. Manitoba, where a cold, wet winter and spring produced historic flooding, ended the year with one of its driest summers on record and more days hotter than 30°C than in the previous three years combined.

"I remember talking to one farmer," Environment Canada weatherman David Phillips told a Portage la Prairie news outlet, "and he said, 'I could have applied for flood insurance and drought insurance at the same time.' It just sort of added to the bizarreness, the weird and the wildness and the wackiness of what the weather had been."[42]

We have little doubt that weather observers will be saying much the same thing for years to come. Increasingly volatile mood swings in the climate—our ultimate provider of water—will drive escalating spikes in food and commodity prices, disrupt other water- and weather-dependent economic activities such as tourism and energy production, and incur mounting losses to water-related disaster damage. Rising individual and business losses are likely to contribute to volatility in politics as well.

Underpricing the health and environmental risk of ecosystem and water degradation on a global scale has brought us climate change, invisible molecular threats to our health, and a reckless extraction of energy and other resources that we know we cannot sustain. As our species confronts an existential rebalancing of its accounts with nature in the next quarter-century, Canada holds ecological assets of great value but is unequipped to use them wisely—or even to know what condition they are in and what benefits they are able to provide.

If wasting our water and allowing it to become dirty and contaminated was profitable in the old economy of nature surplus, in the new one of nature scarcity it won't be affordable. Burning through our natural capital may have made us rich once. Now it's probably making us poorer, and it will certainly do so in the future.

EIGHT

How About Healthy?

PROVINCES, as we've noted more than once, are the front-line defenders of most Canadians' water. But not of all Canadians'. Provincial jurisdiction ends at the boundary of First Nations reserve communities. Within their borders, the *federal* Crown has constitutional responsibility for ensuring essential public services such as safe, reliable water and sanitary waste disposal. There is no better place to take the measure of how well the federal government truly fulfills its oft-voiced commitment to protect the safety and security of Canada's water.

By any standard, it has done appallingly.

If you are a Canadian living in one of these communities, the odds that your tap water may be unsafe are nearly one in three.[1] Roughly one community like yours in six is living under a water warning. There's a good chance it's been that way for years. Then again, even running water that must be boiled may put you ahead of your neighbours: in reserve communities served by the federal Crown, the chances that water comes into the house in buckets are *ninety times* those of other Canadians. By the federal government's own admission, roughly five thousand homes in places where it is the sole public authority lack basic tap water and indoor toilets. Ottawa has conceded itself, in international filings, that "[t]he incidence of water-borne diseases is several times higher in First Nations communities, than in the general population, in part because of the *inadequate or non-existent water treatment systems*."[2] (Emphasis added.)

"We have water fountains in the community store," Ian Knott, a band councillor in northern Manitoba's Wasagamack First Nation, told CBC Radio in 2011. "For sewage, we still use outdoor washrooms."[3]

Later that year, Attawapiskat, a community of 1,800 on a river of the same name that flows through northern Ontario into James Bay, became a symbol of national disgrace when the Red Cross had to step in to provide humanitarian aid to scores of families living without running water in trailers, canvas and plywood shanties, and even tents as winter temperatures plunged. (It subsequently became a charged icon of both federal dereliction and First Nations' exhausted patience when the community's chief, Theresa Spence, began a hunger strike within sight of Parliament Hill to demand a meeting with the federal Crown's senior figures—Prime Minister Harper and Governor General David Johnson—escalating the Idle No More movement of protest and resistance.)

At Pikangikum, another northwestern Ontario community under federal stewardship, 95 percent of nearly four hundred homes were without indoor plumbing. The federal government installed a water treatment plant there in 1995, but it was connected to fewer than two dozen homes. That's probably just as well: its intake pipe was placed downstream from a sewage lagoon. A provincial medical team sent at the community's request to investigate Pikangikum's plight in 2006 found what one of its members described as "a level of neglect that almost appeared purposeful," marked by a heightened incidence of urinary and gastrointestinal infections, as well as eye/ear and skin infections—all of which "could be attributed to the lack of an adequate and safe water supply system."[4]

Several thousand more Canadians obliged to rely on federal standards of service in northern Manitoba face similar conditions. In the communities of St. Theresa Point, Garden Hill, Red Sucker Lake, and Wasagamack, the majority of homes lack piped water and indoor toilets. Residents dip water from a lake (contaminated with everything from spilled snowmobile oil to dog feces) and carry it home in a bucket; for waste, there are slop pails and pit privies.[5]

We could go on. Researchers conducting a national inventory of water services at 571 First Nations communities as recently as mid-2011 revealed that *more than a quarter* of all homes in these communities lacked piped water. Fifteen percent relied on trucked water or water hand-carried from another source. The portion of homes relying on water deliveries reached a third in federally serviced communities in Alberta. The share without indoor plumbing of any sort peaked in Manitoba, at 6 percent.[6]

That study may have lowballed the scale of the neglect. A survey of 290 reserve water systems in 2009–10 concluded that more than half (53 percent) were at "high risk" of delivering unsafe water; another 18 percent were at "medium risk."

The Harper government responded to the crisis at Attawapiskat by blaming the community. Federal statements accused its band council of mismanaging the funds it received to pay for water services—an assertion that was not only deeply undercut by the existence of very similar conditions in scores of other communities under federal stewardship but was also found by the Federal Court, in a ruling in August 2012, to be "unreasonable in all the circumstances" facing the Ontario reserve.

Ottawa-based human rights lawyer Paul Champ saw a more cynical motive at play in the government's rationale for generations of failure to ensure that citizens living under its jurisdiction enjoyed sufficient safe water and sanitation. "Even those Canadians who don't see themselves as being racist or having racist stereotypes are definitely susceptible to that frame that first nations mismanage money," Champ suggested. "I think those are regrettably very deeply rooted stereotypes in Canada. This government played on that."[7]

It's true, as federal apologists also pointed out, that many reserve communities are remote from other centres. The implication that this represents a barrier to providing safe and secure water, however, is disproved by the accomplishments of the same government, which found it quite possible to deliver hot showers and even Tim Hortons coffee and doughnuts to its expeditionary soldiers in the unserviced deserts of Afghanistan.

Moreover, the excuse of remoteness cannot be made for the quite different health problems experienced by another Canadian community subject to the federal Crown's standard of care.

The Anishinabek community of Aamjiwnaang is a tiny oblong of real estate squeezed between the Ontario city of Sarnia, hectares of petrochemical refineries, and the international St. Clair River. Since the early 1990s, parents here have welcomed fewer and fewer infant boys into life. By the first decade of the new century, two girls were born to the community for every boy, an astonishing and almost unparalleled divergence from the normal gender ratio at birth of about 105 boys to every 100 girls.[8] Families in the community organized three teams of girls for baseball but only one of boys; the boys' hockey team folded for lack of players.

Is it something in the water? The air? The exact vector may be immaterial: what enters the air almost invariably enters the water, coming down to earth with precipitation or settling on land surfaces to be absorbed into groundwater. Residents of Aamjiwnaang describe "ash"-falls of white powder from a local refinery and waste industrial mercury lying so thickly in a local stream that enterprising youngsters panned it like gold for selling. By whichever route of exposure, however, researchers say that stray molecules from the chemical works around the community are most likely behind its gender imbalance. "It's hard to imagine what else it could be, it's such a glaring anomaly," remarked Devra Davis, an epidemiologist at the University of Pittsburgh who studied the small Canadian community as part of a larger inquiry into the possible effects of exposure to industrial chemicals.

We applaud the success of Canadian engineers and utility workers in delivering ample fresh water that won't make you immediately sick to hundreds of millions of taps every day. That is no small accomplishment.

But it also provides a misleadingly narrow snapshot of the safety of our water today or its security tomorrow. And it is not only the unfortunate few Canadians directly exposed to federal water stewardship who are at risk. Eighty percent of Canadians live in river basins that we share with the United States—another realm of federal jurisdiction. The large, navigable, and fish-bearing waterways from which many communities draw domestic water, and more draw economic and recreational value, are likewise under federal authority.

Pollutant challenges we thought were mastered a quarter-century ago are back, creating an annual "dead zone" in Lake Winnipeg rivalling that in the Gulf of Mexico. The pollutants of a hundred years ago have meanwhile been vastly eclipsed in potency, variety, and ubiquity by a new class of synthetic molecules. Many of these are also persistent, mobile, and bioaccumulative. They may travel long distances, show up in unexpected places, and collect and concentrate over time in the bodies of people and wildlife. They also have exotic effects that make a temporary fit of runny bowels look mild by comparison.

In one of the most perturbing of these, the "lost" boys of Aamjiwnaang appear to be among a legion of unborn males around the world. A paper on which Devra Davis collaborated found a gender imbalance in U.S. births between 1970 and 2002 equivalent to 135,000 "missing" American boys; Japan "lost" 127,000 boys during roughly the same time. As she and her authors put it: "Males are being culled."[9]

The question "Has putting our water at risk for the sake of economic gain made us *healthier*?" receives a different answer depending on where you look.

Canada's expansion and enrichment over the twentieth century coincided with great improvements in the containment and treatment of "old" contaminants. Much improved municipal liquid waste treatment has dramatically reduced the fecal pathogens and organic and other chemical components in released sewage that contribute to oxygen depletion in receiving waters. Public policy has also made measurable progress in reducing environmental releases of lead, dioxins, and furans from pulp and paper mills; certain pesticides, such as DDT; and the gasses that contribute to acid rain.

Those improvements, replicated across the developed world over the last 120 years, have encouraged some analysts to theorize an environmental equivalent to what's known as the Kuznets curve. In the original hypothesis, first expressed by economist Simon Kuznets in 1955, inequality initially rises in a society as its per-capita income increases, and then it declines again—graphed conceptually as an upside-down *U*. In a similar fashion, advocates for an "environmental Kuznets curve" suggest that pollution initially rises as a society industrializes (Canada in the first half of the twentieth century) and then falls as the society becomes wealthy enough to afford pollution controls and its economy shifts away from industrial to service pursuits (Canada post-1960).[10]

The assertion of an environmental Kuznets curve lends credence to the argument of some developing nations that their economic needs demand a period of leniency in environmental standards—similar to the one that Western countries enjoyed early in their industrial era— the damage from which can be made good later when those societies have more resources. Our own prime minister makes much the same case, in effect, when he insists that environmentally destructive energy projects must proceed immediately—while environmental repair and protection can be postponed.

Kuznets's original curve, the one that purported to find a decline in income inequality as a society's per-capita income rises past a certain point, has suffered lately. In light of rising inequalities in wealth in Canada, the United States, and elsewhere, as staunch a defender of global free markets as the World Bank conceded, in a 2011 paper by its chief economist, that "the famous Kuznets Curve [in income inequality] is not supported by the evidence."[11] It reached the same negative conclusion about the proposition that societies will automatically grow their way out of a polluted environment ("—no Kuznets curve here").[12] It's true, the World Bank team observed, that most developed countries, such as Canada, have contained the worst excesses of local water and air pollution from their past. "But this is not true of local pollutants with invisible or long-term impacts (e.g., pesticide accumulation), global pollutants (e.g., greenhouse gases), or the destruction of bio-diversity," the World Bank stated. "These get worse with higher income."

It is deeply as well as sadly ironic that many of the remote communities exposed by federal dereliction to the most primitive of water-borne health risks are also surrounded by some of the most unpolluted water bodies on the planet. But if remoteness offers no assurance of pure water for Pikangikum or St. Theresa Point, neither has adjacency to some of Canada's wealthiest southern addresses kept Aamjiwnaang's males safe from chemical "culling."

Some old hazards still threaten the safety and security of Canada's water, while the new pollutants of the twenty-first century are everywhere.

Many Canadian shoppers are familiar with the Tropicana brand of orange juice. In January 2012, Tropicana's owner, PepsiCo, revealed that its internal testing had detected low levels of an agro-industrial fungicide, carbendazim, in its OJ. It tested its juice after learning that competitor Coca-Cola Co. had found the same fungicide, in similar amounts below U.S. federal product-safety thresholds, in its Minute Maid juice imported from Brazil.[13] Carbendazim has been linked to infertility in mice and "degenerative changes" in the testicles of Japanese quail;[14] it has been banned for use on fruit crops in Australia.[15] It was present in the companies' products in trace amounts only, and the juice remained on the shelf.[16]

Polybrominated diphenyl ethers (PBDEs) are used in everything from cars to computers to clothing, to reduce their risk of bursting into flames. They're members of a larger class of chemicals known as POPS (persistent organic pollutants) for their capacity to resist decay in the environment. PBDEs have been detected since the early 1990s in the breast milk of Inuit mothers living in northern Quebec, thousands of kilometres from industrial centres. By 2003, the chemicals' presence in tested mothers' milk had risen by 40 percent.[17]

Carbendazim and PBDES are a small sampling of the thousands of high-potency engineered molecules employed in modern production facilities or available in the consumer and medical marketplaces. The total number of these compounds in economic circulation rises to 100,000 in some estimates.[18] Many Canadians are aware of the prevalence of such synthetic compounds. What is less widely known, and shockingly underappreciated, is that they are largely invisible to even the best contemporary water treatment plants. These remove biological pathogens from drinking water and strip them, along with heavy metals and excessive organic content, from liquid waste (sewage) before releasing it back to nature. They were never designed to filter out pharmaceutical or other exotic synthetic molecules, and they generally don't.

Thus, almost every exotic molecule that enters the flow of water continues to flow through the remainder of the hydrological system—passing unhindered through municipal waste treatment plants into the environment, where it may well be drawn up into another water-system intake, again pass unaffected through treatment procedures meant only to remove infectious agents from drinking water, and eventually be consumed by someone in a glass of tap water.

The federal Crown's dereliction of its duty to protect the few communities where it alone holds that responsibility may leave "only" a small number of Canadians in out-of-the-way and powerless places under conditions more reminiscent of the turn of the last century than this one.

Exercising the same standard of stewardship toward the exotic pollutants now entering the water cycle puts every citizen in the country at risk.

Let's consider the variety of ways that water may become unsafe to human or other life.

The U.S. Environmental Protection Agency (EPA) ranked the most significant "stressors" degrading America's streams. These turned out to be, in declining order: silt and sediments, nutrients, biological pathogens, metals, synthetic pesticides, suspended solids, and salinity.

Some of these enter surface water in municipal sewage. Others are by-products of modern farming or industry. Silt and sediments are the result of erosion and natural weathering, typically exacerbated by human activity. All, in one way or another, make water some combination of unappetizing, dangerous to consume, or unhealthy to contact for both humans and wildlife.

To those we might add the effects of climate change. Longer, hotter, drier summers are amping up the invisible effect of evapotranspiration, extracting greater volumes of water from lakes, streams, and artificial reservoirs. The removal of that water leaves behind greater concentrations of complex synthetic chemicals along with traditional pollutants in the diminished volume of water that remains for human, aquatic, and wildlife communities to draw on. Low summer stream levels are often accompanied by soaring water temperatures as well— an additional stress factor that can be lethal to some fish. When rainstorms do relieve the drought, they are frequently more intense than in the past, scouring fields and urban land surfaces where pollutants have built up and sluicing their concentrated contaminants into rivers, reservoirs, and water tables in toxic bursts.

Nutrients, suspended solids, silty sediments, and heavy metals are generally effectively removed by well-functioning drinking water treatment systems. They pose relatively little risk of illness to most urban Canadians, though people relying on shallow wells may be exposed, and their combined effects on ecosystems are beginning to present other health threats to human communities.

Myriad other compounds—whether active ingredients or by-products of the manufacture and use of everything from computer circuits to personal care products—infuse urban and remote environments alike. The great majority of these were commercialized to exploit some chemical or molecular reactivity. Many remain reactive in the residual products that reach our taps. Their potential to mix unsupervised in waste streams, to mix and mate with each other to form altogether new compounds with unknown potencies, is an acknowledged but barely studied risk. Virtually none of these materials are intercepted by existing treatment technology at either end of water's flow through the human economy and physiology. Although most eventually decay in nature, each new flush delivers a pulse of fresh exotic compounds to our waterways. These are accumulating as a growing component of our personal and environmental chemistry.

Several studies between 2007 and 2010 detected anti-inflammatories ibuprofen and ketoprofen, the antidepressant venlaxafine, beta blocker propranolol, and numerous other prescription and over-the-counter drugs in municipal waste water entering Ontario's rivers.[19] Concurrent studies identified anti-inflammatories in the open water of Lake Erie, antidepressants in Lake Ontario, anti-epileptics in both, and, in Lake Michigan, detectable values of nicotine.

The water of the St. Lawrence River tested positive for a dozen prescription drugs, including antibiotics and drugs used to control seizures.[20] An examination of Fraser River water for clues to the decline of its salmon revealed more than 200 industrial, pharmaceutical, and pesticide chemicals, as well as a variety of potently toxic dioxins.[21] Tests done on water from streams in 30 American states, for the presence of pharmaceuticals or household, agricultural, and industrial chemicals, found at least one product in more than four-fifths of the 139 streams examined. More than half contained 7 or more chemicals. Even ocean water off the coast of Oregon has been found to have the added buzz of 45 nanograms of caffeine in every litre.[22]

What's in nature's water has a habit of finding its way into our taps as well. A study of public drinking water supplies in twenty-eight American cities uncovered a small pharmacy's worth of prescription drugs—from anticonvulsants to mood stabilizers—in the treated tap water of all but three of them.[23] Philadelphia set the record, with a tap-water cocktail of no fewer than fifty-six pharmaceuticals or by-products.[24]

Subsequent research by the U.S. EPA, reported in 2010, detected hexavalent chromium (the carcinogenic heavy metal brought to the big screen in *Erin Brockovich*, a movie about an industrial whistle-blower) at an average concentration three times recommended limits in the tap water of thirty-one out of thirty-five American cities from

Boston to Honolulu.[25] Triclosan, an antibacterial agent used in soaps and surgical scrub rooms but stalked by experimental evidence that it disrupts endocrine function in test animals, showed up in the urine of three-quarters of Americans tested by the Centers for Disease Control.[26]

Recent studies break the threats these compounds pose to human health into two or three broad and not mutually exclusive general categories, each bearing its own acronym. Natural heavy metals such as lead, arsenic, chromium, and mercury are in the category of persistent, bioaccumulative, and toxic pollutants (PBTs), along with by-products of fossil fuel combustion and those persistent organic pollutants (POPs) mentioned earlier. Many of these are formulated in pesticides specifically to be fatal to plants, insects, fungus, or other life forms.

A second basket of new threats is believed to account for Aamjiwnaang's missing boys. Endocrine disrupting compounds (EDCs)[27] are compounds that mimic the chemical signalling action of natural hormones that all living creatures, including humans, rely on for orderly development—for instance, signalling to the maturing body that it's time to switch puberty on or off.

Yet a third category, volatile organic compounds (VOCs), sweeps together a broad family of molecules mainly refined from or created in processing fossil hydrocarbons but having in common their origins in organic feedstock and a tendency to gasify into the atmosphere. Benzene is one of these; it is often a by-product in petroleum refining, a common industrial ingredient, and associated with elevated risks of leukemia and other blood cancers.[28]

VOCs, by their nature, don't stick around. High levels of exposure typically occur only over extended proximity to some industrial activity that generates or employs them, more often by inhalation or dermal contact than ingestion by drinking. But they can also contaminate water. Sampling by the U.S. EPA found benzene, toluene, acetone, and hints of diesel fuel in well water in a Wyoming community at the centre of a gas extraction boom.[29]

PBTS pose their greatest threat over time. Chronic exposure to these compounds in amounts too small individually to induce noticeable discomfort, immediate impairment, injury, or death (even, in some cases, below the threshold of human detection) may still do physiological or neurological damage. Mercury (a naturally occurring element) and man-made DDT (the villain of Rachel Carson's *Silent Spring*) are two classic examples of PBTS. The insecticide DDT has been banned from most uses in North America for decades, but other PBTS are accumulating around us.

Researchers testing eggs laid by thick-billed murre (a variety of duck with the black-and-white dress code of a penguin) in the remote Canadian Arctic between 1975 and 1995 reported that the amount of mercury in the eggs' shells doubled over that time. Colleagues testing the eggs of seagulls around Lake Ontario documented an even more shocking *"65-fold increase"* in the amount of flame retardant they contained over an even briefer period of eighteen years (1981–1999).[30] (Emphasis added.) Positively stratospheric concentrations of bioaccumulative PBDEs have been recorded in Puget Sound, just south of Vancouver: their level in the meat of harbour seals (a frequent meal for orca whales) has been doubling "every 3.5-4 years."[31]

EDCs, meanwhile, are increasingly believed to act at very low dosages of exposure if these coincide with vulnerable developmental moments, such as conception or puberty, when an individual's body is particularly susceptible to a faux hormone signal. They are suspected in a broad spectrum of epidemiological anomalies—many of them involving disruptions of gender, gender ratios, pregnancy, genitalia formation, and other aspects of reproductive function.

Some EDCs come by their endocrine mimicry by accident. Polybrominated biphenyls were designed as another class of flame retardant. They were not supposed to cross the placental barrier in pregnant women. Yet according to the U.S. National Institutes of Health, they do, producing "significant adverse effects on normal pubertal development" for the children later on.[32] Other compounds in the same category intentionally meddle with the hormones of target species; it's how they do their job for us. The herbicide 2,4-D, for example, is a synthetic plant hormone that triggers uncontrolled, disorganized, and eventually fatal cell growth in its targeted species. Many of these active compounds rely on molecular mechanisms that are similar across many species (the very reason we test drugs meant for people on other animals), so it is not surprising to find they may also jiggle human chemistry.

The list of reproductive effects associated with elevated occupational exposure to some of these compounds is long. Grain farmers exposed to pesticides were found to have experienced higher rates of abortion and preterm births. Farmers exposed to combinations of herbi-, fungi-, and insecticides produced 21 percent fewer boys than girls. Birth defects (including urogenital defects) were 25 percent more common among infants born to parents who had applied agrochemicals to corn and soybean crops than among parents in the general population.

Some of these effects have been identified with time of exposure. In one study, conceptions that coincided with spring applications of herbicides were more likely to miscarry than pregnancies commenced in other seasons.[33]

"Pesticides penetrate both maternal and paternal reproductive tissues and organs," observed Theo Colborn and Lynn Carroll, the zoologist and entomologist[34] who surveyed the research cited above, "thus providing a pathway for initiating harm to their offspring starting before fertilization throughout gestation and lactation." Endocrine disrupting pesticides have been detected in human amniotic fluid, blood, placenta and umbilical cords, ovarian follicular fluid, and semen.[35]

Other EDCs have the same power to disrupt the body's natural signals. Flame retardants are in this category, as are many of the ingredients in pharmaceuticals, cosmetics, and personal care products such as lotions and shampoos. The ubiquity of these compounds, and the unpredictable, though not random, timing of their effects on differently susceptible people, make it difficult to demonstrate a conclusive cause-and-effect relationship between a specific compound and a particular pregnancy that ended in miscarriage or any other single health effect.

Whether these compounds *are* hormones (in synthetic form), behave like them, or otherwise disrupt their effect, they all upset the real thing's critical natural functions. "All vertebrates have similar sex hormone receptors, which have been conserved in evolution," former British government advisor Gwynne Lyons wrote in a report summarizing the "known or suggested" effects of chemical contamination on wildlife.[36] All creatures with backbones, that is to say, respond similarly to endocrine chemistry: what is bad for birds and bears is also likely to be bad for human girls and boys.

"There truly are no safe doses for chemicals that act like hormones," commented Laura Vandenberg, a biologist at Tufts University near Boston who with colleagues reviewed hundreds of epidemiological studies on the effects of environmental exposure to low doses of hormones and endocrine disrupting compounds.[37]

The omnipresence of these chemicals and their engineered potency make them prime suspects in a global epidemic of gender-bending aberrations observed in wildlife as well as people.

"Population statistics indicate that fertility, reproductive success, and male/female live birth ratio are declining in the industrialized world," Colborn and Carroll observed.

In Canada, those researchers found that "[a] clear shift... toward fewer male births began to appear in 1970." Poring through statistics going back to 1930, researchers determined that by 1995, the shift in sex ratios had amounted to a decline of 2.2 males for every 1,000 live births nationally over the previous quarter-century. The Atlantic provinces lost the most males: 5.6 baby boys for every 1,000 births. At that rate, and if no further shift in sex ratio has occurred in the years since, some 850 boys went "missing" from Canadian maternity wards in 2010.[38] Estimates of the shortfall in male births around the world reached 250,000 "unborn" boys as of 2007.[39]

Other boys are missing fully functioning parts. International surveys have documented a rising incidence of cryptorchidism (undescended testicle) and hypospadias (in which the urethral opening is along the shaft or at the base of the penis rather than its tip) in Britain, the United States, and several Scandinavian countries. The incidence of cryptorchidism in England and Wales doubled over a thirty-year period in the second half of the last century.[40]

Male sexual health appears to be under attack in other respects as well. Sperm rates in industrial countries have declined in country after country studied, along with sperm vigour. Testicular cancer is occurring roughly twice as often as it did in the 1970s.[41]

None of these worrisome trends has been conclusively linked to the rising incidence of EDCs in the environment, but some findings are strongly suggestive. University of Toronto uro-oncologist Dr. David Margel compared the use of birth control pills, whose active ingredient is a type of the female hormone estrogen, to rates of male prostate cancer in eighty-eight countries. He found a positive relationship: the places with more prostate cancer were also places where the most oral contraceptives were used.

"We think this is environmental," Margel theorized. Not all the estrogen in a contraceptive tablet is metabolized. Some is excreted with the woman's urine "into the water, into our food chain. Although the amount one woman would secrete is minimal, when millions of women take it for a long period of time, it may have an environmental effect."[42]

Women's sexuality and anatomy are not immune from the rising tide of real and synthetic hormones and act-alikes infusing the environment either. The onset of female puberty has been occurring earlier for at least two generations, but recent research indicates that this shift may be accelerating. A comparison of the development of two cohorts of girls, one in 1991–93, the other in 2006–08, found that girls in the latter group started to develop breasts a year younger than those fifteen years earlier.[43]

Adult Canadian women have experienced a startling 25 percent increase in the incidence of breast cancer since the mid-1970s. "The majority of cases cannot be explained by the current known or suspected risk factors," wrote a team of researchers based at the University of Western Ontario. However, they added: "Factors that increase cumulative estrogen load have been found to increase risk.

Increasing evidence suggests that synthetic chemicals, particularly those that mimic estrogen, may increase risk by acting as endocrine disruptors." The team suggested this after its own research found a correlation between living on a working farm in western Ontario during puberty (a setting where agricultural chemical exposure was fairly routine) and a woman's heightened chances of subsequently developing breast cancer.[44]

Researchers in Los Angeles compared the blood of 1,240 newly pregnant women for the presence of perfluorinated compounds (PFCS), an industrial chemical used in stain repellant for carpets, among many other purposes.[45] They then inquired into how long it had taken each woman to become pregnant. Women in the quartile with the highest PFC count in their blood took on average a year longer to conceive than those in the lowest fourth of the sample. Several of the women in the high-PFC group ultimately resorted to in vitro fertilization to conceive a child.[46]

In Florida, as many as 40 percent of "male" cane toads in agricultural counties were found to be hermaphrodites. So, in Canada, were a smaller number of polar bears.[47] University of Calgary researchers, as mentioned earlier, have discovered that dace minnows in some portions of the Oldman and Bow Rivers have become nearly unisex, with males vanishing.[48] Lyons's summary, for a British foundation, reported observations of abnormal testes in fish, frogs, turtles, birds, bears, mink, sea lions, whales, and panthers; other physical deformities in the genitalia of alligators, otters, and polar bears; and precursor proteins to egg-laying in otherwise male fish, amphibians, and birds.[49]

Concluded Lyons: "The basic male tool-kit is under threat."

The threat may be greatest where the largest number of Canadians live: around the Great Lakes. One reason is historical, another hydrographic.

Much of North America's twentieth-century industrial boom centred on the lakes' basin. In Canada, it stretched from Lake Superior's pulp and paper mills, past Sarnia's expanding petrochemical complex to Hamilton (steel), Toronto (manufacturing of every kind), and Oshawa (cars), on Lake Ontario. In the U.S., it created some of the century's mightiest industrial complexes, in Chicago, Detroit, Cleveland, and Buffalo. Waste flowed unchecked into the lakes for decades from refineries, factories, slaughterhouses, chemical and steel plants, and municipal sewers. Many of the worst effluent streams from industry have been contained in the last half century. Still, most of what has happened in the Great Lakes has stayed in the Great Lakes: the toxic detritus of previous years is still with us.

A great deal of that poisonous legacy is at least relatively static: suspended or congealed in bottom sediments and mud. These are most heavily contaminated in current and former industrial harbours, where the cost of cleaning them up can pose a barrier to desirable redevelopment of derelict shorelines. But mobile contaminants also persist in the lakes' water.

Only about 1 percent of that vast volume of liquid flows out down the St. Lawrence or is evaporated into the air every year. The rest is "resident," for as long as two hundred years in Lake Superior or as briefly as three years in Lake Erie.[50] Those are estimated averages. Certain parcels of lake water may be more transient. Others, particularly at depth, dwell longer in one place. In both, continuous streams of persistent chemicals from human waste accumulate and concentrate.

Surveys of "areas of concern" identified under the mid-'70s Canada-United States Great Lakes Water Quality Agreement (GLWQA) documented a staggering *101 different synthetic chemicals* in lake water. While levels of DDT and PCBS declined in gull eggs after their use was restricted in Canada and the United States, no corresponding decline occurred in key fish species. Lake trout and walleye continued to show elevated levels of the long-lasting POPS. According to the 2001 Environment Canada review that made the disturbing determination, it "reflect[ed] continued emissions from urban areas and recycling of contaminants within the lakes."[51]

"Numerous studies of fish consumers in the Great Lakes," the study's authors added, "suggest that exposure to contaminants . . . causes disturbances in reproductive parameters and neuro-behavioural and developmental deficits in newborns and older children."[52]

In 2006, in the lead-up to the first renegotiation of the Great Lakes Water Quality Agreement since 1987, the Canadian Environmental Law Association and three other environmental NGOs reviewed progress in cleaning up those "areas of concern" in the lakes ecosystem. Of forty-two "hot spots" identified for priority attention, a total of three had been fully restored in nineteen years. Thirty-nine remained on the to-do list.

Some threats once considered defeated were back. Anoxic "dead zones" had reappeared in Lake Erie, while growing areas of southern Lake Michigan had been reduced to "biological desert."[53] Raw sewage releases to lake water were still "frequent and commonplace." Botulism had broken out several times among birds and fish in Lake Erie—further evidence of populations under stress.

Although the cause is not known, "various species of [Great Lakes] fish now suffer from tumors and lesions, and their reproductive capacities are decreasing," the NGOs stated, quoting from an Environment Canada web document. "Of the ten most valuable species of fish in Lake Ontario, seven have almost totally vanished."[54] (The cited web page no longer appears on Environment Canada's site.)

If the health of species that live in water is an indicator of that water's safety for humans, there is reason for worry elsewhere as well. Most conspicuously under threat is the last of Canada's great basins: the Mackenzie.

Guy Thacker has lived his entire life at the junction of the Mackenzie's two most important southern tributaries. The tugboat operator and sometime trapper lives at Fort Chipewyan, on the edge of a vast interior wetland as rare in its way as the Serengeti.[55] Here, at the west end of Lake Athabasca, the river of the same name mingles with the Peace before their combined waters continue to the sea down the

Slave River. Thacker has watched the delta and its rivers change for five decades.

Their aquatic equilibrium was first disrupted when British Columbia installed one of the world's biggest dams on the upper Peace River in the 1960s. Filling and maintaining Williston Lake behind the W.A.C. Bennett Dam permanently altered the timing of high and low flows in the river system downstream. That has had profoundly damaging consequences.

Chatting in his backyard workshop, Thacker explained that beaver, to name just one delta species, customarily secure their lodges on small creeks during the autumn, entering them at freeze-up with the expectation of spending a snug and dry winter inside. They were unprepared for the unnatural and unseasonable release of millions of gallons of water far upstream, as B.C. Hydro opened up the turbines at the Bennett Dam to light and heat homes in Vancouver. When that pulse of water reaches the Athabasca Delta, Thacker says, "the whole Slave rises six, seven feet, backs up in all these little creeks. The beaver have settled in, they aren't expecting it, so they drown."[56]

Lately, Thacker has seen equally dramatic change come to the delta's namesake tributary. Running his red-and-white barge tug M V *Atha* up the Athabasca to Fort McKay, in the shadow of the oil sands mines, every couple of weeks during the summer, he has noticed its stream is much shallower than in the past, in some places "only three feet deep, some places two and a half." To haul his barges and boat over newly exposed shallows, Thacker has taken to carrying a tracked backhoe on every voyage.

He frequently spots oil slicks descending the river. "It never used to be like this," Thacker says. "With all these new oil plants along the river, obviously it's coming from their places."

Chapter 5 catalogued some of the evidence that spurred the Alberta and federal governments belatedly in 2012 to begin to set up a credible and comprehensive research program to document that imputed connection—or disprove it. Many experts, however, consider the prima facie case to be made already.

"Today, deformities such as tumors, deformed spines, hematomas, deformed eyes and mouths are fairly common" in the Athabasca's fish, says David Schindler, the limnologist whose media tactics at last prompted the overhaul in pollution monitoring in the region. "One can only conclude that something has happened to greatly increase fish deformities sometime between the 1970s (when the oil sands industry was very small) and now."[57]

Today's threats to water safety are numerous, are easily hidden in the background, and may pack an outsize punch to the soft targets of hormone-sensitive bodies. The sources of exotic chemicals are global as much as local. They are typically invisible rather than visible. And their effects are chronic and long-term rather than acute and immediate.[58]

Linda Birnbaum directs the United States' National Institutes of Health's National Toxicology Program.[59] In 2010, she noted four distinguishing characteristics of the endocrine disruption threat for the U.S. House of Representatives Subcommittee on Energy and Environment:[60]

Low dose: Natural endocrine signals have profound effects on development at minute concentrations. It's therefore plausible to suppose that even low doses of chemical exposure may produce dramatic disruptions in normal function or development.

Multiple effects: Hormones direct the activity of most of our organs and processes. Disrupting that signalling system may therefore induce a wide variety of different symptoms, some of which mask their origins in endocrine contamination.

Persistent effects: The effects of endocrine disruption may not appear for years after exposure. In particular, hormone signal-dependent growth and development may be altered long after someone was exposed—and even in children of those who have been exposed.

Ubiquitous hazard: "[C]hemicals with endocrine disrupting activity are widely dispersed in our environment, often at levels plausibly associated with biological effects; exposure to humans is widespread."[61] Exposure can occur through inhalation, ingestion, or dermal absorption from air, water, food, or soil and through the use of everyday consumer products like skin cream and shampoo.

These new threats attack the safety of our water today and imperil its future security through a thousand ports of entry.

Some continue to be released by industrial plants or facilities. Others are sent into local waterways when precipitation rinses excess or residual agricultural chemicals from farm fields—an effect that is escalating with the new climate's more intense downpours. Precisely how much each of these contributes to the pollutant mix in drinking water is a matter of debate and varies with local industry, farm activity, and landscape.[62]

Other sources are more remote: toxins released into the air over Asian factories ride the circumpolar jet stream to settle from the sky over northern Canada. The persistent quality of PBT compounds allows them to build up in certain places, such as the sediments in an industrial harbour. When those are disrupted by natural or human action, such as dredging that harbour for redevelopment, those contaminants are remobilized to the environment in what has been dubbed a "grasshopper" pollution effect.[63]

Yet the most prolific source of exotic chemicals in Canadians' environment may be our own lifestyle. From car wax to drain cleaners, hair restorers to skin conditioners, daily prescriptions to once-a-year weed-and-feed on the lawn, the twenty-first-century consumer goes through tons of carefully compounded and blended chemical mixes in an average lifetime. Much of these products' content is inert filler. Some ingredients are natural or derived from natural products. But to achieve their many useful purposes—and avoid undesirable outcomes, such as a wax going runny when warm or caking when dry—chemical engineers draw on a vast array of active materials.

Some of these working constituents (in car wax, for example) eventually get washed into a road drain. Others (skin conditioner, pharmaceuticals) stay with us until we wash them off or excrete them. Then they too enter a drain.

About one-quarter of Canadians are served by individual or small community well systems. Most of these households also make use of a septic tank and drainage field to dispose of their personal and liquid waste. They are already at heightened risk of exposure to conventional contaminants in their drinking water because of the large proportion of rural individual septic systems that malfunction, contaminating the groundwater source of their wells. These households are also more at risk than city dwellers when heavy precipitation leaches contaminants from actively worked farm fields nearby. Either crop chemicals (fertilizers, herbicides, fungicides, and pesticides) or the combination of fecal pathogens, antibiotics, and veterinary pharmaceuticals that are eliminated with livestock manure may enter their wells. Conventional tests may confirm that coliform counts in the tap water of those households are low enough to make the water safe to drink. They typically do not detect more complex contaminants.

Urbanites can generally be confident that traditional pathogens are effectively filtered out of, or destroyed in, the water they receive from municipal mains. But they're little better defended than their rural cousins against diffuse agents of more subtle physiological disruption. Disinfecting agents (typically chlorine, but other technologies are also used) employed to neutralize microbial pathogens in drinking water treatment plants may react with some new classes of chemicals but not others. As the U.S. EPA and Environment Canada conceded in a joint statement in 2009, "drinking water facilities do not in general remove all contaminants."[64] The proof of this admission lies in the range of pharmaceuticals turning up in tap water across North America.

Waste treatment plants have come a long way from their early "screen, settle, and release" incarnations in most of Canada. Yet the amount that municipalities have invested over the decades to maintain sewage treatment infrastructure is a mystery even to governments.

When the Canadian Council of Ministers of the Environment tried to work out the number in 2008, its researchers found it "very difficult to determine."[65] The report was more certain in saying that, as of 2003, more than half (58 percent) of the sewage treatment infrastructure in the country was nearing the end of its projected service life of twenty-nine years. The same report estimated that federal, provincial, and territorial governments had spent a combined $2.88 billion in the years 2000–07 to improve sewage infrastructure, over and above whatever amount municipalities had spent.[66] Those senior governments had committed additional billions to the same purpose over the following years, spending that was expanded by additional billions in recession stimulus spending.

Sadly, these vast public sums only brought lagging treatment systems more into line with contemporary standards of tertiary treatment against traditional pathogens. There was little choice: no demonstrated technology exists to strip exotic chemicals from water on the scale required by a city or at a price taxpayers are likely to stomach.

Sewage "treatment is complicated by the introduction of synthetic chemicals and pharmaceuticals and personal care products to the waste stream," the NAFTA Commission for Environmental Cooperation wrote in a 2011 special report.[67] "Wastewaters from homes or business can contain mixtures of detergents, surfactants, disinfectants, pharmaceuticals, food additives, pesticides, herbicides, industrial chemicals, heavy metals, and other synthetic materials." The ability of conventional treatment processes to break these down, the report noted, "is limited for many [toxic new] substances and nonexistent for others."

A pharmacologist at the University of Adelaide's Research Centre for Water Quality and Treatment who examined the same question was even more unequivocal about the exotic compounds of greatest concern: the gender-bending ones. "Neither basic wastewater treatment nor basic drinking water treatment will eliminate the estrogens, androgens or detergent breakdown products from water," Ian

Falconer concluded, "due to the chemical stability of the [molecular] structures."[68]

Nonetheless, some of the money spent in the last decade to upgrade Canadian sewage management did valuable work, reducing the amount of urban liquid waste that continues to be dumped raw and untreated into receiving waters in Canada—an event that happens more often, and in greater volume, than many Canadians might suppose.

Most of Canada's municipalities that now collect domestic, commercial, and light industrial liquid waste for disposal treat that sewage at least to a so-called secondary level. That removes suspended solids and dissolved organic matter to reduce the waste liquid's biological oxygen demand—an indicator of its impact on downstream water quality. But a surprising amount of that sewage never reaches a treatment plant at all, particularly in older and eastern cities, where so-called combined sewers are more prevalent.

These were installed in the first generations of urban sewer servicing, as economy measures. They combine storm drains—where rainwater goes when it disappears through a grate at the curb—with sanitary drains—where your flush goes—in a single collection tunnel, usually separated by a continuous wall that forms two channels in the sewer tunnel. Under normal operating conditions, the two channels lead to separate outflows: storm water back to the environment, sewage to a treatment plant. The trouble arises when a heavy downpour of rain, running off into street drains, overwhelms the storm water channel, tops the dividing wall into the sanitary channel, and forms one current of diluted sewage.

Two consequences ensue. Large volumes of diluted sewage are released to the environment through outfalls meant to convey only relatively clean storm water. The same fetid blend follows the half of the channel meant for sanitary flow to a sewage plant. There, however, the sudden flood encounters treatment processes optimized for volumes of full-strength sewage, not a torrent heavily diluted with rainwater; the mismatch sharply reduces treatment efficiency.

Around the Great Lakes such overflows are weekly occurrences. A study of twenty lake cities in the first decade of the twenty-first century estimated that their antiquated sewers released 100 million cubic metres of untreated waste a year into adjacent lake water.[69] That's enough to fill the Toronto Rogers Centre stadium to its retractable roofline and empty it into the Great Lakes *every six days*.[70]

Climate change is increasing the occurrence of the sort of heavy rain that causes combined sewer overflows. Even so, that volume may be less today. According to Ontario's environment commissioner in 2011, about half of the hundred Canadian municipalities around the lakes with combined sewers had at least developed plans to reduce the overflows.[71] They either installed separate sewers for storm and sanitary flows or, often the cheaper choice, dug huge holding tanks where combined storm water and liquid waste can be collected and held until it can be accommodated at a treatment plant.

As we've noted, however, even when every drop of liquid waste is fully treated by a modern sewage treatment works, many of the new exotic contaminants it was never designed to remove pass through and back to receiving waterways. But that's not the only route our chemical castoffs take to get back to our lips.

Much primary and secondary sewage treatment is concerned with removing solids and suspended organic matter from waste water, usually by settling or what civil engineers call flocculation, in which chemicals are added to encourage suspended particles to clump together for easier removal. Either process leaves a residual sludge that must still be disposed of. A few Canadian sewage treatment plants use the sludge as a feedstock for biogas energy recovery. Most disinfect it, dry it, and sell it as a kind of coarse fertilizer. Much of Vancouver's residual sewage sludge, for example, is trucked to the provincial interior, where it's used to help re-establish vegetation on mine sites undergoing restoration.[72]

But of the residual sewage sludge created countrywide, the disinfected and (mostly) neutralized concentrated solids from 35 million Canadians' bowels and showers and shop drains, about half winds up on farm fields where Canadian food is grown.[73] Applications of such biosolids as fertilizer are subject to regulation in most provinces (and prohibited in Newfoundland and Labrador), but as in other dimensions of Canada's Balkanized water responsibilities, actual requirements vary across the country.[74]

In any case, once biosolids are on the soil, the next rainfall will provide a mechanism for residual and persistent exotic molecules in the biologically deactivated sludge to re-enter the hydrological cycle.

A century's investment in sewage treatment notwithstanding, the volume of known pollutants that we continue to release from our homes and businesses into the environment is significant.

In Canada, municipal waste treatment facilities are required to report their releases and "transfers," including sludge sent for disposal on fields. Their American and Mexican counterparts are not. Other differences in the three nations' data systems make it difficult to draw direct, apple-to-apple comparisons. Nonetheless, across broadly similar Canadian and U.S. lists of reportable chemicals, Canadian municipalities reported the release of more pollutants to the environment in 2006, in absolute volume (96.56 million kilograms), than the ten most-polluting American industrial sectors *combined* (95.03 million kilograms).[75]

This volume of sewage entering waterways directly or indirectly adds to the surplus of nitrogen and phosphorus leaching from farm fields. Together they contribute to what is becoming recognized as a global overload of chemical nutrients in aquatic settings. Not all of it travels by water. More nitrogen is produced as a by-product of fossil fuel combustion or vents to the atmosphere during agricultural application.

Like the PBTs that drift from China's crowded cities to Canada's Arctic outposts, "biologically-active nitrogen associated with human society is being transported in the atmosphere to the most remote ecosystems on the planet," according to fisheries scientist Daniel Schindler (son of David Schindler). The University of Washington researcher and colleagues sampled sediments beneath lakes from the western United States to northern Europe. Employing the same method that revealed rising contamination in the Athabasca Delta, they documented a measurable increase in nitrogen content beginning in about 1800—roughly at the start of the Industrial Revolution. In a striking parallel to the increasing concentration of atmospheric greenhouse gasses, human releases of nitrogen have doubled since 1950.[76]

When combined with increasing amounts of phosphorus leached from farmland, this is creating an epidemic of eutrophication—the process by which a body of healthy fresh or salt water that once supported a varied aquatic community becomes a scummy, smelly soup of algae and bacteria, devoid of other species and ultimately poisonous to people.

Fuelled by the flood of high-octane nitrogen and phosphorus from human sources, blue-green cyanobacteria are a particular problem in Canada. The aggressive strain easily out-competes other species for the oxygen available in warm, shallow water bodies in the summer, forming filaments that cling to each other and ultimately turning square kilometres of lake into algal blooms of matted, greenish scum. As these eventually die and decompose, the process consumes more oxygen, eventually leaving areas of the water column anoxic—too lean in dissolved oxygen for fish and other complex life to survive.

As their tiny corpses break down, these bacteria release a variety of liver, skin, and neurological toxins strong enough to kill a human. Fifty people did die when water imperceptibly laced with algal toxins was used to treat dialysis patients in Brazil.[77] A survey of lakes across Canada in 2012 found one of these breakdown products, microcystin, in nearly 1 in 10 of the 256 lakes sampled. The potent liver toxin was most prevalent in the shallow Prairie lakes of Alberta and Manitoba—both provinces with high concentrations of livestock.

There is some evidence that as climate change renders waterways warmer, shallower, and more susceptible to such algal blooms, the rising temperature is also intensifying the toxins they release at the end of their life cycle—a double whammy with a vicious sting in its tail.[78]

Certainly, killer lakes and biological deserts underwater are appearing in growing numbers around the globe. A 2007 algal bloom choked China's third-largest freshwater body, Lake Tai, leaving more than 2 million people without drinking water.[79] A 7,700-square-kilometre oxygen-starved dead zone has spread annually in the Gulf of Mexico, threatening its $2.8 billion-a-year fishery.[80]

In Canada, about a quarter of western lakes show early signs of eutrophication. In some, such as Saskatchewan's Qu'Appelle lakes and Alberta's Lac La Biche, the problem is serious. It is encouraged by summers that are growing longer, sucking more water from lakes and reservoirs, and warming what's left behind: superior conditions for algal growth. The affliction is spreading east. It has appeared in Ontario's Lake Simcoe. In 2007, 122 Quebec lakes sprouted massive blooms. In 2008, an algal colony managed to blossom even in the flowing St. Lawrence River, killing fish, birds, and mammals. In the Great Lakes, a spokesman for the International Joint Commission warned in late 2011, "We're seeing things we haven't seen since the 1970s."[81]

The Canadian lake perhaps most at risk of being eutrophied to a biological flatline is Manitoba's Lake Winnipeg, the tenth-largest freshwater lake in the world. It receives precipitation and runoff collected over 900,000 square kilometres of four Canadian provinces and as many U.S. states. About half the excess nutrients entering the lake are estimated to come from beyond provincial borders. The lake's watershed is largely given over to industrial agriculture. Manitoba is the epicentre of Canadian industrial pork production: the number of hogs raised there has quadrupled since 1990.[82] The practice of draining small wetlands to add crop acreage, meanwhile, has reduced the landscape's natural capacity to filter runoff water before it enters the lake's countless tributary creeks and streams.[83] The largest of those is the Red River. The last of several cities whose sewage that river absorbs before entering the lake is Manitoba's biggest and its capital: Winnipeg.

Algal blooms now smother more than half of Lake Winnipeg in most summers, threatening the $100 million-a-year tourism and recreational industry and a $25 million commercial fishery. In 2006, the "pea soup" blanket covered almost the entire lake, presenting its ten thousand cottagers with a front-yard view of a lake gasping for life.

Estimates of the number of distinct chemical compounds in commercial use in North America run from 80,000 to more than 100,000 products. More than 3,000 of those are produced in volumes of more than 450 tonnes a year.[84] About 12 trillion kilograms of chemicals are manufactured or imported into the United States every 12 months.

This suggests a proportionate use in Canada of at least 1 trillion kilograms a year. Were that material the density of sand, it would take a line of six-yard dump trucks stretched nearly twice around the equator to deliver it all. If the timing is right, some of these compounds are biologically active in the human body in amounts of micrograms.

An unknown portion of those millions of kilos of chemicals survive their application in industry or the bathroom shower. They and their breakdown products join other molecules from industrial emissions and agricultural leakage in the same water sources from which we later drink. There they linger.

Many of the gender-bending endocrine disrupters are not removed by our waste treatment systems, and some at least remain to recirculate through the water cycle, augmented daily by the contents of the latest flush.

Over time, many, if not all, of these will break down as a result of chemical action in the environment. But we do not know whether they break down fast enough to keep up with the amounts we are adding to the environment annually. The rising presence of some indicator chemicals suggests that the answer is no and that we are daily ingesting an ever-stronger solution of unpredictably active chemicals.

Prudence might suggest some caution in releasing new synthetic compounds to the marketplace to begin with. Indeed, this may be a textbook case for the application of the precautionary principle that "where there are threats of serious or irreversible damage, lack of full scientific certainty shall not be used as a reason for postponing cost-effective measures to prevent environmental degradation," as it was expressed in the 1992 Rio Declaration.[85]

Instead, Canada's system for defending our water and our bodies against toxic chemicals operates by the principles of "innocent until proven guilty" and "lock the barn door after the horse has bolted." These are products of history and organizational culture. Thousands of chemicals entered into use in the last century with little or no regulatory review. Absent persuasive positive proof that they are doing harm (and in the case of tobacco, not even then), it is deemed economically unjust to remove them from sale. Meanwhile, advancing science has in some cases called old risk assessments into question.

The oversight of pharmaceuticals and other potentially hazardous compounds falls under the jurisdiction of the federal Crown. The 1988 Canadian Environmental Protection Act (CEPA) created a legal foundation for regulating potentially hazardous "discrete chemical compounds, classes of chemicals, emissions and effluents, and products of biotechnology, including microorganisms."[86] Within a year, Environment Canada had established its first Priority Substances List, with forty-four suspect formulations on it.

Since 1994, Health and Environment Canada have identified 23,000 compounds as "chemicals of concern"—CEPA's version of a starter list of potential, not actual, risks. Of those, 4,300 were deemed to need closer scrutiny. By 2006, that number was further whittled down to 500 "priority substances"—putting Canada ahead of some of its peers facing similar challenges.[87] About 200 of those had been reviewed by time of writing, and federal officials hoped to complete all 4,300 formulations deserving a second look by 2020.[88]

Yet despite that apparent activity, a panel of experts convened by the Council of Canadian Academies to review how federal scientists reach their safety determinations reported in early 2012 that "estimates suggest that *toxicity data are lacking for 87 percent* of chemicals on the market."[89] (Emphasis added.) One reason for that is the paring down of professional resources available to the public service.

Target dates notwithstanding, the review process itself appears to favour deliberation over haste. The original 1988 CEPA gave regulators a leisurely five years from the time a chemical reached the "priority" substances list to determine its toxicity—the damage it does to organisms and under what conditions (through inhalation or ingestion, over long exposure or acutely).

Despite that leisurely schedule, the conclusions may be open to suspicion. Federal scientists have limited lab capacity. Most of the "facts" on which they base their determination are therefore conclusions reported by so-called sponsored studies—that is, research paid for by the company seeking the product's approval.[90] Applicants are not required to submit research if its outcome is unflattering to their product.

There is, moreover, the question of whether the testers are looking for the right signals at all. The conventional method is to subject test animals such as fish or mice to a variety of acute and expected in-use levels of exposure to the subject chemical and then see how many die or develop specific abnormalities such as cancers. Vandenberg and her colleagues at Tufts found these to be inadequate to detect the "remarkably common" effects of some chemicals on susceptible hormone systems. "Current testing paradigms are missing important, sensitive endpoints," Vandenberg wrote.[91]

In any event, even when unequivocally proven by conventional measures, high toxicity alone is not enough to keep a substance off the market. A second evaluation determines its "risk" in use. This judgement considers its toxicity in balance with other factors: the likelihood of human or wildlife exposure to the compound and the economic and social value its use conveys.

At the end of this second step, regulators may advise businesses using or producing the substance that they intend to introduce or amend regulations to control its use. More time passes as those are written, circulated for stakeholder comment, revised, and recirculated. Industry groups are free to intervene with political lobbying efforts in support of their products.

More time passes.

Rarely is a product prohibited outright, though restrictions may be placed on its use or handling. Rarer still is the withdrawal of a chemical already in the marketplace, as occurred in the nearly unique example of Canada's 2010 ban on the use of bisphenol-a in the plastic for baby bottles after a review placed it on the "toxic" list.[92]

The philosophy of "smart" regulation, aggressively pressed on civil service managers just as all those grandfathered toxic chemicals were coming up for review, created a further check on any impulse to determine that a particular substance might be too toxic over its possibly long lifetime to be worth the risk. The "smart" doctrine, to recall, required that any proposal to remove or regulate a product, even a toxic one, be assessed for its economic impact, a process inherently captive to the estimates of self-interested vendors and other users.

The combined effect of these factors, environmental legal scholar David Boyd has written, has been that our federal Crown "consider[s] chemicals innocent until proven guilty... Tens of thousands of industrial chemicals have entered the marketplace in recent decades without adequate testing for human and environmental health. In rare cases where governments do apply the precautionary principle, corporations fight back aggressively."[93]

The Harper ministry has conspicuously extended this permissive trend.

A provision in CEPA allows a producer to challenge Environment Canada's provisional determination that a chemical is toxic by requesting that the minister of environment have the finding reviewed by outside experts. In the first three decades of CEPA's existence, no minister subjected his staff scientists to such second-guessing. Then, in 2009, Minister Jim Prentice named a panel to review the case against Siloxane D5, an odourless, colourless material used in cosmetics and personal care products as well as industrial cleaning.[94] In late 2011, the panel found Environment Canada's judgement "flawed," saying "that it used overly-conservative modelling and that it inaccurately characterized the compound's fate in the environment."[95]

In January 2012, Peter Kent, the second minister to succeed Prentice, addressed a Calgary Chamber of Commerce audience salted with oil, gas, and petrochemical executives. "I'm not here to kill your buzz," he assured them. Although his agency remained a regulator, the environment minister wanted his listeners to regard it rather as "a strategic partner," with a "renewed" focus on expediting investment.[96] Four weeks later, Kent annulled his departmental scientists' finding, and declared Siloxane D5 "not harmful to the environment."[97]

While the slow, judicious process of testing the toxicity of each new compound or chemical class inches forward, thousands of synthetic molecules already inhabit the wild, promiscuously exchanging pieces of each other in reactions whose chemical offspring have yet to be closely studied. They are not on the federal Crown's "one toxin at a time" list for testing.

Are environmentalists overreacting? Was Kuznets right, and is it possible that Canada's water has been getting *healthier* for us, even as we've been throwing ever more stuff into it?

If we consider only the narrow measure of our chances of remaining free from gastrointestinal distress after our next glass of tap water, we live in a far safer world than most of our great-grandparents a century ago.

Modern water treatment has largely eliminated old threats such as typhoid and cholera from the closed water systems that service our homes and businesses. Today's systems do a much better job than earlier ones of reducing the environmental burden created by the daily elimination of thousands, if not millions, of human bowels in a confined ecological space.

But the rest of Canada's water, the part not expensively treated and contained at any one moment in our homes' and cities' reservoirs and pipes, is not faring nearly so well. Some conspicuously toxified hot spots in the Great Lakes and elsewhere have been remediated, but the background level of exotic, persistent bioaccumulative or endocrine disrupting compounds appears to be rising.

These enter our water cycle through innumerable channels, but once there, many never leave. Others are believed to break down or interact spontaneously with each other, creating entirely new molecules whose nature and effect can only be guessed at. Many of these pass unchecked into our domestic water systems—and back out again to the wild. Ecosystems and wild species without the benefit of our (partly) purified domestic water show the consequences of these molecules' persistence, accumulation, and unpredictable effects in combination.

The rising concentration of toxins in our water makes it expensive and ultimately impossible to completely eliminate them. Some—and the logic of increasingly polluted water sources suggests a growing number—of those chemical agents will get through defences designed for other, older, and biological pathogens.

And nearly a thousand new Canadian parents who might have brought home a baby boy in the next year will instead bring home a girl.

Seldom does the aphorism that "an ounce of prevention is worth a pound of cure" apply better than to the conundrum of removing some of these compounds from nature once they have been released. Yet our most senior leaders have made it clear that they have no quarrel with the loitering pace their predecessors set for sorting toxins from more inert or fast-decaying molecules.

NINE

No Secret Remedies

O NE SPRING day in 1969, one of the authors played hooky from his last few high school classes to canoe a local stream with a friend.

Spencer Creek begins near the hamlet of Puslinch, west of Toronto, and meanders south across twenty-five kilometres of farm country to drop over the Niagara Escarpment as a picturesque waterfall west of Hamilton. In the millennia before European conquest, it also fed one of the largest marshlands in the lower Great Lakes, a nursery for abundant fish. When European settlers arrived in the nineteenth century, they built water-powered flour and saw mills along the creek above and below the landmark cliff,[1] several near where the growing town of Dundas would later erect its high school.

On this occasion, the teenage truants paddled down Spencer Creek's lower reaches, past sun-dappled backyards and overgrown banks blushing with the first shoots of spring, a passage stolen from *Huckleberry Finn*. At last, their canoe drifted on the slowing current beneath an arched culvert that constituted the creek's estuary.

Beyond it, they emerged into an expanse of calm water the size and rough shape of a football field—the remains of a canal dug through the marsh in the era before railways to bring lake vessels within reach of the mills on Spencer Creek. As they came to rest in the middle of the long-abandoned turning basin, the distinctive aroma of raw sewage filled the boys' nostrils. Beneath the canoe, a thin layer of clear liquid a few centimetres deep supported its weight. Below that, an unguessable depth of suspended material formed an ash-grey false bottom that erupted into turbid vortices at the dip of a paddle. The two canoeists had emerged from the creek into an open-air cesspool. The brick building on the far bank of the canal was the outfall for the town sewers.

A visitor to the same spot today finds a very different scene. A public park, built on landfill, covers much of the turning basin. Effluent from Dundas showers and toilets still flows into the stump of the canal, but it has received three levels of treatment first, in settling ponds and disinfecting chambers. When pulses of storm water overwhelm the town's century-old combined sewers, the mixture of sewage and rain is stored in cavernous tanks until it can be treated.

The marshland, given the name Coote's Paradise in the nineteenth century for its lush diversity of wildlife, has taken small but perceptible steps back toward its former glory with the re-establishment of once extirpated plants. Pike and perch have reappeared.[2] The old canal has become a destination for local birders. Its water may still not be ready for a drinking glass, but it no longer smells like a freshly opened septic tank.

Much has been gained in the past half century. Yet much of the progress, though certainly more than merely cosmetic, has been overtaken by the introduction of new products to the marketplace and the increasing burden of growing communities. Improvements to Dundas's sewage treatment now remove or sterilize most of the phosphorus, sediment, and harmful bacteria it contains. But myriad bioactive waste pharmaceuticals, personal care products, and other household chemicals slip through. Although much of the Niagara Escarpment has been protected from development, the hard roofs and paved surfaces of tract housing and shopping centres have replaced pasture and farmland over much of Spencer Creek's watershed. Along with the rest of southern Ontario, the west end of Lake Ontario is experiencing milder winters and hotter summers, inducing more water to evaporate from streams and lakes into the humid air.

A country with more clean(ish) fresh water per citizen than almost anywhere else on Earth finds itself unprepared for a changed world of insecure nature and deepening global thirst. What to do?

The present authors are not the first to dip their paddles into this subject. In the last decade, at least a dozen groups of highly qualified independent experts have examined one aspect or another of Canada's water policy and practices.

Their examinations have proceeded from perspectives across the ideological spectrum—from the Bay Street–oriented C.D. Howe Institute to the highly corporate-critical Vancouver-based David Suzuki Foundation. Academics, technical professionals, legal experts, and social-policy researchers have all had a go. Their efforts have identified sound common principles for securing the present safety and future security of water for our taps and our wildlife. What is perhaps most striking has been the extent of their agreement—and the wide gap between that consensus and our actual practice.

If the best-informed Canadians on the subject from across the political spectrum are right, here is what we need to do to keep our most important national asset safe and secure.

We need first to take a holistic view of the ways in which we affect water. Whenever we make a decision that has any sort of material component, we need to remember that our water's safety is at stake in that choice. Water needed to manufacture a product is degraded when that product is discarded. Water required for construction is soiled when a building displaces a field or creek.

Likewise, we need to consider water we can't see because it is underground for what it is: an intimately linked part of the larger and continuous body of water that moves ceaselessly through the nation's (and the planet's) hydrological circulation, pooling in aquifers and lakes, moving through streams and subsurface flows, but always ultimately connected. Water taken from a near-surface aquifer may not be available lower in the watershed to maintain important sur-face streams; correspondingly, rivers drawn down by withdrawals, or sloughs ploughed over for field space, will contribute less to aquifers that supply local wells.

Because water's values to nature and humanity are so varied, our choices must also bear in mind how they will affect more than just its volume. They must also take into account water's purity, temperature, and state (ice, steam, or vapour, as well as liquid), and the timing of its availability or flow in nature. Water in plenty can be a nuisance to a farmer during planting season but is dearly sought when the seeds begin to sprout. A manufacturing facility may tolerate some impu-rities in water but not interruptions in its supply. A brewer may not mind an occasional disruption in supply so long as its water maintains a high standard of purity. A wide variety of wildlife is adapted to sea-sonal extremes of high and low water; when that timing is disrupted, as it is, for example, by hydroelectric installations, those species suffer.

For all of these reasons, decisions about water management must engage many voices. Every party that has an interest at risk or whose actions may damage water-productive ecosystems needs to be involved if the decision is to gain the expected benefits without incurring unacceptable costs to third parties or our collective natural security.

This tangled ecology of human, topographical, chemical, and bio-logical factors compels us to treat water in the context of the whole watershed in which it exists, from the tiniest ephemeral creek to the mega-watersheds that drain into the Mackenzie or St. Lawrence Riv-ers. Virtually all water policy experts urge the alignment of public agencies with significant natural watersheds, recognizing that these are nested within each other and that consequently such agencies may also need to be nested within higher-level entities.

Legal scholars Oliver Brandes, Michael M'Gonigle, and col-leagues at the University of Victoria's POLIS Project on Ecological Governance reached that conclusion after reviewing the fragmented landscape of Canada's water governance in 2005.[3] The Conference

Board of Canada did the same after assessing the subject in 2007.[4] Six months later, experts mainly from the NGO community, funded by a consortium of eight environmental policy centres (again including POLIS but also the World Wildlife Fund, Sierra Club, and the Centre for Indigenous Environmental Resources) and the philanthropic Walter and Duncan Gordon Foundation, reprised many of the same arguments to come to the same opinion.[5]

In 2009, the Alberta-based environmental non-profit Pembina Institute, looking at the vulnerability of the Mackenzie River to energy development, urged a bilateral agreement between Alberta and the Northwest Territories to establish "cooperative water management" in its watershed.[6] That same year, a panel of subject experts convened by the Council of Canadian Academies found that managing water in its natural basin was equally essential to protect southern Canada's groundwater.[7]

In the last report it completed before the Harper ministry closed its doors, the National Round Table on the Environment and the Economy (NRTEE) called on the Council of the Federation, Canadian municipalities, First Nations, and the federal Crown to negotiate a charter to "affirm the legitimacy of collaborative water governance."[8]

The Adaptation to Climate Change Team (ACT) at British Columbia's Simon Fraser University was examining the implications of shifting weather patterns for water security when it reached the same conclusion.[9]

By all roads and any point of view, it appears, the best way to manage water in the wild starts with bringing together as many of the people who share its watershed as possible. Other studies have identified key provisos about why some big-table watershed agencies work—and others do not.

Models vary around the world, from Ontario's Conservation Authorities to the water parliaments that have long managed major water supply and sanitation infrastructure in France. But uniformly they are more effective when provided with a collective mandate set to measurable objectives in which participants (which may include local municipalities, industry, or riparian groups; scientific or technical resources; and civil society groups, among others) have clearly stated roles and responsibilities. Agencies that merely share information are a start. But experience in Ontario and France suggests that they accomplish more when they wield adequate resources (water rates fund French *parlements de l'eau*; municipalities partly fund Ontario's Conservation Authorities) and meaningful influence over activities that affect the security of a watershed, as the Conservation Authorities do in reviewing development permits.[10]

Nature in the literal form of topography defines the boundaries of a watershed. Likewise, nature in the ecological sense of the embracing habitat from which our unique life form emerged, and on which it continues to rely, must also be allowed to define the boundaries of our thirst.

On this, the views of the pro-business Conference Board, centrist NRTEE, pro-environment Pembina Institute, and science-based ACT align once again: in allocating scarce water, the first priority must go to ensure the vitality of aquatic ecosystems with adequate in-stream flows.[11] Commercial ambitions must come second to natural security.

These may seem simple precepts. They are not so easily accomplished in the tangled political and jurisdictional landscape of the institutional world.

Large provinces are in a position to manage many of their watersheds without reference to other jurisdictions, as we saw in Chapter 5. A few large Canadian regions share no (or very few) watersheds with others: Prince Edward Island, Newfoundland and Vancouver Islands, and Nova Scotia (apart from a short border with New Brunswick). In every other part of the country, watersheds cross borders, sending water from British Columbia to Alberta and the reverse. All three Prairie provinces occupy parts of the Saskatchewan-Nelson river system. Water flows north into Canada from the United States in Manitoba and Quebec, south the other way in Saskatchewan, Alberta, and B.C. Only half of the basin of the Great Lakes is within Ontario; the other half sprawls across eight U.S. states. Their water fills Quebec's historic *fleuve*, the St. Lawrence.

The geography over which water travels, and the pluralities of "junior" jurisdictions—state or provincial—responsible for it, compel national-level attention as well. Indeed, they are among the reasons why the Canadian Constitution gives the federal Crown authority to provide it. Watershed stakeholders may know their ground, but the aforementioned studies also emphasize the urgent need for the kinds of support that are compatible with even a narrow reading of the federal remit: creating the critical public knowledge on which others, whether in business or provincial governments, may take effective action. "Subsidiarity," the precept that public agents closest to the scene know best, is adrift without direction, standards, and data that are best provided at national scale—by the federal Crown.

The roles that policy reformers have begged Ottawa to play are numerous. They include (with the expert groups that urged them):

- creating and maintaining an advisory national water commission (ACT);

- completing detailed national maps of Canada's aquifers (Council of Academies);

- leading the development of a national freshwater strategy (Gordon Water Group);

- obliging Alberta to suspend oil sands expansion until it reaches an agreement with the Northwest Territories to safeguard water in the Slave and Mackenzie Rivers (Pembina);

- establishing a national public database on best water practices (Sierra Legal/Ecojustice);

- sharply stepping up enforcement of its own existing water-protection legislation (Canadian Academies, Gordon);

- and, far from least, finally enacting binding, enforceable national safety standards for drinking water (Gordon, Sierra Legal/ Ecojustice).

One need, however, has been identified more often, by more of these deeply researched analyses from all over the ideological spectrum, than any other: the immediate urgency of reducing our ignorance.

The rubric that "you can't manage what you don't measure" is overused in expert examinations of why Canadian water policy is so inadequate. It is true all the same. Ignorance about where our water is, how much of it there is, what's in it, and where it's going blinds public water agencies on every scale to looming threats while it conceals untapped benefits from communities and investors.

Nine of twelve major studies and reports on Canada's water made public between 2005 and 2011 urged that more public resources be given to collect data and understand it. An early call envisaged a "sustainability reporting" agency to fill "important environmental data gaps" in what decision makers know about the state of Canada's natural ecosystems and the consequences for water quality and human health.[12]

There have also been calls for the creation of a national public database of water quality indicators and boil-water advisories, in response to contaminant threats to Canadian drinking water; a national water inventory; and the accelerated gathering of basic data about groundwater. The Council of Canadian Academies called for detailed modelling of the critical exchanges between surface and groundwater and monitoring of home wells for more hazards than bacteria count and water level.

In 2010, Ecojustice inquired into how well Canadians were being protected from contaminated drinking water. One study examined contaminant risks, another the enforcement of water safety laws. Both reported shortcomings in the record that made it difficult to determine whether the public was being protected. The environmental NGO fingered inconsistent public disclosure of how well municipal drinking and waste water systems were meeting water safety guidelines and "significant gaps" in the public record of enforcement actions taken against polluters.

The following year, the multi-sector NRTEE called for better metering of the vast quantities of water abstracted and used by

Canada's expanding resource sector. The soon-to-be-dissolved advisory panel urged the federal Crown to develop an ability to forecast water demand and supply, with more refined forecasts available for individual watersheds. Weighing Canada's vulnerability to climate change, also in 2011, scientists at Simon Fraser University called for continuous, comprehensive monitoring and public disclosure of water quality and flow conditions and of their supporting ecosystems. It was much the same mission that several of the same researchers had earlier proposed for an "environmental sustainability reporting" agency.

The key requirements for safeguarding Canada's water that attract strong consensus are:

· View and manage Canada's water resource as one body, above and below ground, co-extensive with critical ecosystems and topographical features.

· Organize governance of water issues within the hydrological perimeters of significant watersheds.

· Create management agencies that bring to the table as many stakeholders in a watershed as practical.

· Give those agencies clear, nationally consistent mandates and measurable objectives for water safety and supply security.

· Dramatically improve nationwide monitoring of water and ecosystem resources and institute public reporting of their stock, condition, and flows (both to inform management choices and confirm progress toward, or retreat from, objectives).

An approach including those elements would assign clear goals to accountable agencies with explicit powers and holistic views of their jurisdiction—much, in fact, as the European Water Framework Directive discussed in Chapter 4 does.

And we need to stop driving with our eyes closed. Ignorance in the face of threats to our natural security cannot be bliss.

Data points alone aren't enough to tell us what the fragmentation of boreal forests for seismic surveys, access roads, pipeline corridors, drill pads, and the other physical changes necessary to energy development does to the water passing through them. Obliging industries to report the toxins they release to the environment in their operations or the exotic molecules embedded in their products is pointless if research is not done to determine the effect of those complex synthetic compounds on wild and human life.

Perhaps the most alarming gap in our natural security intelligence has to do with climate change. One of the most astounding media misses of the past decade was the failure of news outlets to inform Canadians that the most populated parts of their country have been losing water for the past third of a century.

That loss is not trivial. On average, from 1970 to 2004, each year brought southern Canada 3.5 cubic kilometres less water yield—the net amount available for ecological or human economic use over a given geography and time period—than the previous one.[13] That's the loss each year of nearly enough water to supply all 33.5 million Canadians with water for a year.

There is no reason to expect that trend—confirmed by more than a quarter-century of observations and consistent with other emerging climate changes—to reverse. There is considerable reason to fear it will accelerate over the decades ahead. At the existing rate of loss, it would still take most of the rest of the century for southern Canada's water "income" to drop by a quarter. But for regions such as southern Ontario and the dry southwestern prairie from the Rockies to Saskatchewan, where existing water resources are already stretched to the limit, economic demands must adapt to nature's clawback of an increasing share of the water it supplies.

That unavoidable reality presents Canada with an urgent need to better understand the performance of our water-productive and water-dependent ecosystems under conditions of long-term decline in water availability, upward shifts in the seasonal ranges of temperature, and increasingly volatile, violent weather events. Only armed with that knowledge may we be able to adjust our industrial, agricultural, energy-production, and environmental-protection practices so that Canadians continue to enjoy ecological security under very different climate and weather conditions.

We must also reduce the risk to human and wild life from the accumulation of physiologically active compounds in the water circulating back and forth between built and natural environments. Before the rounds of cuts to government science in 2011 and 2012, Health Canada's target for assessing the individual risk of 4,300 substances still on its to-check list was 2020.

Meanwhile, more compounds are brought into use each year, more are added to the environment with each shower and toilet flush, and the compounds already in rivers and lakes decay and re-form into derivatives about which we know effectively nothing.

With adequate resources, we may eventually determine the toxicity of everything we're releasing into Canada's streams and lakes—and even how their combinations and by-products of decay affect us. Already we know that some useful compounds—dry-cleaning fluids, motor lubricants, oral contraceptives—also have deleterious effects and that some clearly pose a greater risk than others.

A small but growing number of jurisdictions has concluded that it's worth the extra effort to retire the most toxic chemicals currently in use as soon as less-toxic substitutes can be developed. Some measures to promote such so-called Green Chemistry policies place sundown dates on the approval for commercial use or sale of certain high-concern compounds. A softer approach requires manufacturers or importers to perform "due diligence" searches for, and give consideration to, alternative ingredients with fewer health or environmental effects.

Realigning water decision making with water's natural geography; equipping the public, business, and decision makers with adequate, timely, and broad water intelligence; closing the most threatening gaps in our understanding of our vulnerabilities—these three tasks are essential to ensuring the safety today and security in an uncertain future of Canada's water.

As several reviews have also noted, additional choices could make those goals easier and cheaper to reach. They come, however, with a catch of our own making. Commonly known as "economic instruments," these rest on sound principles.

One recurs almost religiously in government policy statements, though it is far less apparent in federal or provincial actions. That is the principle of "polluter pays": if you damage your neighbour's property or the environment we all share by releasing noxious material into it, you ought to foot the bill for making good that loss. Another derives from the observation—a commonplace of economic and environmental literature—that the "externality" of environmental impairment to conventional cost accounting, and its corresponding absence from corporate bottom lines, produces a market failure in damage to the public's interest in ecological services. The obvious, much attempted solution is to "internalize" those environmental costs by putting them on financial balance sheets—part of the intent behind levying fines on industry for pollution.

The simplest and most frequently advocated way to internalize one key environmental cost is to raise the price that Canadians habitually pay for water.

Currently, fewer than half the country's homes served by water utilities are equipped with meters to record their consumption. Those without them pay one price for as much water as they can use. Many of the minority of homes and businesses equipped with water meters pay higher rates for water consumption above certain thresholds, but we are unaware of any whose rates reflect *all* the costs associated with providing it—let alone secure its safety and supply into the future.

As the NRTEE observed in its 2011 review of the vulnerabilities of Canada's multi-billion-dollar resource sector to water threats, the country's voraciously thirsty mines, mills, and oil sands bitumen upgraders receive the immense volumes of water they consume or contaminate at even less cost—typically for free.

In telling research, environmental economist Steven Renzetti has demonstrated the consequence. While paying some of the world's lowest prices for water, Canadians use more of it per capita than anyone else except our North American neighbours. Renzetti's survey of developed countries reveals a clear inverse relationship between water rates and consumption. The countries with the steepest water charges also consume the least of it.

Putting a price on the private use of public water—at a minimum, the full price of its future supply and security—would serve several desirable ends. It would discourage waste, removing the all-you-can-eat temptation of goods that come free or at a fixed price with no limits. It would create incentive for large users to invest in process changes or other innovations that reduce water use. To the extent that Canadians used less water, they would also save the vast amounts of energy (and associated costs) it takes to extract, store, treat, deliver, and heat water for our many uses. Lastly, paying an honest price for what comes out of our taps would provide the financial resources to ensure that they continue to run: paying to replace water and waste infrastructure as it reaches the end of its service life, to secure water sources against land-use changes and other "upstream" threats, to neutralize the exotic new molecules in drinking water, and to safely sequester residual contaminants in sewage sludge.

Other economic instruments run the gamut from tax levers to the creation of specialized markets for the right to use industrial quantities of water.

Few municipal property taxes discriminate between properties with lot-to-lot pavement and those with porous lawns and gardens that allow rainwater to percolate into soils. Tax penalties for the first and subsidies for the latter are two examples of ways to better align necessary tax collection with green goals for water and other environmental values.

Historically, Canadian regulation has generally set a limit on the pollution that is permitted from a given industrial or municipal facility. Facilities that exceed their permitted emissions may face penalties. The approach is costly to enforce, "criminalizes" normal business activity, and provides no incentives for industry to reduce emissions any more than required.

So-called pollution fees overcome at least two of those short-comings and reduce the third. These operate by determining the maximum amount of pollution that a particular receiving water body can safely absorb and charging industry for the use of that available public resource. Enforcement is still required to ensure accurate billing, but the high cost and uncertain outcome of judicial prosecution for permit violations is likely to be lower.

The possibility of limiting the total emissions permitted under a pollution fee system like the foregoing introduces another opportunity: the "cap and trade" approach first proven effective in reducing North American releases of the sulphur and nitrous oxide gases that produce acid rain.

In this arrangement, permits to release pollutants up to the environmental cap are distributed to emitting facilities (typically either by auction or based on historical releases). Facilities that reduce emissions to levels below their permitted volume may then "trade" (sell) the surplus permits to others whose permits are insufficient to cover their releases. Permits expire and new ones are required; issuing fewer permits over time lowers the cap, forcing emissions downward. In the case of acid rain, the approach reduced emissions sooner, and far more cheaply, than had been predicted for conventional command-and-control regulation. Cap and trade has, of course, also been advocated (and in Europe applied) as the lowest-cost strategy for reducing greenhouse gas emissions. Ontario's South Nation River Conservation Authority operates a somewhat similar "trading" system, which seeks to cap and reduce phosphorus releases in that watershed by requiring new emitters to pay to "retire" old emissions, through a fund that upgrades manure handling on farms, a known "non-point source" of phosphorus-laden runoff.

A different sort of cap and trade might also be applied to expedite the allocation of scarce water to the most productive use.

At present, in most of the country, permits to use water in large volumes for industrial purposes, including (where they apply) agriculture, are extended or withdrawn by government on an individual basis. Many of these have been in the same hands for decades, but in legal form they remain concessions of the Crown (usually in right of a province). Typically, they entitle the permit holder to withdraw a specific maximum volume of water from its source over a period of time. There may also be other restrictions, such as not lowering a surface pond or lake by more than a certain amount.

The system provides certainty of supply for some water users at the expense of others. Holders of legacy permits face little incentive to use water more efficiently. In parts of Alberta and British Columbia where existing supplies are fully permitted, even new industries wishing to innovate more water-productive products or services may be prevented from doing so. Unable to support the kind of innovations that will be most crucial and most profitable in a water-stressed world, those region's economies will suffer.

The "first in time, first in right" water licensing in force in western provinces means that available water goes first to fulfill the permits of longest standing (first in time), potentially leaving sharply reduced amounts or even nothing for "junior" licensees, regardless of which licence holder will produce more from the water used. Water may flow to a wasteful producer of low-value products, while a highly efficient user, producing much more valuable products, goes without.

Eastern provinces adopted varieties of "riparian" water law. Inherited from Britain, which has more people and less geography, this variant allows landholders along a river bank (hence "riparian") to use as much water as they like—so long as the stream flows essentially unimpaired and unaltered to the next neighbour downstream. It was this condition that the Kalamazoo Vegetable Parchment Company failed to respect in the case described in Chapter 3.

Moreover, permits issued long ago to remove specified volumes of water from western streams, even if those volumes were modest when the permits were issued, are unresponsive to long-term reductions in southern Canada's water income. In parts of southern Alberta, the amount of water that could be drawn from rivers under licences assigned in some cases more than a century ago exceeds the amounts now flowing through the watershed. This mismatch can only become more acute, and affect more places, as southern Canada dries out.

Allowing water permits to change hands more freely addresses some of these problems. The innovator who finds a way to get more value from a litre or acre-foot (the antique metric still in use in some places) of water can share some of that added value with an incumbent user who releases permitted water from a less efficient purpose to the more productive use. In drought, the ability to draw the greatest economic benefit from available water carries advantages for society as a whole. If permits entitled holders to a certain *share* of available water rather than a certain *volume*, as is done in parts of Colorado, this "trade" could be accomplished under a "cap" that rose and fell with the water estimated to be available in any given year or season.

There are cautions to be raised around such water exchanges, however. When every drop of water removed from a river under an agricultural licence is put to work, the result may be more "efficiency" in generating per-litre profit but less water than the same licence left in the river before, when producer "inefficiencies" left a significant amount of "wasted" water to slip back into the environment.

International experience suggests that the economic advantages of water exchanges need to be backed by strong measures to ensure that the public's pre-eminent interest in vital, productive ecosystems is preserved. Otherwise, water-hoarding, rent-seeking, and other undesirable behaviours will tempt those in a position to pursue them at potentially great environmental and public cost. One potential check against such unintended negative outcomes is a concept we'll explore in depth in the next chapter: the doctrine of public trust.

Yet another form of economic instrument that can be put to the service of water security has less to do with the water than with what happens around it. Payment for ecoservice arrangements recognizes that landscape management choices—whether to plow a field or leave it in pasture, whether to let a forest stand or cut it for timber, whether to drain a marsh for development or leave it alone—have a bearing on the water those landscapes produce. These arrangements deploy a variety of mechanisms for consumers of that water—industry or municipalities—to reward private landowners for activities that will secure the supply and quality of water their land generates.

For these many presumed benefits, a number of studies have investigated the adoption of economic instruments to better connect Canadians' water choices to our pocketbooks.

The strongest Canadian advocates of harnessing environmental ends to economic incentives are housed at the University of Ottawa. Its Sustainable Prosperity group is led by economist Stewart Elgie and counts former national Reform Party leader Preston Manning among its advisors, alongside resource industry lobbyists, former federal deputy ministers, and top academics. It is preoccupied with rectifying the pervasive moral hazard tempting Canadians to overuse their underpriced environment.

"Where market prices omit environmental costs and benefits," Sustainable Prosperity's mission statement argues, "rational economic decisions lead to environmental harm, as well as to economic distortions and inefficiencies." In short, capitalism wastes the environment because it's cheap. The group's answer is "'getting the prices right'... adjusting market prices to include environmental costs and benefits."[14]

In 2011, the Ottawa group released a "state of knowledge" report, entitled *Sustainable Prosperity*, about some of these economic instruments. It reviewed examples of alternative water pricing, pollution pricing, water exchanges, and payments for water-related ecoservices to see how they might accomplish the goal of "environmental pricing reform" for Canada. It found that none were simple to implement. Nonetheless, some models did offer "reasonable success stories." In particular, the group saw promise in "scarcity pricing" for water during periods of low water supply and in trading permits for the use of water held in stock, so to speak, in storage reservoirs. The researchers emphasized that such permits should be based on shares of seasonally available water, rather than fixed volumes.

"Theory, and international policy experience," the report concluded, "suggests that using market-based instruments together with traditional regulation can achieve desirable water-policy outcomes at a lower economic cost than regulation alone."

The pro-market Ottawa think tank's endorsement came with caveats. Some had to do with limited government capacity to design and administer price-rectifying economic policy instruments. But a greater "barrier," it suggested, was Canadian attitudes. "The 'cultural, social and even spiritual importance that many Canadians assign to water,'" it observed, quoting a previous analysis, "poses a particular challenge" to the introduction of economic measures to protect and preserve that water.

Indeed, apprehension about the potential commodification of water makes many Canadians unreceptive to any discussion of water in economic terms. Nonetheless, the Conference Board of Canada saw potential in specialized markets to allocate water more productively (after first satisfying in-stream needs and "social priorities").[15] Likewise, the expert panel assembled by the Council of Canadian Academies to study groundwater found "considerable evidence that greater use of economic instruments such as water prices, abstraction fees and tradable permits has potential to promote more-sustainable groundwater use."[16]

The panel was less optimistic about price- or market-based incentives for reducing groundwater contamination—mainly because of the difficulty of assigning responsibility for the diffuse non-point sources of much of the pollution creeping into groundwater, such as road runoff during rainstorms. That group, too, commented on the "institutional and political" barriers to introducing ideas of market exchange in the same breath with water.

The obvious connection between the low price that Canadian homes and industries pay for water and our spendthrift use of it cannot be overlooked, however. The NRTEE, in its 2011 examination of resource industry exposure to water supply shocks, urged that it be billed for water based on the volume taken, with the money directed to maintain the watersheds that produced the water. Former Reform leader Manning, Victoria's POLIS policy centre, one of the authors of this book,[17] and many others have also argued that all of us who use water, with humanitarian exceptions, need to bear the full cost of securing its future safe supply.

The authors of a 2006 report card that gave the federal Crown an F for its multiple failures to protect our drinking water had one "hopeful observation" to make. "There is at least one and sometimes several, provinces where each of these individual aspects of drinking water protection is done well."[18]

Ontario's Conservation Authorities are models of watershed-based management that have been emulated, at least in spirit, in other provinces. Its source-water protection rules, designed to keep landscape pollutants out of wells and groundwater, are similarly progressive.

Alberta has undertaken water inventories of its major river basins and pioneered, with extreme caution, the market exchange of water-withdrawal permits in the South Saskatchewan River system. It, along with Nova Scotia and Yukon, have made it mandatory for municipal water providers to meet the full suite of federal Guidelines for Canadian Drinking Water Quality, covering microbiological, chemical, physical, and radiological qualities.

The evolution continues. British Columbia's century-old Water Act was under review as this was written. One feature that was conspicuously open for discussion was the "first-in-time, first-in-right" seniority system for allocating fixed volumes of water from provincial streams and lakes to locked-in users.

Alberta's government, facing the increasing need to stretch declining natural water supplies in the country's driest province across a growing economy, considered expanding its experiment in giving markets a role in allocating some (limited) water. The subject sparked duelling views.

Water Matters, an Alberta-based environmental NGO, and Ecojustice released a proposal to expand market exchanges of permitted water withdrawal rights, based on fixed shares but fluctuating amounts of water available for removal from Alberta rivers after ecological needs were satisfied.

Jeremy Schmidt, a geographer cross-trained in ethics and philosophy, took a different view in an analysis for the non-partisan Parkland Institute in political economy at the University of Alberta. Schmidt doubted "that either 'efficiency' or the satisfaction of 'preferences' through markets can solve Alberta's water problems." Instead, Schmidt advocated communitarian frameworks for negotiating water use. One might establish water as a "common-pool resource," in which many groups and individuals may hold a variety of rights in "private, public or... different forms of communal tenure." Another would recognize a public trust in water, which must be reflected in use decisions that protect public interests "greater than the sum of private interests."[19]

A growing number of cities have introduced volume-based pricing for municipal water—the simplest and least controversial form of economic leverage to reduce waste and raise funds to pay for improved water security. Several provinces require large users to report the volume of water they take out of surface sources—lakes and streams. Fewer insist on knowing what's pumped from underground, despite the linked nature of surface and groundwater. Only one—Nova Scotia—bills industry for the water it uses (others have tried and backed away after meeting resistance).

Canada's developed-country peers have gone further on almost every front. Chapter 4 explored the European Water Framework Directive, with its explicit mandates, target dates for achieving measurable water quality goals, and plans for accomplishing them that recognize natural geographies ahead of national, state, or canton borders. France, Germany, and the Netherlands have all levied pollution fees for decades, mainly as a way to fund the construction of water and waste treatment infrastructure.

Even in those countries, however, there is some way to go to meet Sustainable Prosperity's goal of fully pricing pollution. France's emissions taxes have been estimated to recover only about half the measurable cost of the environmental damage that polluters cause.

Australia, a close constitutional cousin of Canada within the British legal heritage, experienced unprecedented drought in its most important agricultural watershed, the Murray-Darling, in the first decade of the twenty-first century. The region's states overcame rivalries and embraced water exchanges to make the most of what little water they did get. By one estimate, areas where farmers were allowed to trade water among themselves—with higher-value, more-efficient producers able to buy or lease permits from less-productive operators—experienced less than half the economic loss from the drought than they would have suffered without that freedom.[20]

Simpler forms of economic leverage have found their way into tax rates in the United States. There, as of 2012, some four hundred cities and utility districts were charging higher water and sewer service rates to customers who paved a high proportion of their property—thus adding to the estimated 10 trillion gallons of untreated runoff from urban surfaces that enter U.S. waterways every year.[21]

Europe's REACH program provides incentives and requirements for industries to replace the harshest and most hazardous exotic compounds in use with more benign substitutes. In 2012, the European Commission provisionally added six more chemicals to the thirty-three already on its "priority hazardous" list of compounds that must be eliminated from use within twenty years. The latest products put on the commercial equivalent of death row in Europe included persistent organochlorine biocides heptachlor, dicofol, and quinoxyfen; a bromine-based flame retardant; and dioxin and dioxin-like polychlorinated biphenyls (PCBS).[22]

At almost the same time, California's Department of Toxic Substances Control (DTSC) issued draft regulations to implement that state's 2008 so-called Green Chemistry initiative. The draft rules ordered chemical manufacturers doing business in the state (and, if they failed to comply, importers and even retailers) to review their use of roughly three thousand identified "chemicals of concern." Businesses using any of them would have eighteen months to tell authorities which less-toxic compound they planned to substitute for the "chemical of concern" or offer a good explanation for why they were sticking with the more hazardous formula.[23]

If the explanation does not satisfy California's DTSC, the proposed regulations would allow it to prohibit the sale of products containing a listed toxin. The Green Chemistry initiative also taps the power of shame as part of its enforcement strategy. Its draft regulations included authority to make public a rogue's gallery of violators (formally, a Failure to Comply list), revealing details about toxic compounds that remained in their products.

The tactic leveraged earlier experience with the United States Toxic Release Inventory. It requires identified industries to report significant releases of several hundred listed compounds to the U.S. federal government. When it disclosed that some publicly traded firms were contributing large volumes of toxic pollution to the environment, their share prices dropped sharply. The companies whose market value dropped the most, studies determined later, were also those that subsequently reduced emissions the most. The subsequent rebound in their reputation was reflected in the recovery of their stock's market price.[24]

Finland has adopted a similar strategy, with a central database where competitors, civil society groups, or individuals can find out what environmental permits are issued to individual firms, as well as their reported discharges to air and water and their solid wastes.[25]

This brief survey of the variety of ways that other places have taken action to defend their water highlights another missing piece in our natural security pointed out by several of the last decade's studies: our failure to learn.

In studying the difference between the European Union's Water Framework Directive (WFD) and Canada's water management regime, water scholar Emilie Lagacé highlighted the WFD's Common Implementation Strategy. It organized subject-area working groups, drawn from all its member countries, with the explicit mission of sharing their expertise. The groups, Lagacé found, "increased trust and interpersonal relationships [and] facilitate[d] the flow of information and joint research" from EU states with higher capacities to those with less.[26]

POLIS, Sierra Legal Defence/Ecojustice, and the Gordon Water Group have all recommended that Canada's fragmented federal and provincial agencies would benefit from a similar formal silo-busting process.

We have not commented on two measures widely advocated as necessary to the defence of Canada's water: a declaration by the federal Crown that water is a human right and additional statutory bans on the bulk export of water.

On the first, we are of two slightly different views. One of us (Pentland) generally supports the recent declaration by the Canadian federal Crown of a human right to water as a possibly beneficial gesture. The other (Wood) finds little in the record of declared "human rights" to support expectations that extending them to water will accomplish much and in any case dissents from the view that humans enjoy "rights" in nature at all, as distinct from civil rights protected by a society of laws.

On the second, the authors concur that the laws of physics and economics are likely to render those of Parliament moot.

Existing statutes in nine of the ten provinces ban the diversion of water from their major watersheds, with minor and well-defined exceptions. The century-old Canada-U.S. Boundary Waters Treaty prohibits removals from boundary waters by either signatory without the prior approval of the International Joint Commission. (What America does with rivers that cross the border and don't come back, like many in British Columbia, is beyond Canadian influence.) An interstate charter with congressional imprimatur prohibits bulk transfers out of the Great Lakes basin, except in very narrow circumstances and small amounts. At the time of writing, Parliament was also considering a private member's bill that would further prohibit diversions of water either from or into rivers that flow across the international border.

Future governments facing a different political climate could over-turn any of these safeguards against bulk water exports, of course. We nevertheless support them, if only because we find they help to silence proposals that otherwise distract us from more pressing water issues.

Geography and energy, by contrast, cannot be repealed. South-ern Canada has no water to spare. In fact, it is losing the water it has previously enjoyed, and its strongest centres of economic growth—Alberta and southern Ontario—are the first to hit the wall of "no more to go around." Under no conceivable circumstance (other than out-right military menace, which would similarly render legal injunctions moot) will it be in the political interest of any southern-tier provincial government to permit the diversion away of water already oversub-scribed by Canadians.

Hydrological circumstances are different in the North. Records and forecasts both indicate that higher latitudes, including northern Brit-ish Columbia, are receiving more precipitation than in the past. Several schemes dreamed up in the last century proposed to move northern Canadian water to imagined markets in the U.S. southwest. But set aside the near-certain overwhelming popular sentiment against any such plan. By any envisaged route, the enormous expenditure of money, energy, and materials required to move such a mass of water so far, and so far up over several mountain ranges, would make the final product more expensive by far than water obtained in any other fashion. In a nature-scarce world, there essentially isn't enough energy or cement to build the thing.

In short, although these issues worry many Canadians, they are peripheral to the failures of fragmented, misaligned governance, patchwork standards, weak enforcement, and willful ignorance that constitute the real gaps in our natural defence.

The existence of a strong expert consensus around the steps that would give meaningful protection to the health and safety of Canadi-ans' water does not mean they will be taken.

Our leaders know what should be done. The groups surveyed here and others have been pointing out for a decade or more what we need to do. Between 1995 and 2009, senior advisors to a succession of federal environment ministers tried nearly a dozen times to draft some of the best suggestions into policy—and to interest political leaders in enacting them.[27] None succeeded. Some ideas were unpopular or ran counter to partisan ideology. More met resistance from incumbent political power centres or vested economic interests.

Reasons not to proceed with change are easy to find. The suggestion of basin-scale management units runs up against provincial, municipal, or other in situ governing bodies that seldom relinquish authority willingly to new entities. Putting the biological needs of instream ecosystems first becomes harder when it means putting aside human economic wants. Requiring consumers to pay the full cost of securing their water supply for the present and future meets resistance from social groups concerned about access for the poor and from industry accustomed to paying nothing for water (and whose competitors in other jurisdictions may continue to receive water for nothing). Other firms are reluctant to retire products or processes that have made agreeable profits over the years without immediately killing or injuring anyone, on the strength of speculative connections between their chemical ingredients and genetic abnormalities.

There is one action, however, repeatedly identified as essential for any subsequent reform, policy, or decision to be effective—that happens also to escape most of these reasons for inaction: institution of a comprehensive, current, and detailed inventory of our built *and natural* water infrastructure.

The multiple demands on Canada's water mount. Some are more compatible than others. Some have higher costs in lost ecoservices. Some uses, to be practical, earn our national and individual bank accounts a better return than others—on or off the books of conventional economic accountings. Whoever must choose where to direct water, or where to direct capital to take advantage of water, must wrap their decision making around a dynamic web of interacting variables, from timing and temperature to cost and availability.

"Financial markets, investors, regulators and analysts can all refer to reliable and regularly refreshed core data like consumer prices or regional hiring rates," economist Renzetti observed after encountering a dearth of information on which to estimate water's contribution to Canada's wealth. "The unprecedented stakes now riding on choices about water accentuate the need for similarly refined and robust reporting on its flow through the economy."[28]

This means monitoring water stored in snowcaps and water tables, the condition and flows of surface water, the amounts being withdrawn and returned, where and when that is happening, and what's been added to the water when it rejoins the natural cycle, all in as close to real time as technology allows.

These are skills Canadians excel at, and the price of the necessary hardware is plummeting. This country has long boasted some of the world's leading mapping skills—the benefit of so much geography. It's also led in remote sensing of the earth's surface, with companies such as MDA Corporation, formerly MacDonald Dettwiler, built on the economics of observations that cover vast areas of ground far more quickly and more thoroughly than field expeditions. An agency with a somewhat parallel mission in medicine is the independent, non-profit Canadian Institute for Health Information (CIHI), which creates databases, carries out in-depth analyses, and prepares expert reports to help legislators and other stakeholders better understand health care issues.

Other countries are again ahead of us in establishing an ecological intelligence capacity. Britain has completed a comprehensive inventory of the economic and hydrological value it receives from every ecosystem in its territory (admittedly, very much tinier than Canada's). But the United States, with a comparable acreage to cover, does far better through the combined reporting of the National Oceanic and Atmospheric Administration (NOAA) and National Aeronautics and Space Administration (NASA), the second of which has established the Earth Observatory, with its own website. Norway's government is bound by legislation not only to report to citizens on the state of its various "national capitals"—including natural capital—but to increase them all over time.[29]

We are in an unprecedented time. Nature, once overwhelmingly abundant, is running out. Climate is shifting around us at a pace beyond anything our planetary home has experienced since the last ice age. We are entering a different world, with a more energized metabolism that will produce cascading effects on Canada's natural assets—our forests, fields, tundra, and marshlands—and the water-yield income we enjoy. These changes may even be beyond our capacity to manage. But no strategy for weathering them can hope to succeed without the closest attention to their critical indicators.

Geographer Jared Diamond recounts how Japan, facing catastrophic deforestation in the seventeenth century, reversed the trend in the eighteenth, thanks largely to an inventory of its public forests that counted every tree by its species, size, and quality.[30] Our situation is equivalent. We could do worse than learn to count our trees—and lakes, rivers, and aquifers.

It is astonishing that a country that became one of the world's richest thanks largely to its natural resources and that claims the second-largest territory on the planet and one-seventh of its renewable water[31] should be so blasé about the health of such a fortune. It is all the more surprising when disrupted climate and deepening global ecological overdraft threaten even Canada's natural security.

Canadians do not lack means, motive, or opportunity to secure our water. What we have lacked is *political will.* And it has been most flaccid where it is needed most—at the top.

No country or federation has erected a perfect defence against every potential assault on its water. The European Union, in many respects a model of progressive watershed management, can descend into silliness, as when its Brussels mandarinate declared that water might no longer be described in packaging as a healthy beverage.[32] The U.S. Environmental Protection Agency's binding national standards notwithstanding, America's water continues to suffer a variety of injuries. Its taxpayers suffer the costs. The city of Baltimore is spending $2 billion to replace leaking sewers and water mains that in some places run centimetres apart, cross-contaminating each other's contents. Even that investment will not restore Baltimore harbour to a place you would want to swim in by the city's optimistic goal of 2020.[33]

But at least those federations, responsible for large and challenging geographies, our closest international peers, are trying. Canada is not.

Our national default strategy of leaving the defence of water to the provinces has produced uneven results that consistently test below international standards.

The reasons are little mystery. Provincial governments, like governments everywhere, harbour deeply rooted fears that good stewardship of their environment will drive away investment, business, and jobs. The governments of Ontario and Quebec admitted as much in a 2009 Trade and Cooperation Agreement. In article 11.3.3 of the agreement, the two provinces undertake that: "No Party shall encourage trade or investment by weakening levels of protection already afforded in its environmental laws, in particular, as an encouragement for the establishment, acquisition, expansion, ongoing business activities or retention in its territory of an enterprise."

Weibust and other researchers have demonstrated repeatedly that environmental regulation triggers neither capital flight nor investor reluctance. It scarcely matters. The reluctance of provincial leaders to act in ways that might be perceived as putting their citizens at an economic disadvantage vis-à-vis their neighbours reflects a well-known phenomenon of first-mover disadvantage.

When several players compete for a market or resource, even actions that would be in the best interests of all the participants may not be taken individually, because to do so would also, in the short term, raise costs or otherwise reduce that first mover's competitive position. In addition to the risk of putting the first jurisdiction at a disadvantage, to the extent that its actions did protect or restore a common asset—a shared water body, for example—the efforts also benefit "free riders," which reap improved conditions at no cost.

These "first mover" or "common action" problems are nothing new. The problem is implicitly acknowledged in the British North America

Act, Canada's founding constitutional document. It assigned fisheries to the federal Crown partly to avoid damaging competition among Atlantic provinces (and also because the presence of American fishermen in Canadian waters was a burning issue at the time).

Nova Scotia encountered the paradoxical problem within its own jurisdiction in the long tug-of-war between Halifax and Dartmouth and several surrounding suburbs over the sewage effluent that for decades progressively polluted the magnificent natural harbour they all share. While cities inland invested in waste treatment to protect their waterways, Halifax and its neighbours continued to flush their toilets more or less directly into the harbour, often leaving the floating evidence to rankle noses and tarnish the region's tourism image.

Even as residents deplored the decline in the harbour's water, however, no one municipality was prepared to place a comparatively greater burden on its taxpayers by investing in upgraded sewage treatment. Not, that is, until the competing communities were effectively "federalized" as a single municipality in 1996. With the first-mover problem out of the way, the former rivals at last acted together to build collection and treatment facilities for the combined communities' wastes that began operating in 2008.

Europe's sovereign member states partly resolved their common-action and free-rider problems through the Treaty of Amsterdam (see Chapter 4). In it, they agreed to pay significant financial penalties if they failed to meet common regulatory standards and other requirements established through the European Union. Canada's provincial governments have not been willing to submit themselves to the same discipline.

There is another reason why the Constitution assigned management of Atlantic fishing to Ottawa, hundreds of kilometres from salt water. As the late prime minister Pierre Trudeau, justifying Ottawa's role in a much later fisheries dispute, once tartly observed: "Fish swim."[34]

Rivers flow. The water that collects in the Rocky Mountains crosses three provinces and two northern territories. When the upstream and downstream management of those rivers comes into conflict, only the federal Crown is in a position to mediate or ensure an equitable outcome.

This is no academic problem. Upstream development in the Peace-Athabasca-Mackenzie river system has been shown to imperil wildlife and water downstream. There, the government of the Northwest Territories, after some of the most extensive consultations with its citizens ever conducted in Canada, has set the brave goal of keeping the Mackenzie's water "substantially unaltered in quality, quantity, and rates of flow."[35] How that will be accomplished in a watershed the size of western Europe is the subject of ongoing negotiation among the jurisdictions along its length. Handicapped by location, money, and power, the downriver Territories can look to only one referee to insist that negotiations remain fair: the federal Crown.

As other jurisdictions have found, a meaningful defence of a territory's natural security must ultimately engage the priority attention of its top national leaders.

Weibust has demonstrated, in her comprehensive study of environmental protection in federations like (and unlike) Canada, that centralized standards and enforcement offer the most effective and economically optimal way to protect water and other ecoservice capital assets. The Constitution confers on the federal Crown more than adequate authority to protect the public's interest in safe, secure water and stable, resilient, and productive ecoservices. It cannot credibly claim to be in doubt about the measures it could take. And there are some urgent roles that only the federal Crown can fulfill.

Yet it is missing in action.

We are not the first to say so. A partial list of others who have offered the same indictment includes the Canadian Institute for Environmental Law and Policy ("lack of Federal government leadership is a significant barrier, producing uncertainty and challenges for businesses"[36]); the Gordon group of water experts ("The federal government is systematically failing to represent the common interest of the Canadian public"); and the University of Calgary Institute of

Resources Law researchers Owen Saunders and Michael Weng, who forecast that "as Canada's waters come under more stress in the next few decades, the federal government's stance of deferring to provincial interests in areas of legitimate national interest [in water quality and quantity] will become increasingly untenable."[37]

In turning its back on Canada's water, our federal Crown is failing to defend the most vital of all national assets: the living habitat that sustains us, underwrites our health, and constitutes our greatest source of potential wealth in the human age of nature scarcity.

This is a delinquency Canadians cannot and must not accept.

TEN

~~~~~~~~~~

Magna Carta Natura

WHILE THIS manuscript was in preparation, two young friends became new parents. Let's call their daughter Olivia (not her real name but evidently the most popular girl's name in Canada these days).[1] Olivia will celebrate her thirteenth birthday the year the present century rolls over the clock on its first quarter. By then, its talismanic trends will be as evident in events as the radio and the automobile were by 1925.

What will Olivia's world look like?

Some of its features we can anticipate. Absent wholesale breakdowns of essential economic and political systems, we will likely still be enjoying many of the fruits of twentieth-century invention: cars, electric lights, effective medicines, the Internet. The flavour, scope, and, most especially, the price of our daily choices may be radically different, however. And in some ways, Olivia will wake up on her thirteenth birthday to a world quite different from today's.

Swollen by accumulating heat, the global tropics have expanded north and south, pushing subtropic and temperate zones toward their poles. Polar zones have contracted. All this repositioning of global atmospheric activity has redirected the aerial jet streams that drive

day-to-day weather across Canada and around the world, redistributing rain, snowfall, and evaporation around the map and the calendar.
The world is still coming to terms with how new weather patterns are
also redistributing wealth.

Olivia can't understand why her grandparents describe violent
swings from stuttering winter to sweat-drenched summer as "weird,"
however. She has grown up with them. Her teachers try to convey
how the world will continue to change. American news is filled with
accounts of farm families from northern Texas and Oklahoma abandoning what's being called the New Dust Bowl. In Africa and Asia,
famine has thrown once-"developing" countries back into poverty and
reduced others to lawless bandit regions.

Canada, they tell her, has mostly been a winner in this redistribution of the weather. Air masses moving across warmer oceans
are picking up more water than a century ago and dropping it on
northern British Columbia, Labrador, and northern Quebec. But
Olivia's Prairie cousins tell her that their family's farm has suffered
from recurring soggy springtimes and bone-dry, searing summers.
The family's crops have shrivelled without rain, sharpening feelings
against neighbours who have access to irrigation water.

In Ontario, where Olivia lives, few kids spend summer outdoors
anymore. Humidity saturates the air. Municipal waste outflows
maintain a trickle of water in the most important streams and reservoirs, but conservation authorities have struggled to keep swimming
areas free of toxic algae. The leaden humidity of summer is broken
by thunderstorms that often graduate into tornados. The previous
July, a twister cut a swath of destruction a kilometre wide across the
city of London. Water warnings are pretty common, but few people
still drink from the tap in any case. Olivia's parents restrict her to
water bottled in the North, which is relatively free of gender-bending
metabolites.

Olivia recalls the last few winters as hitting in January with fero-
cious blasts of cold and heavy snow and lasting for about ten days. She
did her science project last year on how ice used to cover most of the
Great Lakes in winter, acting like a lid to keep their water in them.

That hasn't happened in her lifetime, and now the exposed surfaces of Lakes Superior, Michigan, and Huron give up their water all winter long to dry winds blowing across them from the continental interior. Central Ontario's "snowbelt" has been getting that water back in record dumps of white stuff. A winter or two ago, one huge snowfall collapsed the roof of a friend's cottage.

Meanwhile, the water in Ontario's lakes continues to drop, especially in the fall. Olivia's mother is helping to design controversial plans to deepen navigation channels on the Great Lakes.

The North appears constantly in the news. People living around the oil boom at Norman Wells, along the Mackenzie River, display fish with deformities and complain about their mealy meat. Time-lapse satellite videos on the Internet show lakes in Nunavut that appear and disappear. Every September, Olivia's school holds a clothing drive for families that lost homes in the season's boreal firestorms.

Beyond her thirteen-year-old interest in boys and bands (some things don't change), Olivia's world is struggling in other ways that worry her parents more than her. They remember that when Olivia was a newborn, most of the talk about the cost of climate change came from industries opposed to paying to avoid it. But that was before insurers began buckling under damage claims from weather disasters. Then came the human catastrophes of rolling crop failures in India, Russia, Argentina, and North America. The global surpluses of grain that once mitigated local harvest failures have been consumed. Famine proceeds unchecked. Populations in some countries are plummeting.

World GDP stalled in the late 'teens and is trending downward. A growing share of it represents repairs and rebuilding rather than investment in new products or production. World leaders are taking the opportunity of the quarter-century milestone to hold a global summit. They hope at last to take serious steps to slash greenhouse emissions.

Some of their ideas are far more radical than anything considered tolerable when Olivia was born: rationing of air travel, permanent cuts in electrical supply to retire fossil-fuelled generation, a quadrupling of shipping costs for out-of-season produce. And still scientists warn that even those measures will not immediately slow the cascade of change disrupting Canadians' natural security.

And now, as Olivia extinguishes the last candle on her cake, a new alarm buzzes across the world's browsers. Ecologists have identified a thinning out of nature around the globe. Once-complex webs of many species are degrading into simpler collections of more durable but often more primitive organisms. For example, pale and spineless jellyfish pulse in parts of the ocean where fish of many colours used to swim. Now scientists warn that terrestrial ecoregions, such as Africa's Sahel, America's high plains, and the interior conifer forests of British Columbia, are likewise crashing toward simpler and less productive states.

Olivia serves her cake. Her parents try to push aside their fears for her future.

Wealth, as we understand it, is more than the number of digits to the left of the decimal point in a bank account. We include in our understanding of wealth financial assets, of course, but also one's health, in all its dimensions of physicality, mental and emotional satisfaction with life, meaningful work, and supportive social connections.

Wealth requires a measure of security. In 1994, the United Nations Development Program described the seven types of security that human beings seek. These are: economic security, food security, security of health, environmental security, personal security, security of our community, and political security.[2] Security is enriched by what we might describe as the spiritual essential: a sense of personal connection, exchange, and interdependence with the wider body of life that shares our habitat. It is for this last sense that people universally seek out and value nature, whether roughing it in the wild or nibbling a biscotti and drinking a latte in the shade of a city park.

But none of this—no wealth or comfort, from personal hygiene to the latest generation of web experience—is available without water. Water has always been a requirement of industry, an input factor of production so basic its availability is often simply assumed. It has been a source of kinetic power for Canadians from the age of Lachine's water wheels to the great hydroelectric installations of the twentieth century. Its absence has brought down civilizations, from ancient Mesopotamia to the Maya of Central America.

Water is no less essential to the ecosystems that, in another of those critical earth-system feedbacks, also secure its safety and supply. Those natural systems, in turn, form and sustain our own biological setting as a species. Their health determines ours. We are only as secure as our habitat.

More than ever in the twenty-first century, water is wealth, and healthy water reflects a healthy human habitat. Together, these realities define what we have termed "natural security." And in the twenty-first century, this kind of security will be increasingly threatened, and tougher to preserve, than the internal order and political frontiers that fall under the familiar rubric of "national" security. It little matters how well guarded our borders are from unauthorized incursion if the landscapes within them collapse from drought and contamination.

Yet we have seen that our existing arrangements for the defence of Canada's natural security are weak, incomplete, uninformed, and failing. International comparison tells us we should not be surprised. Wherever "junior" jurisdictions such as states, provinces, or Swiss cantons have shared economic arenas with others they perceive as competitors, environmental stewardship has suffered. Governments have repeatedly surrendered the public interest in clean water to industry protests that protection cannot be afforded—despite good evidence that this is untrue.

In fact, in an era of permanent and deepening nature scarcity, the opposite is true. We cannot afford *not* to protect our water.

But our "collective action" problem, beholden to provincial trepidation, inhibits even measures that would demonstrably benefit citizens. Small and poorer governments struggle to defend their environmental security against richer and larger populations upstream and upwind. Ontario, with no Canadian rivals to consider in the Great Lakes basin, cares better than most of its counterparts for its terrestrial hydrological assets but is content to ride free on American investment to restore the Great Lakes.

When Europe's states encountered the same problem, they agreed to submit to the external discipline of the Treaty of Amsterdam (see Chapter 4). This ingenious diplomatic instrument binds signatory sovereign states to pay fines that can rise into the hundreds of millions of euros if they fail to abide by EU mandates. Canada's provinces might do the same, building on the vehicle of the Council of the Federation. Given the provinces' reluctance to accept even the slight obligation to meet binding national safety standards for drinking water, we cannot consider that a likely outcome.

The United States, facing the same lack of collective action in the mid-twentieth century, invoked constitutional authority to "federalize" environmental protection with landmark legislation, including the Safe Drinking Water and Environmental Protection Acts. These were subsequently strengthened and, for the most part, robustly defended against ideological attacks.

The Canadian Constitution grants its federal Crown, as we have noted before, powers substantially similar to those of its Republican American counterpart. But rather than wield that authority to defend Canadians' environmental interests, generations of federal leaders have accepted the shackles of what has been termed the "political constitution"[3]— a polite term for cowardice in the face of provincial recalcitrance and rivalry. While successive (and, strikingly, mainly Republican) presidents instituted and sought to enforce national standards for safe water and air in the United States, Canada's leaders performed a dance of promise, bluster, retreat, and betrayal.

To each new eruption of public alarm, whether over polluted beaches in the 1960s or today's oil sands, the federal government of the day has made brave commitments to defend Canada's aquatic resources. In substance, however, these have seldom amounted to more than modest support from the sidelines for whatever measures the provinces were taking (or not) on their own. When the federal Crown's rare exercise of its power—for example, in defence of fish-bearing waters—brought it into conflict with the provinces, Ottawa called off its troops.

The flood of enthusiasm for globalization and unfettered markets over the quarter-century that preceded the financial crisis of 2008 gave both Liberal and Conservative ministries further reason, were any needed, to dismantle what few defences our natural security had briefly enjoyed.

Arguably the most invidious betrayal of Crown guardianship has been the failure to provide for an adequate natural intelligence capacity. Without robust monitoring of our water and supporting natural systems, Canadian public agencies, private businesses, and voting citizens can neither detect nor counter imminent environmental dangers. Imagine a parallel abdication of the Crown's responsibility for ensuring the nation's military defence. It is as if Ottawa were to let every surveillance satellite go dark, close down every maritime radar station, ground every air patrol, bring every coast guard and navy vessel back to port, and send every border-service agent home.

Canadians simply cannot know the extent or seriousness of their losses. That, of course, may be one reason no federal government has provided Canadians with such an accounting.

All of these trends have accelerated since Prime Minister Stephen Harper's ascent to power. In early 2012, reluctantly and under intense pressure from its own trade diplomats and senior scientists, numerous experts, and scores of environmental groups, the Harper ministry undertook anew to improve its monitoring of pollution from one priority area: the oil sands developments in northern Alberta. But the federal Crown's partners in the plan are the oil industry itself and Alberta's strongly pro-industry government. We wish the new plan well, but the experience of decades dilutes our optimism.

Meanwhile, other important natural defence assets have been scrapped, including science facilities in Ontario that studied how pollution and climate change affect lakes, and in the Arctic where those changes are having their most dramatic effects and liberating untold quantities of water once permanently frozen. A research program that we noted in Chapter 8 had been tracking the spread of industrial contaminants through the Canadian marine environment was eliminated completely.[4]

Legislative amendments in the spring of 2012 stripped from the venerable Fisheries Act crucial provisions that for decades required the federal Crown to protect not only commercially valuable fish but also the habitat that supports all aquatic life. New language prohibited only "serious harm" to "fish that are part of a commercial, recreational or Aboriginal fishery"—while granting the federal fisheries minister discretion to allow that as well.[5] That autumn, further amendments withdrew tens of thousands of smaller Canadian lakes and streams—an estimated 99 percent of our inland waters—from the coverage of the 130-year-old Navigable Waters Protection Act.

This is not what Canadians want.

Progressive business leaders, highly oriented toward metrics, have pointed out the rashness of attempting to manage ecological resources with inadequate information.

"[E]nvironmental assets that provide the 'services' that make life possible... are at least as important to the future economy as factories and machinery," the National Round Table on the Environment and the Economy noted in 2003. "To ensure development opportunities for future generations, Canada needs to track and consider all these important types of capital in making economic decisions. Otherwise we risk significantly depleting key human and natural assets without even being aware of it."

In 2005, the International Joint Commission consulted publics across the Great Lakes basin about the renewal of the Great Lakes Water Quality Agreement. More than four thousand groups and individuals responded. Summarizing their views, the IJC noted that most "wanted all levels of government to reinvigorate their efforts" to improve the lakes' water.[6]

Financial shock and recession have not blunted Canadians' desire to better protect their natural security.

"In Canada, two-thirds of respondents (66%) think their federal government is paying too little attention to the environment," the international Angus Reid Public Opinion group reported in mid-2010.[7]

A 2011 survey funded by the country's largest financial institution found that nine out of ten Canadians foresee seriously damaging consequences for their prosperity "if nothing is done to improve the management of water resources in Canada."[8]

Canadians know how to protect our water and defend our natural security. We have told our leaders that we expect them to do so with vigilance and vigour. Yet they have not.

We regard this as a failure of sovereign duty of the first order.

In the past, the implications of this failure were merely unnecessary public cost and inconvenience. Now they are much, much greater. In an era of deepening ecological overdraft, Canadians must do more than plead with our governments.

We must oblige our leaders to acknowledge that in being entrusted with the exercise of Canada's sovereignty, they also hold a duty to the public interest and that no interest is higher than Canadians' natural security.

The law serves all (or at least ought to), and every Canadian has a stake in it. Moreover, the law is not static but evolves.

The documents that today are consolidated under Canada's Constitution Acts, 1867–1982, have much to say about the respective spheres of federal and provincial Crown *powers* but little at all to say about Crown *responsibilities*. Citizens are presumed to owe the Crown a duty of loyalty and obedience to laws. The Crown, on the face of our founding constitutional document, the 1867 British North America Act, owes the citizen nothing.

That is fully in keeping with the medieval origins of the legal tradition of which Canada is a part. Legal scholars and constitutional antiquarians trace that lineage to the absolute monarchs of the Middle Ages, whose authority was rooted in bloodlines, bloodletting, and a claimed divine title and who brooked no constraints at all. The ghost of that absolute power lives on in the widely appropriated legal concept of "sovereign immunity," in which a sovereign state by definition can commit no wrong and hence may not be sued.

But contemporary society has moved beyond rule by the brawler with the biggest sword, as our rich body of law fully recognizes. And even "immune" sovereigns are sometimes constrained.

The American Constitution, born out of rebellion against the British monarch, is explicit in accepting its authority as a grant from "we the people." In practice, U.S. governments have been as quick as any other to embrace the unaccountability that sovereign immunity conveys. Even so, the fundamentally democratic framing of America's founding document embeds a reciprocal duty of the governing to the governed that, as we shall see, has practical implications.

Canada achieved its national independence without decisive rebellion. Our Constitution Act was framed instead in the shadow of monarchy. On its own terms, the powers it allocates flow from the blood descendants of the god-kings of yore, rather than from "we, the people."

In the everyday sense, of course, that is no longer how Canadians regard the Crown. Rather, we use the term interchangeably with words or phrases denoting the public interest. "Crown" land in this country is what others call "public" land. Whereas public prosecutors in the United States file charges against a criminal defendant in the name of "the people," in Canada they do so in the name of the Crown. Once, flesh-and-blood monarchs considered themselves the physical embodiments of their realm. Their diminished descendants today are hereditary players in a metaphorical pageant in which the physical crown embodies the nation, a notion that itself is coterminous with its people.

The Canadian Crown, to put it simply, is us: the Canadian public.

Legal historians trace this shift in perceptions of the Crown's anchoring moral identity to the British Parliament's increasingly muscular assertion of its sovereignty in the first half of the nineteenth century. Before that period, monarchs retained and often exercised the right to countermand the "advice" they received from Parliament.

Influenced by Enlightenment philosophies and the social upheavals triggered by industrialization, and encouraged by a succession of weak Hanoverian kings, the initiative passed from monarch to Parliament.

In the conventional view of the moral basis of contemporary constitutional monarchy, Parliament is the authentic seat of national sovereignty. It merely delegates the administration of that sovereignty to ministers of the day—to governments. These serve only so long as they hold the confidence of the people's representatives in Parliament. The latter may revoke that confidence, bringing a government down, or establish offices like that of the Auditor General to oversee government's performance.

The idea that Canada's senior political leaders are to serve the interests of its people, embodied in the Crown, and not the reverse, is reinforced again in the nomenclature and custom of government. In contrast to the unitary American presidency, at once head of state and government, our most powerful elected position is no more than the "first minister"—a term that in the old English from which it is adopted meant roughly the same thing as "first servant." The principal administrative divisions of the federal bureaucracy are known as "ministries," once again implying a primary duty of service.

Political initiatives pass into law only when the monarch's proxy (we might say "the people's" proxy), the Governor General, assents to legislation. Acts and regulations are expressed formally as the will of the "Governor [General] in council." In a similar conceit, that office-holder ceremonially introduces each new Parliament with a speech from the throne describing what "my Government" proposes to do. This phrasing, like the requirement for royal assent, expresses the essential underlying principle that the political bench serves the Crown—once an individual tyrant, in our time the embodiment of the Canadian public—and not the other way around.

The same sense used to be made explicit in a term that has gone out of fashion in recent decades: "public servant." The term that has largely replaced it, "public-sector employee," sacrifices, intentionally or not, a subtle presumption of responsibility.

In practice, of course, most Canadian governments have considered victory in a general election all the moral justification needed to do whatever leaders have believed to be—or believed they could justify as being—in the national interest. "Winning" government has mostly been about *getting* to do things and much less about *having* to do them. Sovereign immunity ensured that no liability was attached for failure.

Although power, moral authority, and constitutional symbolism may not align perfectly in our semi-medieval governing arrangement, leaving first ministers and cabinets with few effective checks, law and theory do agree on some of their essential duties. Maintenance of the country's currency is one such obligation of a national sovereign; we have seen recently in Europe the consequences of surrendering it too impetuously. Representing Canada's interest in international arenas such as the G20 or United Nations is another undisputed historical role for the sovereign Crown. Likewise, providing for the border defence of the realm and its internal order. (These last two obligations the Harper ministries have taken up with enthusiasm.)

These duties reflect the existential requirements of a functioning modern state: a currency reliable enough to support commerce, internal and external security, and working relationships with the neighbours. But the list is not exhaustive. In the era of nature scarcity, the biological underpinnings of Canadian society—the safety of our water and of the ecosystems that secure its future—are endangered. Habitat is not an ideological choice or a consumer preference: it precedes all other requirements of the human organism. There can, as a result, be no superior obligation of a responsible sovereign than to preserve the ecological means of a people's survival.

This is what "national security" means in an age of nature scarcity. It is the essence of our *natural* security. And, we assert, Canada's federal Crown bears an onus for its defence that it may no more shirk than it may the sovereign duties to keep money sound and the borders guarded.

This is increasingly clear to some of the least sentimental of analysts. In 2011, the Canadian army conducted a study of security threats likely to require a military response by 2040 (roughly the decade in which our young friend may become a mother herself). It concluded that the greatest dangers will arise from shortages of water and fossil energy and the impacts of a changing climate on societies.[9] In a similar exercise, the U.S. National Intelligence Council, in an unclassified assessment of future security threats, warned in 2008 that "growing energy, food, and water constraints; and worries about climate change" would be primary drivers of conflict by 2025.[10]

International investors have reached the same hard-nosed conclusion. At a New York conference on global risk in early 2012, professional fund managers with a combined $26 trillion under their administration warned that companies needed to be much better prepared to mitigate the effects of resource exhaustion and climate change on their businesses. "There is a genuine risk in our portfolios related to climate and sustainability," declared keynote speaker Kevin Parker, the worldwide head of Deutsche Asset Management, with more than $1.9 billion in its care. If investment professionals do not insist that portfolio companies plan for such risks, Parker added, they could be accused of "a dereliction of our fiduciary duties."[11]

Just as, we believe, may be national leaders who turn their backs on natural defence.

The idea that government may, even within a constitutional monarchy with its ghosts of absolutism, owe a particular and explicit duty to the governed is neither radical nor new.

It has ancient roots, was a norm of British law in the days of Adam Smith, and finds judicial confirmation in the United Kingdom of today. Echoes of the idea can be found in the jurisprudence of our legal cousins in the Commonwealth: India, New Zealand, and Australia. The United States, which shares much of its legal DNA with Canadian common law, has expressed the idea in the public trust doctrine, examined below.

In Commonwealth jurisdictions like our own, the idea is more often captured in the phrase that Parker employed: a "fiduciary duty." This, in law, is the obligation of an individual or agent in a position to exercise exclusive discretion over an interest belonging to another party, to administer that interest, in trust, for that party's benefit. These two ideas—of trust and fiduciary duty—are intimately bound up in law and ethics.

The paradigmatic example of a fiduciary duty falls on a person holding funds in trust, say for a minor. But the duty may also arise out of insubstantial and even speculative interests, such as the unobtained financial return on funds that a trustee failed to invest. It may apply to more than one beneficiary, whose financial needs or preferences may differ. On the other side of the relationship, the individual in a position to exercise such an exclusive degree of control over someone else's interests may be subject to a fiduciary duty even when it is not written down in a contract. That applies, for example, to the person keeping their bowling club's bank account. Under the onus of a fiduciary duty, they may use that money only for the club's benefit, not to take a personal shopping trip.

The application of this concept to government long precedes the Commonwealth. The laws of ancient Rome held that some features of the landscape—air, rivers, sea, and seashore—were common property for the use of all citizens. Magna Carta, the shorthand name for not one but rather a series of concessionary "charters" and guarantees forced upon King John of England and his successors in the thirteenth century, confirmed that ordinary citizens had the right to use Crown land for public purposes such as fishing and navigation. Until Parliament became the primary arena of redress for public grievances, eighteenth-century British justice relied heavily on what was known as the law of offices—a common-law tradition that regarded public offices as positions of "trust and confidence concerning the public," with fiduciary-like duties to the citizens they served.[12]

The pre-modern French civil code perpetuated the Latin notion of common property with respect to navigable waters and streams. It came to New France in the seventeenth century and endures to this day in Quebec and Louisiana. The Quebec Act of 1774 preserved its notions of common property in Canada.

The fiduciary duty is amply supported in private law—the legislation and jurisprudence that govern agreements among individuals, companies, organizations, or other private parties and that sort out who owes what to whom when those agreements go sour. Large bodies of precedent and analysis lay out the duties that the paradigmatic trustee described above owes to the minor whose money she manages.

A small but growing number of legal theorists, and some jurists, see fiduciary duty to be at the heart of legitimate democratic government as well. In lay terms: if government does not exist to serve the public good, what is it for? Sovereign rule may be either for the benefit of a few or for all; and if it is for all, no better description applies to the duty then incumbent on governments than "fiduciary."

Evan Fox-Decent, a legal scholar at McGill University, has teased out the history, foundations, and applicability of fiduciary duty to the realm of public law (the companion branch to private law, which embraces the workings of government) in *Sovereignty's Promise: The State as Fiduciary*, one of three titles shortlisted in 2012 as that year's best in Canada on political theory.[13] He finds several of the conditions that produce a fiduciary duty in private law clearly present in the relationship of individuals to the Canadian Crown.

At the core of these is that ordinary citizens have an interest in the extent, protection, and administration of legal rights (expressed in laws and regulations) which they cannot administer directly but must entrust to the agents of government. "Legal subjects, in other words, are in a position of *de facto* and *de jure* dependence on the state for the provision of legal order," Fox-Decent notes.[14] That dependence, he observes, arises inevitably from the state's assumption and exercise of sovereignty—and equally automatically triggers at least a potential fiduciary duty on its part toward its citizens.

"The conditions inherent to sovereignty disclose a free-standing and overarching fiduciary relationship between the state and each person subject to its powers," Fox-Decent concludes.

In the McGill scholar's view, the provision of basic legal order alone may not raise that potential to an actual fiduciary duty. "For the interest . . . to enjoy the protection of fiduciary law," he writes, it "must embody a substantial or vital interest that is entrusted to a party who has discretionary power of an administrative nature over [that interest]."

Those conditions occur, however, every time a citizen encounters the apparatus of the state, from the day his birth is recorded until his estate is probated at death. It was just such a fiduciary duty, Fox-Decent argues, that doctrines such as the law of offices addressed in the past by establishing the obligation of public office-holders to treat people fairly. And although the McGill scholar finds that other forms of accountability, notably the political accountability of Parliament, have eclipsed the state's fiduciary duty in the last two hundred years, they have not extinguished it.

The fiduciary duty endures, in other words. Fox-Decent holds, with Thomas Hobbes, that "the Office of the Sovereign, (be it a Monarch or an Assembly,) consisteth in the end [i.e., purpose], for which he was trusted with Sovereign Power, namely, the procuration of the *safety of the people*."[15] (Emphasis in the original.) In modern terms, we entrust our safety to our sovereign—the federal Crown. In the era of ecological overdraft, that safety relies far more on our natural defence than on the number of air patrols our forces fly over the Northwest Passage.

What Fox-Decent's deep historical, legal, and philosophical analysis draws our attention to, however, is that the Crown's fiduciary duty to the public exists even when political leaders of the day fail to perform it.

There is one other way in which the ancient and enduring fiduciary duty of sovereigns to the governed is worth examining. In contrast to the breaking of a political promise, breach of a fiduciary duty carries an implied right of action by the injured party. When the trustee runs off with the inheritance, the victimized orphan may sue to recover her money.

Something very much like that has happened frequently over the last 125 years in the United States, under what is known as the public trust doctrine. Its most-cited application was in 1892, when the U.S. Supreme Court found in *Illinois Central Railroad Co. v Illinois* that the city of Chicago could not convey a large portion of its harbour and land underlying it to the railway.

Public trust doctrine draws on legal tradition going back to those Roman antecedents. It holds that certain natural assets—primarily but not exclusively involving waterways and access to them—are the common property of all of a country's present and future citizens. Governments hold that property in trust, and they therefore bear a fiduciary duty to preserve and protect its value for all of those beneficiaries, now and into the future. As the U.S. Supreme Court emphasized, moreover, in ruling that Chicago was not within its powers to alienate the public's interest in its harbour, "the state can no more abdicate its trust over property in which the whole people are interested, than it can abdicate its police powers in the ... preservation of the peace." [16]

Plaintiffs, many of them motivated by environmental ends, have invoked the public trust with growing frequency in the last half century to bring action against American state, federal, and local government agencies that failed to protect aquatic ecological resources.

Perhaps its most celebrated modern application had its roots in the same murky events that spawned the movie *Chinatown*: the extension of Los Angeles' aqueducts in the 1940s. Reaching deep into the mountains 480 kilometres north of the city, engineers captured and diverted water from four of five freshwater streams that fed a remote salt lake in a closed valley. Amply watered, Los Angeles boomed, spreading irrigated lawns and golf courses across the southern California desert. Mono Lake, a geological holdover from an earlier epoch believed to be among North America's oldest water bodies, at an estimated 500,000 years, shrank by half. Its salinity doubled. That in turn affected the brine shrimp and alkali fly larvae that lived in the lake water and provided food for a million migratory birds a year.

In 1979, the National Audubon Society and a committee of self-appointed stewards of Mono Lake filed suit against the Los Angeles Department of Water and Power. They argued that the environmental damage done by its diversions from the Mono Lake watershed violated the public trust, and they asked the courts to order that they be reduced. In 1983, the California Supreme Court agreed and instructed the state water board to reconsider the volumes of water Los Angeles could take from Mono Lake's basin (in the end, diversions were reduced but not eliminated; Mono Lake regained some but not all its former extent).[17]

The public trust doctrine is more often relied on by American states themselves, typically to secure compensation or a change in behaviour from some industry or other party that is putting a natural asset at risk. The state of New Jersey, for example, sued the Jersey Central Power & Light Company for damages when power plants the company owned were held responsible for killing fish along the state's shoreline. In ruling for the state, the court confirmed that New Jersey possessed a "right and the fiduciary duty to seek damages for the destruction of wildlife which are part of the public trust."[18]

In 2011, two newer California environmental groups, together with five legal minors through their guardians, invoked the public trust and government's fiduciary duty in an effort to arrest climate change. In their pleading, the non-profit Kids vs. Global Warming and WildEarth Guardians called the U.S. District Court for the Southern District of California's attention to "more frequent heat waves . . . reduc[ed] summer water flows, and increase[ed] irrigation needs," among other injurious consequences of "warming due to human-induced global energy imbalance." They asked the court to "determine [that] the Public Trust Doctrine applies to the current climate crisis and issue appropriate equitable relief."[19] Nearly two dozen leading American professors of law signed an amicus (friend of the court) submission endorsing the groups' legal argument.

Although he was neither party nor amicus in that case, McGill's Evan Fox-Decent has also written in support of a citizen's right to "an atmospheric trust." As he argues it, "a fiduciary theory of public authority" obliges sovereign states to protect "a sustainable environment capable of supporting independent lives [that] individuals have reason to value."[20]

Although the public trust doctrine has found its fullest expression in the United States, it has been acknowledged in other jurisdictions as well, including some closer to Canada's own legal tradition.

British courts have found that local authorities in Birmingham and the London borough of Bromley were under an unwritten fiduciary duty to their taxpayers.[21] In 2002, India's Supreme Court cited British jurisprudence in finding that the state of Himachal Pradesh, high in the foothills of the Himalayas, had violated the public's trust when it conveyed twenty-seven bighas (about ten hectares) of public land along a rushing river to a motel company. In its judgement in *M.C. Mehta v. Kamal Nath*, the court ordered the land transfer voided, the motel demolished, and the riverbank restored.[22] Australia's High Court has invoked its citizens' "public right" to standing in court when "an interest of the general kind which the relevant public right was intended to safeguard or protect" is at issue.[23]

Canadian courts have resisted arguments asserting a fiduciary duty on the Crown. But they have not rejected them entirely.

The clearest judicial confirmations that such duties exist have come in cases involving First Nations claims against the Crown. The landmark precedent was set in 1984. That year, the Supreme Court of Canada found that the federal Crown had breached a fiduciary duty when, acting on behalf of the Musqueam First Nation in 1958, it leased 170 hectares of prime Vancouver real estate belonging to the Musqueam for use as a golf course, without fully explaining the terms of the lease to the band. Subsequent Supreme Court rulings have amplified the scope of the Crown's fiduciary duty to First Nations to reflect inherent aboriginal rights, in particular, by mandating that their holders be consulted about developments that may impact traditional territories.

The justices of the Supreme Court in 1984 were pointed, however, in asserting that the Crown's fiduciary duty to First Nations citizens was unique—"*sui generis*," as they put it—and without equivalent elsewhere in Canadian public law. This assertion was based on the nation-to-nation relationships established by treaties between the British Crown and various First Nations before Canada came into existence and the long aboriginal occupation of and claim to unceded landscapes where treaties had not been signed (as in most of British Columbia, including Vancouver).

With full respect to the legal scholarship of the Supreme Court bench, we find it difficult to see how the Crown can reasonably be held to a different standard of duty of care for some citizens than for others. (This works both ways, we might add, as in the federal Crown's failure to bring water services in First Nations communities to the same standard that other Canadians enjoy.)

The Court has also contemplated the existence of potential toeholds for the "fiduciary theory of authority" outside of the *sui generis* legal universe of First Nations law. Two decades ago, a forest company working on Crown land in the British Columbia Interior started a controlled fire to get rid of slash left over from its operations but failed to make sure the fire was fully extinguished. The following spring, its lingering embers erupted into a blaze that destroyed 1,500 hectares of forest, including environmentally sensitive riparian areas. A dispute arose between the province and the forest company over how much the latter should pay the former in compensation for the lost forest. The company, Canada Forest Products Ltd. (Canfor), was prepared to compensate the province for some share of the market value of the destroyed timber. But, echoing American states such as New Jersey, British Columbia held out for more, arguing that Canfor should also compensate the provincial Crown, as representative of the public's interest, for the additional value of the incinerated sensitive ecosystems. When the two could not settle, the dispute reached the Supreme Court of Canada.

The court's decision, handed down in 2004, dedicated several paragraphs to the question of whether Canadian provinces can, like American states, "sue as a representative of the public to enforce the public interest in an unspoiled environment." Writing for the majority, Justice Ian Binnie cited both *Illinois Central* and the Romans yet again. He also found support for the proposition in English law from the thirteenth century—when "[b]y legal convention, ownership of such public rights was vested in the Crown." After considering the American public trust doctrine as well, Justice Binnie concluded that "no legal barrier" stood in the way of the province's claim to compensation for "environmental damage to public lands"—an implicit affirmation of the existence of a public trust-like interest.

For other reasons (mainly having to do with the absence of a reliable way to place a value on the destroyed ecosystems), Binnie concurred in the majority decision that in the particular circumstances of the case, Canfor's liability did not extend beyond what it would have owed any other landowner for lost timber. Nonetheless, he made a point of identifying—if not resolving—several "important and novel policy questions" the case had raised. "These," the justice observed, "include the Crown's potential liability for *inactivity* in the face of threats to the environment, [and] the existence or non-existence of enforceable fiduciary duties owed to the public by the Crown in that regard."[24] (Emphasis in the original.)

The key elements to note in Justice Binnie's speculative comments are the phrases "liability for *inactivity*" and "enforceable fiduciary duties owed... by the Crown." Both hint at an answer to the root problem frustrating Canadian efforts to safeguard our most precious natural asset: the refusal of successive national governments to defend the public's existential interest in a healthy and resilient water supply. If the Crown owes a fiduciary duty of care for the "public trust"—those assets held in common for all Canadians, present and future—that is a duty that citizens may also have standing to ask the courts to enforce.

The court has cracked open the door for arguments based on the Crown's fiduciary duty in other cases outside the *sui generis* silo of First Nations law. In one instance, more than a thousand retired Canadian soldiers, including many who were disabled and some who had served in World War I, sued the federal Department of Veterans Affairs as a class for its failure to protect the value of funds it had held in trust for the veterans. Instead of investing the sums, the Crown had merely held the money, allowing it to be eroded by inflation. In a unanimous decision, the Ontario Court of Appeal held that the federal Crown's fiduciary duty to the vets required more. The Crown appealed to the Supreme Court. In 2002, it confirmed that a fiduciary duty did exist for the Crown, though it based its finding on the narrow fact that the plaintiffs in the case had a clear property interest in the financial return they might have enjoyed had the Crown invested their money properly.

Nevertheless, the idea that powerful state institutions may be called to account when they fail their duty to the public is finding echoes outside the academy and a handful of courts. No less rock-ribbed a figure than the commissioner of the Royal Canadian Mounted Police, Bob Paulson, acknowledged in 2011 that members of his storied force had so abused their authority over a decade of high-profile scandals, including the killing of a confused Polish traveller and recurring sexual harassment of its female officers, that the loss of public trust put its future in doubt. "I tell you, one day, there is going to be the removal of the Stetson if we don't get this straight," Paulson told the *Globe and Mail*.[25]

If Canada's iconic Mounties can contemplate dissolution for violating the public's trust in the delivery of internal order, we must wonder about the vulnerability of political leaders who fail to protect its natural order.

The public trust doctrine enjoins governments to "preserve and continually assure the public's ability to fully use and enjoy" its common property resources. It is well established that water is one of these. We would say their scope must also include the life-supporting ecosystems that make human use and enjoyment possible.

That doesn't mean water resources may never be exploited. Under the public trust doctrine as it has evolved south of the border, governments may "recognize and convey" proprietary interests in respect of common property—but only provided that the public interest is not "substantially" impaired. Much the same occurs now in Canada when provincial governments issue licences granting individuals or businesses the right to use Crown resources for hunting, trapping, fishing, or guiding. Provincial wildlife authorities typically restrict these by season or, in the case of hunting and fishing, bag and catch limits, to preserve the long-term viability of the ecosystem.

We can reduce the emerging health threats associated with newer forms of water pollution. We can preserve the ecosystems that give our species essential life support. We can do so in ways that will make us wealthier, both across the full spectrum of social capital and meaningful prosperity *and* in the hard-dollar terms of the GDP.

On the experience of the past, however, that will not happen if we leave our water's safety to a feckless federal Crown. Our water and the wealth it supports will be secure only when citizens are able to compel the Crown to fulfill its sovereign duty to preserve the life-sustaining attributes of water, air, and oceans and to collect the necessary intelligence to assure Canadians that they are protected.

Most simply, Parliament could enact into law an unambiguous acknowledgement of the federal Crown's duty to protect Canada's natural security. With that must go two companion obligations: first, to provide the public with sufficient timely information about Canada's natural inventory for people to be confident that the Crown is fulfilling its trust obligations, and second, but no less important, a presumption of "right of standing" before the courts for every Canadian to litigate any failure of the Crown to meet those obligations.

This is not to imagine an impossible-to-achieve legislative ideal. The state of Michigan has had these provisions on its law books since 1995:

(1) The attorney general or any person may maintain an action in the circuit court having jurisdiction where the alleged violation occurred or is likely to occur for declaratory and equitable relief against any person for the protection of the air, water, and other natural resources and the public trust in these resources from pollution, impairment, or destruction.

(2) In granting relief provided by subsection (1), if there is a standard for pollution or for an antipollution device or procedure, fixed by rule or otherwise, by the state or an instrumentality, agency, or political subdivision of the state, the court may:

(a) Determine the validity, applicability, and reasonableness of the standard.

(b) If a court finds a standard to be deficient, direct the adoption of a standard approved and specified by the court.[26]

Several elements of the Michigan statute deserve special notice. The first is that it grants standing to "any person" to bring an action in the court having jurisdiction to protect the "air, water, and other natural resources" that are in the public trust from impairment or destruction. It further explicitly empowers the court to review any standard, rule, or procedure of any state or local public agency. And, if that rule is insufficient to protect the public trust, the court may compel the agency to change its policy and even direct what that change must be.

These are significant powers. It may be anticipated that Canadian legislators, fearing to unleash a wave of nuisance suits triggered by the application of "any person," might be loath to grant them. Certainly the Harper government, already displeased with the extent of opportunities Canadians enjoy to put industrial development under scrutiny, is unlikely to extend them. But courts are, by definition, arenas for judgement and discretion. In more than a decade and a half since Michigan adopted its legislation, that state has not been immobilized by frivolous suits based on the presumed right of standing of citizens in public trust cases.

Nor does such an acknowledgment encumber the government of the day in choosing how to meet its obligation. If a Conservative ministry believes a wholesale embrace of free-market remedies can defend natural security, let it implement them—*so long as it also closely monitors the results* and reports them candidly to Canadians. If a more left-leaning ministry wishes to revert to an older model of "command and control" regulation of industry, experiment with pollution "rents," or mandate the retirement of some toxic chemicals, the same would apply.

It may be objected that Parliament is unlikely to enact such a law. But elections can change parliamentary minds. There may also be other avenues to the same ends. David Boyd, a professor of environmental law at Simon Fraser University, has argued from the example of constitutionally enshrined environmental rights in other countries for the addition to the Canadian Charter of Rights and Freedoms of a "Right to the Environment," conferring similar entitlements.

In Chapter 4 we saw that more than forty nations have adopted the Aarhus treaty. This 1998 Convention on Access to Information, Public Participation in Decision-making and Access to Justice in Environmental Matters places signatory governments' environmental stewardship under the discipline of their own people. It requires member states to adopt the two critical instruments we have identified here: routine and credible environmental reporting to their citizens and the acknowledgement that every citizen (in the treaty's case, even foreign citizens) has an interest in their environment that carries a presumed right to bring the state's performance of its stewardship before the court for review.

As an alternative to the kind of legislation we advocate above, Canada could do worse than adopt and ratify the Aarhus Convention.

But if Fox-Decent is right, and the fiduciary duty to preserve the value of a public trust in common property adheres to the Crown as an inherent and inalienable attribute of sovereignty, then it endures regardless of other statutes. It cannot be extinguished and awaits only activation. As with other overlooked, neglected, or contravened legal responsibilities, it is the role of the courts to call attention to the lapse and enjoin delinquent parties to meet the requirements of the law.

As Fox-Decent put it in an interview with us, "it only takes one judge" who recognizes and affirms the Crown's fiduciary duty to bring it to light and begin the process of giving it traction in policy.

What is essential is that Canadians acquire the legal means to put our federal trustees on notice that they may no more shirk their duty to natural security than they may abandon the dollar or the national borders.

Society's progress from witch-burning to civil rights reflects, in part, the slow evolution of conventional wisdom about the limits of acceptability.

We may be on a similar trajectory of change in our relationship with water—though in view of most Canadians' physical distance from nature, we are inclined to doubt it. In any case, our circumstances cannot afford the leisurely pace of evolving social standards.

The lesson of corporate example is that small but explicit statements of purpose may have large and cascading consequences. We do not need to wait for the culture to change before we change our practices. Catalytic policy interventions can also change cultures.

This has been evident throughout history. A small change in the rules alters a multitude of actions. The most famous example may be the Magna Carta, whose central concession, that the power of an obscure island monarch in northern Europe during the Dark Ages had limits, continues to resonate through the legal systems of countries around the globe. More prosaically, Canadians encounter daily the safety and convenience that are the result of decisions made decades ago to require seat belts in automobiles and commercial packaging in both official languages.

Other inflection points likewise introduced important values to our nation's legal infrastructure without determining any specific outcome. The extension to women of the right to vote, in the early decades of the last century, is one example (even though it took nearly another half century to extend the franchise to every adult Canadian regardless of race). The establishment in 1982 of the Canadian Charter of Rights and Freedoms is another. Enunciated more than three decades ago, it continues to affect public and private decisions, and Canadians' liberties and security, in myriad ways.

These changes were not won by mass movements—not even the suffragette movement could accurately have been described as that. They certainly didn't require wholesale conversions of Canadian attitudes. Like most such advances, they happened because a *sufficient* number of people, with vision and resources, persuaded the leaders of their day that what they sought was morally irresistible and, in the moment, politically achievable.

Eight centuries ago in England, the leading "stakeholders" of their day—the senior barons and clergy, leaders of the guilds that constituted the age's industrial lobby, the reigning king—met in tents set up in a meadow and departed with a charter of the rights of free men under the Crown. The rights were limited and almost immediately repudiated, but the precedent endured, embodied in generations of law.

From the less picturesque setting of conference halls and meeting rooms in Ottawa, Prime Minister Pierre Trudeau and the provincial leaders of his day emerged with a charter of freedoms that has become a model to the world of how to reconcile personal liberties, human dignity, and the requirements of public order in a modern state.

Our freedoms are established. Our borders guarded. But our natural security is exposed and vulnerable.

"Power concedes nothing. It never did and it never will," nineteenth-century American reformer Frederick Douglass famously remarked. "The limits of tyrants are prescribed by the endurance of those whom they oppress."

Our leaders are hardly yet tyrants, but Douglass's aphorism no less aptly describes the dynamics of their neglect. It too will be limited only by the patience of the neglected.

Canadians should have no further patience for leaders who neglect their public trust. It is time to demand that the federal Crown acknowledge and accept its fiduciary duty to protect Canada's natural security, to show proof that trust is secure, and if it fails, to accept the discipline of the courts.

Call it a new Great Charter, a *magna carta natura*, for the security of the state in a human age.

ELEVEN

Healthy, Wealthy, and Secure

BEFORE THE Sahtu Dene set aside their nomadic life for the settled community of Déline, teepees provided convenient portable shelter. Today, most of the community's frame bungalows still boast a backyard teepee as well, a shelter for summer cooking, ceremonial sweats, and the passing on of oral history. A giant wooden teepee gives a distinctive roofline to the band's office, where Danny Gaudet keeps a desk.

Brisk, burly, and busy, Gaudet is a part-time house builder as well as his community's lead negotiator with federal and territorial governments. As a negotiator, Gaudet's priorities are the well-being of Déline's six hundred people and that of the pristine lake beyond them. But he is fully aware of how the south's model of development has degraded both its water and the ecosystems that provide and protect it. Gaudet wants to see a different standard for the North, one that protects its living web of species and biological productivity in its present robust state. In doing so, he believes he is standing up not only for the interests of his indigenous nation but also for the wider Canadian public, which is no less dependent on the natural security those ecosystems provide.

"If they die, we die," Gaudet succinctly states. And, he adds, "if we don't smarten up, we're going to destroy everything. We're doing it already." He is confident he is not alone in recognizing that threat. "The farmer in Saskatchewan, in New Brunswick, he thinks this way and he's not aboriginal."[1]

In assessing any outside proposal for development of the vast expanse of territory the Sahtu Dene hold west and north of Great Bear Lake, Gaudet has a simple environmental standard: "Here's your baseline: How it looks today. You've got to maintain that. Come up with a plan for how you're going to do that."

The wider world has yet to discover the water in Great Bear Lake, but the rest of old Ayah's prophecy is well on its way to coming true. In much of the southern world, escalating human demands threaten or exceed limited sources of safe water. Urban and industrial development abrade the hydrological productivity of ecosystems, putting those regions' natural security at risk.

Where there is water in the human age of scarce nature, there will be wealth and, very likely, avarice.

The Far North's wealth of water, intact natural ecosystems, and other resources is the object of rising international commercial and strategic interest as climate change relaxes the region's reputation for more or less permanent winter. The Sahtu Dene of Déline aren't the only northern residents who greet this new attention with ambivalence. Jobs and income are welcome in a region where many remote communities have young populations and limited opportunities for work. But people are aware of the price those opportunities may exact on the landscape that many residents of the North, not only its First Nations and Inuit, revere.

In 2011, after meeting with every community in the Northwest Territories, its government announced a radical departure from five centuries of de facto and de jure water policy as practised under colonial and post-colonial Euro-Canadian administrations. These, as we have seen, progressed from early neglect to a variety of measures meant to contain and limit the pollution in water—whether at the tap or in the wild—to some tolerable level.

In its *Northern Voices, Northern Waters* strategy, the aboriginal-majority government of the Northwest Territories recognized the fundamental importance of water to natural security and the prosperity it enables. "Clean and abundant freshwaters," the *Northern Voices* preamble noted, "ensure healthy, productive *ecosystems*. These are essential to the social, cultural and economic well-being of people."[2] (Emphasis in the original.) Rather than debate how much of that comprehensive wealth to sacrifice in pursuit of cash incomes—the typical terms of environmental discourse in much of the south—the territories' goal is the preservation of its water "substantially unaltered in quality, quantity, and rates of flow" and of all the "spiritual, cultural, public health, recreational, economic and ecological values" that water secures.

"We finally understand what aboriginal people have been telling us," Northwest Territories minister of environment and natural resources Michael Miltenberger has said. "If we don't protect the land, the water, and the animals, they won't look after us. We're going to pay a price, and it will be incredibly brutal and painful."[3]

Whether the Northwest Territories' ecological line in the sand will survive its multiple geographic and institutional challenges remains to be seen.

Although vast (and possibly growing) volumes of water fall on the Territories directly, its most important waterway is the Mackenzie River, the ultimate conduit to the sea for whatever contaminants leach from Alberta's oil sands. In 2010, the territories entered negotiations with upstream governments—Alberta, British Columbia, and Saskatchewan—to work out a common management plan for the great river and its tributaries in those provinces. Under a preliminary agreement, signed in 1997, mandating the negotiations, the three provinces had agreed to restrict their activities only so far as not to "unreasonably harm" the downstream territory. Territorial minister Miltenberger acknowledged that he faced a skeptical audience for his stated objective of using the river management plan to secure the Northern Voices' goal of preserving the river "substantially unaltered."

In addition, Canada's Constitution allows for only two institutional incarnations of the Crown: federal and provincial. Other subsidiary units of public administration—municipalities, territories—exist as legal creatures of those senior orders. As such, they do not hold the full suite of powers that define federal and provincial jurisdictions. Municipal governments deploy only the powers that provincial Crowns permit. Likewise, Canada's northern territories are, in effect, constitutional wards of the federal Crown (as were its western ones until their admission to Confederation as provinces). Territorial governments operate by the conditional delegation of power, not on the strength of independent constitutional standing.

That fundamental relationship has changed in the past two decades. In Nunavut and Yukon, the federal Crown negotiated historic agreements to "devolve" province-like jurisdiction and authority to the territories' legislatures. At the same time as the government of the Northwest Territories was in talks with its powerful upstream neighbours about the Mackenzie, it was moving forward in equally consequential negotiations with the federal Crown about the powers it would be allowed to wield in its own so-called devolution deal.

The overlapping talks spotlit the multiple needs for an active and responsible federal role in the protection of this country's water and related ecosystems—the constituents of Canadians' natural security. (We should note that as this volume was going to press, negotiators for the Northwest Territories privately expressed guarded optimism that many, if not all, of its objectives would be met in the agreement expected to emerge later in 2013.)

The river Canada knows as the Mackenzie is described by its Dene name: *Dai Cho*, the "Great River." It is the terminating artery for the water that flows from a fifth of the country. Its outflow is the most significant physical input to the Beaufort Sea, a major but poorly studied influence on the wider Arctic Ocean. It is a river, in other words, on a scale that clearly meets the test of national interest. It is also fish bearing, navigable, and interjurisdictional—all characteristics that place a fiduciary duty on the federal Crown to ensure and defend the ecological integrity of the entire basin.

Complacency about Canada's water is unjustified. Our most populous southern regions are getting and keeping less of it every year. What circulates through our terrestrial waterways is increasingly stressed by heat, human and ecological needs, and contaminants.

It is true that urban Canadians, and even most rural residents, enjoy tap water that is the envy of billions of people in developing countries. The odds of developing diarrhea from a drink of water here are remote. But not zero. We found in Chapter 2 that if Vancouver, a city with one of the country's best-protected water sources and some of its newest service mains, is representative, then "something in the water" makes nearly 200,000 Canadians sick enough every year to visit their doctor or ER—amounting nationally to more than 500 such visits *a day*.

We also saw that Canada falls at the bottom of international comparisons of water stewardship. In repeated comparisons with our peers, developed countries in the Organisation for Economic Co-operation and Development (OECD), Canada has placed no higher than twenty-fourth out of the twenty-five to thirty nations compared (depending on the year of study). Our poor score—despite a large and relatively unpopulated geography—has been identified by one study after another as our own doing: the result, as one frank assessment put it, of "poor policy."

In Chapter 3, we traced the history of that policy. We were reminded that the founding document of Canada's Constitution, the 1867 British North America Act, was more implicit than explicit in allocating responsibility for the protection of the new Dominion's water. Provinces received exclusive responsibility for regulating most on-the-ground activities that have an impact on water: commerce, municipal services, land use, resource extraction. But the federal Crown retained jurisdiction over waterways big enough to float a boat and those supporting fish life—together, effectively any river or lake in the nation—as well as residual authority to secure any objective that is in the national interest.

For a century, apart from legislating some measures to protect fisheries and other powers incidental to keeping shipping channels open which had potential environmental application, governments administering the authority of the federal Crown were happy to leave water management to the provinces. Canada's centennial brought a spike in popular awareness of the degraded condition of the environment—by then odorously and even visibly apparent in many urban waterways.

The 1960s brought the first intimations of the limits and fragility of natural security. Books like *Silent Spring* and *The Limits to Growth* described a world being invisibly poisoned by, and logically incapable of sustaining indefinitely, the human economy's increasing material demands. The scope of popular concern for the environment graduated from preoccupation with local issues—a particular polluted stream or recurrent smog—to a dawning awareness of systemic ones, such as the rise in waterborne background chemicals.

By the new millennium, a succession of governments, both Liberal and Conservative, had put in place an array of federal legislation buttressing and extending the embryonic powers contained in laws of long standing like the Fisheries and Canada Shipping Acts.

The year 1968 saw the introduction of the Guidelines for Canadian Drinking Water Quality—suggestive only, then as now. The Canada Water Act, legislated in 1970, gave the federal Crown explicit authority to take direct management of watersheds at particular risk and provided funds for Ottawa to work with provinces to better understand and plan for their waterways' security. In 1987, on the heels of a thorough canvas of expert and stakeholder opinion across the country, Conservative environment minister Thomas McMillan tabled a comprehensive, integrated federal water policy. It recognized water's central economic importance—in addition to its ecological and cultural dimensions—and sought to leverage that value into significant investments in the protection of Canada's water sources and drinking water supply.

Those early initiatives were followed by a series of acts with more specific focus. The Canadian Environmental Protection Act, passed in 1988 (amended in 1999), gave the federal Crown authority to weed out toxic and dangerous chemicals from the thousands in commercial, industrial, or residential use. In 1992, the Canadian Environmental Assessment Act required that developments that might impair natural values under federal jurisdiction (those aforementioned fish- and traffic-bearing waterways, as well as land in the North, held in trust for First Nations or on military installations), be scrutinized for their potential damage.

The following year, Parliament created the National Pollutant Release Inventory (NPRI), which required most industries to report emissions of specified compounds above certain thresholds. The inventory covered major oil sands and gas-processing plants immediately, but smaller facilities were not brought under its mandate for another decade. Pollutants released to tailings ponds at oil sands operations remained uninventoried until 2006. As of early 2011, according to an Environment Canada spokesperson, "Oil and gas exploration and drilling activities are currently exempt from reporting to the NPRI."

Most recently, Prime Minister Harper's Conservative government added an Environmental Enforcement Act in 2009. Responding to long-standing criticisms of weak enforcement of federal environmental legislation, it consolidated under one title offences that had previously been dotted across nine other acts and provided stepped-up penalties for those found guilty of committing them. The act also exposed individual corporate office-holders for the first time to personal liability for their organizations' environmental crimes under certain circumstances.

While Canada was erecting its array of protections for water at the tap and in the wild, as well as deterrents against their contamination, other countries were doing the same.

America, after witnessing the environmental decline of the first half of the twentieth century on even greater scale than Canada, got tired of waiting for its states to shed their first-mover phobias about competitive disadvantage and federalized responsibility for the essential public assets of clean air and clean water. Acts by those names, and a third—the Safe Drinking Water Act—enabled the U.S. government to establish mandatory, enforceable standards for determining whether air and water were clean or safe enough—and, where they were not, to take action to restore them. The same era created the Environmental Protection Agency to secure compliance with those acts, with its mission emblazoned in its name.

Europe recognized the collective character of effective water management early on. Two centuries ago, its states pioneered the world's first multinational riverine agency to coordinate traffic on the Rhine—and later to protect it. After military competition proved catastrophic in the first half of the twentieth century, Europe's states spent the second half pursuing peaceful integration. The coalescing proto-federation's first efforts featured initiatives to align its members' water-protection policies.

The European Union came into formal existence in 1993. In 2000, it adopted the world's most advanced regime for the protection of water, aquatic ecosystems, and the terrestrial and groundwater features that connect them. The European Water Framework Directive set a target date (of 2015) for all of Europe's waterways to meet explicit "chemical" as well as "ecological" standards to be considered of "good" quality. It further required former national combatants to set aside lingering antipathies in order to develop integrated plans to reach those goals in every European watershed.

A feature of Europe's federation that is missing in our own gave those mandates traction. Although the WFD does not directly bind Europe's various national citizens, member states that fail to enact legislation that does reflect its terms in binding form may face punitive discipline under the 1997 Treaty of Amsterdam.

Whereas Europe and the United States made defence of their natural security a responsibility of their highest political authority, Canada, its panoply of federal acts notwithstanding, did the opposite.

Our federal Crown possesses constitutional backstop powers not very different from those wielded by the government of the United States. Its authority is arguably greater than any that the European Union's fraught executive possesses. The old-as-Confederation Fisheries Act gave the federal Crown adequate power to defend every ephemeral stream big enough to support a fingerling. The Canada

Water Act gives the Crown specific authority to defend a particularly endangered watershed. The 1987 water policy laid out a bold goal to better reflect the value of productive hydrological assets in our economic decisions.

It never happened. We saw in Chapter 5 that no federal government ever reached for the most potent statutory weapons contained in the 1970 Water Act. Attempts by successive federal ministries of different partisan sentiments to inveigle the provinces into enacting consistent national drinking water standards faltered and failed. By the turn of the century, the Liberal government of Jean Chrétien was moving in the other direction. It reached federal-provincial "harmonization" arrangements that surrendered enforcement of the Fisheries and other federal acts to provincial agencies. Where they were signed, the federal Crown disarmed its own enforcement and intelligence capabilities.

Canada's environment commissioners—independent agents under the Office of the Auditor General who report to Parliament, not to the government of the day—have repeatedly condemned this vapid defence of Canada's water. In 2009, Commissioner Scott Vaughan excoriated the Crown for failing so completely to protect the health of waterways under the Fisheries Act that it could not even say what its actual legal responsibilities were.

Alberta has been a conspicuously early and eager adopter of each new cooperative federal gesture that devolved into incremental surrender of federal capacity. Thus, it provided an instructive study in the effectiveness of these gestures—or, as the facts revealed, not. Since the province signed its equivalency agreement with the federal Crown in the late 1980s, oil sands and natural gas development have transformed its northern boreal landscape. Expanding fossil fuel extraction has released a diffuse cloud of air- and waterborne contaminants into the headwaters of the Mackenzie River.

Prior to 2012, the federal Crown offered routine assurances that the environment was also being fully protected. Its confidence rested on the word of an "independent" industry-dominated agency to which Alberta had entrusted monitoring of the oil sands' impacts.

The agency's credibility became strained, however, when independent scientists revealed rising concentrations of toxins in Athabasca River water and downstream sediments. It began to crumble when several expert panels castigated the program under which it operated as incapable of detecting incremental or cumulative degradation of water, air, and ecosystems—or even of confirming whether oil and gas companies were keeping environmental promises made to secure their operating permits. Credibility finally collapsed entirely under the outrage and ridicule prompted by a media display of grotesquely deformed fish taken from the sullied Athabasca.

As we wrote this in mid-2012, current Conservative environment minister Peter Kent announced that he and his Alberta counterpart had each tasked senior deputies to work together to institute a new regime to track the gas and oil industry's impact on the Athabasca region's water and wildlife resources.

The credibility of Kent's new commitment was strained, however, by other announcements in the months that preceded and followed it. In one of the most far-reaching, the Conservative government in which he served amended the historic Fisheries Act to relieve itself of further responsibility for protecting the habitats in which fish live. Other actions slashed at the science and technical expertise of supporting agencies on the front line of defence of Canada's water. The conducting of environmental reviews of energy projects was removed from the agency created for that purpose in 1992 and assigned instead to another, which was mandated to enable as well as regulate the industry proposing them. In the House of Commons, government majorities abruptly terminated committee inquiries into the reassignment of environmental reviews and the impact of fossil fuel development on the Athabasca-Mackenzie watershed. Conservative members also ordered that testimony and research gathered over a year and a half be destroyed—unseen by the Canadian voters whose taxes had purchased the information.

Even before Prime Minister Harper declared the rapid expansion of fossil fuel development a "national priority" higher than natural security, and his minister Joe Oliver intemperately denounced dissenting

Canadians as "radical," it was apparent that the incumbent government was focussed on economic objectives above all else.

Summary economics seemed to bear out the wisdom of Harper's statement—superficially at least. The oil and gas sectors' $20 billion in annual spending, which multiplied as it moved through the hands of suppliers and subcontractors from Vancouver Island to Newfoundland, has made a powerful contribution to Canada's GDP in the last decade.

But the shortcomings of the GDP are legion. Alternative measures show that Canadians' financial gains have been deeply offset by our losses of personal time, social connection, and, significantly for this study, natural capital.

Meanwhile, the world's fundamental economic equations are not what they were in the 1960s. The trade-offs made in the 1980s between national sovereignty and the supposed benefits of liberalized global trade receive much critical attention, but they are the lesser of two profound changes. Far more significant has been the transition from an economy enjoying a global surplus of natural resources and ecoservices to one straining against the limits of the first and in overdraft on the second. This unprecedented reversal has called into question our policies, practices, and previously unchallenged premises. In this new circumstance, environmental costs once dismissed as too trivial to count loom large; ecological services long taken for granted are being reappraised.

A full-spectrum accounting of our national wealth would, for example, discount the significant contribution that agriculture makes to Canada's GDP by its GED: the gross environmental damage it does to waterways, lakes, and infrastructure through the release of sediments and field chemicals. In an illuminating case, U.S. researchers discovered that the ecological and public health costs of producing electricity from coal or gas exceed that energy's contribution to GDP.

The offsetting positive contributions that intact ecosystems make to the economy, largely through services related to water, are also coming into focus. Credible early estimates in Britain and elsewhere suggest that these values in Canada could reach into the tens, if not hundreds, of billions of dollars.

In considering in Chapter 7 whether our federal Crown's decision to put conventionally measured economic gain over protection of natural services is making Canadians richer, we also noted the opportunities that are always present in periods of transition. Shortages of essential natural services and resources must make them more valuable to consumers and industry—their scarcity overturns much of conventional economics, but not the logic of supply and demand.

At the same time, as Michael Porter identified two decades ago, well-designed environmental mandates can have positive economic outcomes for regulated businesses. They spur innovation and help to identify and remedy process inefficiencies. These can translate, as Canadian researchers have shown, into greater productivity and potentially higher profit in subsequent years.

This virtuous effect is already evident in other resource arenas. Germany's enthusiastic embrace of low-carbon energy sources, particularly solar energy, has made it a growing green-energy superpower, with few of the natural assets that Canada's vast territory boasts. Yet despite our blue-drenched national map, Canadian businesses are handicapped in the $500 billion (forecast to soon reach $1 trillion) global market for water-related goods and services. When water is available to industry in effectively unlimited quantities at literally no cost, and no credible, current, or high-resolution intelligence exists to track its state and flow in any case, companies have neither motive to innovate new technology or business processes nor the means to demonstrate their advantages to the global marketplace.

Most Canadians are at less risk of immediate illness after drinking a glass of water today than they were a century ago. But we discovered in Chapter 8 that avoiding nausea and vomiting is not quite the same thing as being safe. The natural biological pathogens that plagued the early decades of the last century are "old school" compared with the bioactive molecules accumulating in the environment of the present one.

Some of these are natural but are released in unnaturally large quantities by human activity—as mining operations, for instance, may unintentionally release arsenic, cyanide, and other toxic compounds into waterways. The volatile and persistent hydrocarbons drifting downwind and downstream from oil sands developments are likewise "natural" but now enter the Athabasca in far greater concentrations than when their only extraction activity was at the foot of eroding riverbanks. Other chemicals of new concern are synthetic; an estimated 23,000 are in wide circulation in industry, business, and Canadian homes.

Techniques adopted over the last century to neutralize the natural pathogens that cause gastrointestinal distress, cholera, and typhoid are ineffective against most of these new compounds. Many are beginning to show up in sources of drinking water and at the tap. Studies in Canada and the United States identified scores of pharmaceuticals, from birth control hormones to anti-epileptics, in public water supplies.

Epidemiologists are closing in on the capacity of many of these compounds to mimic the effect of human hormones as the most likely cause of a worldwide imbalance in sex ratios and a surge in male genital defects. Extrapolating from a study conducted when the concentration of such EDCS (endocrine disrupting compounds) was almost certainly lower than it is today, we estimated that nearly a thousand Canadian baby boys are "missing" from the traditional statistical norm each year as a result of a documented decades-long drift in newborn sex ratios.

The same gender-bending effects are appearing in wild populations, from polar bears to minnows. Meanwhile, biological nutrients of little direct consequence to human consumers, entering waterways from farmland, concentrations of livestock, and municipal waste treatment plants, nourish resurgent algal blooms in lakes both great and small. These are creating biological deserts in such treasured natural assets as Lakes Erie and Winnipeg. With rising temperatures and longer summers, scientists warn, the neurotoxins released when the blooms eventually decay is becoming more potent.

Water is the currency of natural security. It determines the vitality, resilience, and productivity of our life-supporting habitat. That relationship is reciprocal and recursive. The quality of water that our ecosystems receive has a decisive influence on their health and productivity. Among their most essential "products" is a reliable supply of safe water. And the quality of that water is, in turn, among our best clues to the health of the sheltering habitat we rely on no less than any other animal species.

The intimacy and ubiquity of our relationship with water implies lessons for how it is best managed. In the past two decades, more than a score of expert inquiries and internal policy reviews have sought to identify the best practices for Canada's natural defence today and in the future. In Chapter 9, we recapitulated their consensus:

· Manage water in the geography that nature dictates: by the watershed.

· Involve everyone with a stake in or impact on that watershed.

· Take no more water than nature can afford and no more than it resupplies.

· Set explicit standards for what constitutes good water.

· Equip those watershed managers with clear mandates, effective resources, and measurable objectives.

· Hold managers and policies to account with detailed, timely reporting on the state of water inventories and the health of water-productive ecosystems.

Our senior national leaders know all this, or should know it. There is no excuse for inaction.

In the vanished world of the Holocene, it appeared that wealth could be extracted and transferred from nature to the human economy without exhausting the planet's supply. But we know that is no longer so. We even know roughly when our species passed into an altogether new relationship with its habitat. Evidence from scores of natural systems reveals that since the 1980s we have lived in a new age: the human age of the Anthropocene.

This age is marked by, among other qualities, an unprecedented overdraft of human demands on Earth's biological and geophysical services. In this context, the continuation of our society's biological viability is no longer something we can take for granted. And our leaders' neglect of it is a dereliction that Canadians can no longer afford—and ought no longer tolerate.

Our federal leaders have been able to avoid taking up the defence of Canada's water and natural wealth because of an artifact of constitutional history. A thread of the absolutism once wielded by English monarchs who imagined themselves anointed by God runs through our legal traditions still. Canada's Constitution Acts are long on what the Crown is *entitled* to do, in its federal or provincial incarnations, but short on what it *must* do.

But there are some things that Canadians justly do expect from their national sovereign. We described them in Chapter 10: defence of the realm from invasion, maintenance of domestic order and a sound currency, the conduct of relations with other states.

Much legal tradition, a growing body of contemporary analysis, and a somewhat smaller one of judicial precedent add to this list another inalienable obligation of sovereignty: the preservation and defence of the public's vital interest in essential common assets. Water has been the pre-eminent example of this public trust.

We saw that citizens in the United States, Britain, and other Commonwealth nations have invoked this public trust doctrine repeatedly, holding public agencies to a duty to preserve water resources for future generations. Public agencies have used it to secure compensation from environmental violators that damaged their citizens' trust fund of ecosystems and waterways.

The doctrine may strike some as a radical departure from Canadian practice. But we have seen it in action here. We have provided the example of a decade-old provision that entrenches the public trust—and a citizen's right to call his or her government on its failure to protect it—in the statutes of the state of Michigan. And we noted with approval the standard set by the government of the Northwest Territories in undertaking an institutional and political duty to preserve for perpetuity its residents' water "substantially unaltered in quality, quantity and rates of flow."

The Crown embodies the Canadian public. Ministers, even the *prime* minister, serve the interests of the Crown—the public—not the reverse. It is time that Canadians restored that responsibility and demanded that it be met in defence of our water and the wealth we derive from it.

We have called for the enunciation of a new Great Charter—a *magna carta natura*—to frame and enforce that sovereign obligation. We believe it could create one of those inflection points that have occurred throughout history: a small and discreet intervention that changes the direction of choices for decades or even centuries thereafter.

This may seem an impractical idea to many. The more pragmatic will perhaps dismiss it as anachronistic, extreme, improbable. It may be all of those. But we cannot afford to limit our options to the conventional. We are no longer in a conventional time.

In this human age, our supply of clean, safe water—the foundation of all wealth everywhere—will depend entirely on the protection of hydrologically productive ecosystems. This is the meaning of *natural security*.

The girl we have called Olivia is a real child. We ourselves are grandfathers. When our leaders abandoned the defence of Canada's natural security, it is her future and our own grandchildren's that those leaders chose to sacrifice.

They owe us more.

ENDNOTES

~~~~~~~~~~~~~~~~~~~~~~~~~

CHAPTER 1

1 Prince of Wales Northern Heritage Centre,
   http://pwnhc.learnnet.nt.ca.
2 Personal communication with Déline resident, May 26, 2010.
3 Maev Kennedy, "Copper Clue May Solve Mystery of Doomed
   Victorian Arctic Expedition," *Guardian*, October 28, 2009.
4 Paul Harris, "Population of World 'Could Grow to 15bn by 2100,"
   Guardian, October 22, 2011.
5 Global Footprint Network, http://www.footprintnetwork.org.
6 Some commentators have recently challenged Hubbert's theory
   by pointing to a surge in U.S. production of unconventional crude and
   natural gas; this is an apples-plus-oranges elision that misrepresents
   the case.
7 Meena Palaniappan and Peter H. Gleick, *The World's Water
   2008–2009: The Biennial Report on Freshwater Resources*
   (Washington, DC: Island Press, 2008).

CHAPTER 2

1 Interview with Victor Schukov.

2 "Greater Vancouver Boil-Water Advisory Lifted," cbc News, November 27, 2006.

3 "Boil Water Advisory Issued for Lachine, Lasalle," cbc News, October 31, 2011.

4 "Cryptosporidiosis," U.S. National Library of Medicine, National Institutes of Health, http://www.nlm.nih.gov.

5 Hon. Peter Kent, speech to the Economic Club of Canada (Environment Canada, Toronto, on, January 28, 2011).

6 *2011 Canadian Water Attitudes Study* (Toronto: rbc and Unilever Canada, 2011).

7 *Freshwater Quality in Canadian Rivers* (Ottawa: Environment Canada, 2010).

8 *Human Activity and the Environment: Economy and the Environment* (Ottawa: Statistics Canada, 2011), http://www.statcan.gc.ca.

9 "Sustainable Competitiveness," World Economic Forum, accessed October 5, 2011, http://www.weforum.org.

10 Jennifer Blanke et al., "The Long-Term View: Developing a Framework for Assessing Sustainable Competitiveness," *The Global Competitiveness Report 2011–2012* (Geneva: World Economic Forum, 2011).

11 "Human Development Index," *Wikipedia*, http://en.wikipedia.org/wiki/Human_Development_Index.

12 *2011 Human Development Report* (New York: United Nations Development Programme [undp], 2011), http://hdr.undp.org.

13 Including some the authors have participated in.

14 *Charting a Course: Sustainable Water Use by Canada's Natural Resource Sectors* (Ottawa: National Round Table on the Environment and the Economy, 2011).

15 Environment Canada, 2010.

16 James Bruce et al. (expert panel on groundwater), *The Sustainable Management of Groundwater in Canada* (Ottawa: Council of Canadian Academies, 2009).

17   G. Van der Kamp and G. Grove, "Well Water Quality in Canada:
     An Overview," *An Earth Odyssey: Proceedings of the 54th Canadian
     Geotechnical Conference* (Calgary: Canadian Geotechnical Society,
     September 2001).

18   C.G. Schuster et al., "Infectious Disease Outbreaks Related to
     Drinking Water in Canada, 1974–2001," *Canadian Journal of
     Public Health* 96, no. 4 (2005).

19   J. Aramini et al., *Drinking Water Quality and Health Care
     Utilization for Gastrointestinal Illness in Greater Vancouver*
     (Ottawa: Population and Public Health Branch, Health Canada, 2000).

20   5.7 per 1,000 population annually.

21   *Waterproof2: Canada's Drinking Water Report Card* (Vancouver:
     Sierra Legal Defence Fund, 2006).

22   Tim Morris et al. (Gordon Water Group of Concerned Scientists
     and Citizens), *Changing the Flow: A Blueprint for Federal Action on
     Freshwater* (Toronto: Walter and Duncan Gordon Foundation, 2007).
     Disclosure: Ralph Pentland was a member of the reporting group;
     the Walter and Duncan Gordon Foundation supported the research
     for and writing of this book.

23   *Waterproof3: Canada's Drinking Water Report Card* (Vancouver:
     Ecojustice, 2010).

24   Steve E. Hrudey, *Safe Drinking Water Policy for Canada: Turning
     Hindsight into Foresight* (Toronto: C.D. Howe Institute, 2011).

25   *How Canada Performs: A Report Card on Canada* (Ottawa:
     Conference Board of Canada, 2011), http://conferenceboard.ca.

26   "Environmental Performance Index," Yale University,
     http://epi.yale.edu.

27   *Taking Stock: North American Pollutant Releases and Transfers*
     (Montreal: Commission for Environmental Cooperation, 2011).

28   *Taking Stock: North American Pollutant Releases and Transfers*
     (Montreal: Commission for Environmental Cooperation, 1997).

29   *An Update on the Continuing Canadian and United States
     Contributions to Great Lakes–St. Lawrence River Ecosystem*
     (Toronto: Pollution Watch, Canadian Environmental Law
     Association and Environmental Defence, 2010).

30 Author's notes from the event.

31 Chris Wood, "NAFTA and the Unmanning of North America,"
    Miller-McCune (March 2009).

32 *Waterproof 2.*

33 Thomas Gunton and K.S. Calbick, *The Maple Leaf in the OECD:
    Comparing Progress Toward Sustainability* (Vancouver:
    David Suzuki Foundation, 2005).

34 Steven Renzetti et al., *Running Through Our Fingers: How Canada
    Fails to Capture the Full Value of its Water* (Toronto: Blue Economy
    Initiative, 2011).

35 David Boyd and S. Scott Wallace, *Fireproof Whales and
    Contaminated Mother's Milk: The Inadequacy of Canada's Proposed
    PBDE Regulations* (Vancouver: David Suzuki Foundation, 2006).

36 *Human Activity and the Environment.*

37 David Schindler and William Donahue, "An Impending Water Crisis
    in Canada's Western Prairie Provinces," Proceedings of the National
    Academy of Sciences, April 2006, http://www.pnas.org.

38 Gerard Wynn, "World Must Keep Focus on Climate Risk,"
    Reuters, November 17, 2011.

39 Ralph Pentland, remarks to the Canadian Water and Wastewater
    Association workshop on water efficiency and conservation
    (Ottawa, October 18, 2011).

40 Gunton and Calbick, *The Maple Leaf in the OECD.*

41 World Commission on Environment and Development,
    Our Common Future (London: Oxford University Press, 1987).

42 *2011 Canadian Water Attitudes Study.*

CHAPTER 3

 1 Robert Marleau and Camille Montpetit, eds., *House of Commons
    Procedure and Practice, 2000 Edition* (Ottawa: Parliament of
    Canada, 2000), http://www.parl.gc.ca.

 2 Statutes of Canada, Fisheries Act 1868.

 3 Yvon Deloges, "Behind the Scene of the Lachine Canal Landscape,"
    The Journal of the Society for Industrial Archaeology 29, no. 1 (2003).

4 Larry McNally, *Engineers and Waterpower on the Lachine Canal, 1843–1871* (Ottawa: National Archives of Canada, 1992).

5 *Report of Royal Commission on the Leasing of Water Power [at] Lachine Canal* (Ottawa: MacLean, Roger, 1887).

6 Constitution Act, 1867, Third Schedule.

7 Constitution Act, 1867, Sec. 91.

8 Ibid.

9 Many of these sewer lines remain in service today, tracing the course of lost creeks and streams beneath city streets.

10 Michael Cook, "Garrison Creek Sewer," Vanishing Point, http://www.vanishingpoint.ca.

11 "Water Treatment Past and Present," City of Toronto, http://www.toronto.ca.

12 Herbert Brown Ames, *The City Below the Hill: A Sociological Study of a Portion of the City of Montreal, Canada* (Montreal: Bishop, 1897).

13 Statutes of the Province of Ontario, Toronto, 1873.

14 "Early History of Wastewater Treatment in Toronto," City of Toronto, http://www.toronto.ca.

15 Janice Cheryl Beaver, *U.S. International Borders: Brief Facts* (Washington, DC: Congressional Research Service, 2006).

16 *Pollution of Boundary Waters: Report of the Consulting Sanitary Engineer upon Remedial Measures* (Washington, DC: International Joint Commission, Government Printing Office, 1916).

17 Ibid.

18 Mary C. Rossi, "The History of Sewage Treatment in the City of Buffalo, New York," *Middle States Geographer* 28, no. 9 (1995).

19 Inflation factor calculated at: data.bls.gov/cgi-bin/cpicalc.pl.

20 Rossi, "The History of Sewage Treatment in the City of Buffalo."

21 A. Penman, "Wastewater System for the Metropolitan Corporation of Greater Winnipeg," *Journal of the Water Pollution Control Federation* 39, no. 3 (1967).

22 Chris Wood, *Dry Spring: The Coming Water Crisis of North America* (Vancouver: Raincoast Books, 2008).

23 Elizabeth Brubaker, *Property Rights in the Defence of Nature* (Toronto: Environment Probe, 1995).

24 "The K.V.P. Company Limited *(Defendant) Appellant;* and Earl McKie et al. *(Plaintiffs) Respondents,*" Supreme Court of Canada, Ottawa, October 4, 1949.

25 Inflation calculated at: http://www.bankofcanada.ca/rates/related/inflation-calculator.

26 Brubaker, *Property Rights in the Defence of Nature.*

27 "James Bay Project," *Wikipedia*, http://en.wikipedia.org/wiki/James_Bay_Project.

28 Conservation Ontario, http://www.conservationontario.ca.

29 Ibid.

30 *13th Annual Report* (Toronto: Ontario Water Resources Commission, 1968).

31 H.R. Plummer, *A Multiple Case Study of Community-based Water Management Initiatives in New Brunswick* (Fredericton: University of New Brunswick, 1998).

32 *Housing Now*, Canada Mortgage and Housing Corporation.

33 *Interim Report on the Water Pollution of Lake Erie, Lake Ontario and the International Section of the St. Lawrence River* (Washington, DC: International Joint Commission, 1965).

34 Ibid.

35 Brian Oram, "What is Dissolved Oxygen?" Water Research Center, http://www.water-research.net.

36 *Premiers' Conferences 1887–2002* (Ottawa: Canadian Intergovernmental Conference Secretariat, 2002).

37 Martin O'Malley and Justin Thompson, "Prime Ministers and Presidents," CBC News Online, November 22, 2003.

38 *A Guide to the Great Lakes Water Quality Agreement: Background for the 2006 Governmental Review* (Washington, DC: International Joint Commission, 2005).

39 "Clean Water Act," *Wikipedia*, http://en.wikipedia.org/wiki/Clean_water_act.

40 Renamed in 1970: the Canadian Council of Resource and Environment Ministers.

41 William McGucken, "The Canadian Federal Government,
    Cultural Eutrophication, and the Regulation of Detergent
    Phosphates, 1970," *Environmental Review* 13, no. 3/4 (1989).

42 "Canadian Environmental Protection Act, 1999: Regulations
    Amending the Phosphorus Concentration Regulations,"
    Canada Gazette 143, no. 13 (June 24, 2009), http://www.gazette.gc.ca.

43 "Love Canal," *Wikipedia*, http://en.wikipedia.org/wiki/Love_Canal.

44 "Acid Rain in New England: A Brief History," U.S. Environmental
    Protection Agency, http://www.epa.gov.

45 Susan Semenak, "Make Canadians Pay True Cost of Water
    Inquiry Recommends," *Montreal Gazette*, April 11, 1985.

46 Ibid.

47 *Federal Water Policy*, Environment Canada, 1987

48 Ibid.

49 Disclosure: one of the authors, Ralph Pentland, chaired the
    interdepartmental task force that wrote the policy statement
    for Minister McMillan.

CHAPTER 4

1 Randy Newman, "Burn On," Lyrics Depot, http://www.lyricsdepot.com.

2 *The Cuyahoga River Watershed: Proceedings of a Symposium
   Commemorating the Dedication of Cunningham Hall*
   (Kent, OH: Kent State University, November 1, 1968).

3 Inflation calculated at: http://www.usinflationcalculator.com.

4 Ted Nordhaus and Michael Shellenberger, *Break Through:
   From the Death of Environmentalism to the Politics of Possibility*
   (Boston: Houghton Mifflin, 2007).

5 "Cuyahoga River Fire," Cleveland Historical, Center for Public
   History + Digital Humanities, Cleveland State University,
   http://clevelandhistorical.org.

6 *Water Pollution in the United States, Third Report of the Special
   Advisory Committee on Water Pollution* (Washington, DC:
   National Resources Committee, 1939).

7 Inger Weibust, *Green Leviathan: The Case for a Federal Role in
   Environmental Policy* (Burlington, VT: Ashgate Publishing, 2009).

8   Chris Wood, *Dry Spring: The Coming Water Crisis of North America* (Vancouver: Raincoast Books, 2008).

9   Weibust, *Green Leviathan.*

10 *Water Pollution in the United States.*

11 William A. Blanpied and Richard C. Atkinson, "Social Scientists' Contributions to Science Policy during the New Deal," University of California at San Diego, http://www.rca.ucsd.edu.

12 *Water Pollution in the United States.*

13 Weibust, *Green Leviathan.*

14 *Water Pollution in the United States.*

15 Hawaii and Alaska were not yet states.

16 *Progress Report 1939: Statement of the Advisory Committee* (Washington, DC: National Resources Committee, 1939).

17 Weibust, *Green Leviathan.*

18 Ibid.

19 "Cuyahoga River," Environmental Protection Agency, http://www.epa.gov.

20 "Cuyahoga River," *Wikipedia,* http://en.wikipedia.org/wiki/Cuyahoga_River.

21 Ibid.

22 See: James Hoggan and Richard Littlemore, *Climate Cover-Up: The Crusade to Deny Global Warming* (Vancouver: Greystone Books, 2009). Also: Naomi Oreskes, *Merchants of Doubt: How a Handful of Scientists Obscured the Truth on Issues from Tobacco Smoke to Global Warming* (New York: Bloomsbury, 2010).

23 "Toxics Release Inventory," *Wikipedia,* http://en.wikipedia.org/wiki/Toxics_Release_Inventory.

24 Martin Olszynski, "Environmental Damages after the Federal Environmental Enforcement Act: Bringing Ecosystem Services to Canadian Environmental Law?" (unpublished thesis, UC Berkeley, 2011).

25 "Review of Developments in Transport in the ESCAP Region, 2003," United Nations Economic and Social Commission for Asia and the Pacific (UN-ESCAP), http://www.unescap.org.

26 "Paris Sewers," *Wikipedia*, http://en.wikipedia.org/wiki/Paris_sewers.

27 Alexandre Kiss, "The Protection of the Rhine Against Pollution," *Natural Resources Journal* 25, no. 3 (July 1985): 613–627.

28 Ibid.

29 Ibid.

30 Ibid.

31 "1986: Chemical Spill Turns Rhine Red," British Broadcasting Corporation, http://news.bbc.co.uk.

32 W. Giger, "The Rhine Red, the Fish Dead: The 1986 Schweizerhalle Disaster, a Retrospect and Long-Term Impact Assessment (abstract)," Environmental Science and Pollution Research International, May 2009.

33 Ben Page and Maria Kaika, "The EU Water Framework Directive, Part 2: Policy Innovation and the Shifting Choreography of Governance," *European Environment* 13 (2003).

34 "Single European Act," *Wikipedia*, http://en.wikipedia.org/wiki/Single_European_Act.

35 "Maastricht Treaty," *Wikipedia*, http://en.wikipedia.org/wiki/Maastricht_Treaty.

36 M.J. Andrews, "Thames Estuary: Pollution and Recovery" in *Effects of Pollutants at the Ecosystem Level,* eds. P.J. Sheehan et al. (Hoboken, NJ: Wiley, 1984).

37 H.F. Gray, "Sewerage in Ancient and Medieval Times," *Sewage Works Journal* (September 1940), cited in Andrews, "Thames Estuary."

38 Andrews, "Thames Estuary."

39 Ibid.

40 "Royal Commission on Environmental Pollution," *Wikipedia*, http://en.wikipedia.org/wiki/Royal_Commission_on_Environmental_Pollution.

41 "River Thames Wins Major Environmental Prize," *People and the Planet News*, October 13, 2010, http://www.peopleandplanet.net.

42 John Vidal, "Thousands of Fish Dead After Thames Sewerage Overflow," *Guardian*, June 9, 2011.

43 Its full legislative title is Directive 2000/60/EC of the
European Parliament and of the Council of 23 October 2000
Establishing a Framework for Community Action in the
Field of Water Policy.

44 Émilie Lagacé, *Shared Water, One Framework:
What Canada Can Learn from EU Water Governance*
(Toronto: FLOW [Forum for Leadership on Water], 2011).

45 Peter Chave, *The EU Water Framework Directive: An Introduction*
(London: IWA Publishing, 2001).

46 Lagacé, *Shared Water, One Framework.*

47 Chave, *The EU Water Framework Directive.*

48 Ibid.

49 "Europe's Water Ambitions Face Reality Check,"
Global Water Intelligence 11, no. 4 (April 2010),
http://www.globalwaterintel.com.

50 Ibid.

51 Ibid.

52 Hongjun Zhang, *International Experience With Toxic
Chemicals Management* (Washington, DC: World Bank Analytical
and Advisory Assistance Program, n.d.).

53 *The Fight for Substitution Within REACH and What was
Finally Decided* (Toronto: Clean Production Action, 2007),
http://www.cleanproduction.org.

54 Jeremy P. Jacobs, "U.S. Reformers Can Learn Much from
European Regulatory Scheme," *E&E News*, February 29, 2012.

55 David Boyd, *Dodging the Toxic Bullet* (Vancouver:
Greystone Books, 2010).

56 "Europe's Water Ambitions Face Reality Check."

57 Jeremy P. Jacobs, "Lax State Oversight Has Led to 'Weak and
Inconsistent' Enforcement," *E&E News*, December 13, 2011.

58 Erica Gies, "Ocean Sprawl: What Is It And What It Means
for Business," *Forbes*, October 26, 2011.

59 The former members of the European Economic Community,
better known as the Common Market, including France, Germany,
and the Netherlands.

CHAPTER 5

1   William Shotyk et al., "Natural Abundance of Sb and Sc in
    Pristine Groundwaters, Springwater Township, Ontario, Canada,
    and Implications for Tracing Contamination from Landfill Leachates,"
    Journal of Environmental Monitoring (November 9, 2005).

2   Author's personal observations, August 2009.

3   *2011 Canadian Water Attitudes Study* (Toronto: R B C and Unilever
    Canada, 2011).

4   Shawn McCarthy, "Support for Climate Action Still Strong in Canada,
    Poll Finds," *Globe and Mail*, November 30, 2011.

5   Geoff Nixon, "Canadians Favour Tougher Eco-Enforcement,
    Kent Told," CTV.ca News, July 6, 2011.

6   Minister's introduction, *Federal Water Policy*,
    Environment Canada, 1987.

7   David Anderson, speech to the Federation of Canadian Municipalities
    Annual General Meeting (Environment Canada, Banff, A B,
    May 25, 2001).

8   Peter Kent, speech to the Senate Standing Committee on Energy,
    the Environment and Natural Resources (Environment Canada,
    October 4, 2011).

9   Although this may be so, it does not follow that the two are
    equivalent in other respects. To name just one way in which they are
    not, the natural environment could exist without the economic one,
    whereas the reverse is not true.

10 Preamble, Canada Water Act, 1970, http://laws-lois.justice.gc.ca.

11 Herbert Plummer, *A Multiple Case Study of Community-Based
    Water Management Initiatives in New Brunswick* (Thunder Bay,
    ON: Lakehead University, 1996).

12 *Canada Water Act Annual Report*, 1985–86, Environment Canada.

13 Minister's introduction, ibid.

14 Robert J.P. Gale, "Canada's Green Plan" in *Nationale Umweltpläne
    in Ausgewählten Industrieländern* [expert submissions to the German
    Bundestag (Parliament)] (Berlin: Springer-Verlag, 1997).

15 *New Environmental Enforcement Act Cracks Down on Environmental
    Offenders* (Ottawa: Environment Canada, June 18, 2009).

16 *Environmental Enforcement Act Background* (Ottawa:
    Environment Canada, June 30, 2011), http://www.ec.gc.ca/AleF-ewe/
    Default.asp?lang=En&n=A72F150D-1.

17 Chris Wood, "Water House Rules," *Alternatives Journal*
    (December 7, 2010).

18 Hon. Graham Steele, *Estimates and Supplementary Detail for
    the Fiscal Year 2011-2012* (Halifax: Minister of Finance, 2011),
    http://www.gov.ns.ca.

19 *Environmental Bill of Rights, 1993*, Statutes of Ontario, 1993.

20 "Living Water Policy Project," the POLIS Project on Ecological
    Governance, University of Victoria, http://www.waterpolicy.ca.

21 Ibid.

22 "Water Opportunities Act," Ontario Ministry of the Environment,
    http://www.ene.gov.on.ca.

23 Steven Renzetti et al., *Running Through Our Fingers:
    How Canada Fails to Capture the Full Value of its Water*
    (Toronto: Blue Economy Initiative, 2011).

24 "Water. Our Life. Our Future. Québec Water Policy,"
    Government of Quebec, http://www.waterpolicy.ca.

25 "Living Water Policy Project."

26 Inger Weibust, *Green Leviathan: The Case for a Federal Role in
    Environmental Policy* (Burlington, VT: Ashgate Publishing, 2009).

27 Gord Miller, *Engaging Solutions: Annual Report 2010/2011*
    (Toronto: Environmental Commissioner of Ontario,
    November 2011).

28 Ibid.

29 David Donnelly et al., *The Ebb and Flow of Environmental
    Enforcement in Ontario* (Toronto: Canadian Environmental
    Defence Fund, 2001).

30 *Sierra Legal Uncovers 2,500 Violations of Ontario's Water
    Pollution Laws* (Vancouver: Ecojustice, March 21, 2007).

31 James Bruce et al. (expert panel on groundwater),
    The Sustainable Management of Groundwater in Canada
    (Ottawa: Council of Canadian Academies, 2009).

32 *The Great Lakes Water Quality Agreement—Promises to Keep; Challenges to Meet*, Alliance for the Great Lakes Biodiversity Project, Canadian Law Association and Great Lakes United, 2007.

33 Chris Wood, "A Rock and a Hard Place," *The Walrus* (December 2011).

34 Mike De Souza, "'Secret' Environment Canada Presentation Warns of Oil Sands' Impact on Habitat," *Postmedia News*, December 22, 2011. The lower amount is for in-situ production sites; the higher for open-pit bitumen mines.

35 Wood, "A Rock and a Hard Place."

36 Chris Wood, "The Last Great Water Fight," *The Walrus* (October 2010).

37 David Schindler, "Monitoring the Oil Sands," *First Perspective* (July 2011), www.firstperspective.ca.

38 Ibid.

39 G. Burton Ayles et al., *Oil Sands Regional Aquatic Monitoring Program (RAMP) Scientific Peer Review of the Five Year Report (1997–2001)* (Fort McMurray, AB: Regional Aquatic Monitoring Program [RAMP Steering Committee], February 13, 2004).

40 Schindler, "Monitoring the Oil Sands."

41 Catherine Main et al., *2010 Regional Aquatics Monitoring Program (RAMP) Scientific Review* (Calgary: Alberta Innovates—Technology Futures, January 2011).

42 *A Foundation for the Future: Building an Environmental Monitoring System for the Oil Sands*, Oil Sands Advisory Panel, Environment Canada, December 2010.

43 Kevin Timoney and Peter Lee, "Does the Alberta Tar Sands Industry Pollute? The Scientific Evidence," *The Open Conservation Biology Journal* 3 (2009).

44 Christa Marshall, "New Oil Sands Report Sparks Government Review," *E&E News*, September 7, 2010.

45 Schindler, "Monitoring the Oil Sands."

46 Shawn Bell, "Toxic Compounds Increasing in Peace Athabasca Delta," *Slave River Journal*, May 17, 2011.

47 Nathan VanderKlippe, "Oil Sands Toxins Growing Rapidly," *Globe and Mail*, August 9, 2010.

48 Ian Austen, "Oil Sands Industry in Canada Tied to Higher Carcinogen
    Level," *New York Times*, January 7, 2013.
49 Josh Wingrove, "Ottawa Kept in Dark on Abnormal Fish Found in
    Oil-Sands Rivers," *Globe and Mail*, December 17, 2010.
50 Personal communication from Ray Ladouceur, May 19, 2010.
51 Wingrove, "Ottawa Kept in Dark on Abnormal Fish Found in
    Oil-Sands Rivers."
52 Andrew Nikiforuk, "A Smoking Gun on Athabasca River:
    Deformed Fish," *The Tyee*, September 17, 2010 .
53 Wingrove, "Ottawa Kept in Dark on Abnormal Fish Found in
    Oil-Sands Rivers."
54 De Souza, "'Secret' Environment Canada Presentation Warns
    of Oil Sands' Impact on Habitat."
55 *Joint Canada Alberta Implementation Plan for Oil Sands
    Monitoring*, Canada and Government of Alberta, 2012.
56 "Alta.'s McQueen Pushes for Oil Sands Monitoring Funds,"
    cTv.ca News, November 6, 2011, http://www.ctv.ca/cTvNews/
    Canada/20111106/mcqueen-fight-for-oil-sands-monitoring-funds-
    111105/#ixzz1d2vDp4cG.
57 William F. Donahue, "Provincial Government Still Failing Alberta's
    Rivers," Water Matters, November 8, 2011.
58 Ralph Pentland, unpublished.
59 Tim Morris et al. (Gordon Water Group of Concerned Scientists
    and Citizens), *Changing the Flow: A Blueprint for Federal Action on
    Freshwater* (Toronto: Walter and Duncan Gordon Foundation, 2007).
60 *Changing Currents: Water Sustainability and the Future of
    Canada's Natural Resource Sectors* (Ottawa: National Round
    Table on the Environment and the Economy, 2010).
61 Robert Sandford, "Lake Winnipeg: Canada's Great Dead Zone,"
    Water Canada (blog), accessed December 5, 2011,
    http://watercanada.net/2011/lake-winnipeg-canada's-great-
    dead-zone.
62 Jen Skerritt, "Treatment Plant Among Worst," *Winnipeg Free Press*,
    November 24, 2011.

63 Kathryn Harrison, *Passing the Buck: Federalism and Canada's Environmental Policy* (Vancouver: UBC Press, 1996).

64 Peter H. Pearse et al., *Currents of Change: Final Report, Inquiry on Federal Water Policy*, Ottawa, 1985.

65 "Canadian Drinking Water Guidelines," Health Canada, accessed March 9, 2012, http://www.hc-sc.gc.ca/ewh-semt/water-eau/drink-potab/guide/index-eng.php.

66 Randy Christensen, *Waterproof 2: Canada's Drinking Water Report Card* (Vancouver: Sierra Legal Defence Fund, 2006).

67 "Proceedings, Standing Committee on Aboriginal Peoples," Committee Proceedings, fortieth Parliament, third session, http://www.parl.gc.ca/ParlBusiness/Senate/Committees/Committee_SenProceed.asp?Language=E&Parl=40&Ses=3&comm_id=1.

68 *Harper Government Increases Protection for Canada's Water Quality*, Environment Canada, July 18, 2012.

69 "Wastewater Systems Effluent Regulations," *Canada Gazette*, June 28, 2012.

70 *Harper Government Increases Protection.*

CHAPTER 6

1 *Prince Edward Island Population Report* (Charlottetown: Prince Edward Island Department of Finance and Municipal Affairs, 2011), http://www.gov.pe.ca.

2 "100 Largest Municipalities in Canada by Population," *Wikipedia*, http://en.wikipedia.org/wiki/List_of_the_100_largest_municipalities_in_Canada_by_population.

3 *Federal Water Policy*, Environment Canada, 1987.

4 Ibid.

5 "Town of Ponoka Pleads Guilty and is Fined $70,000 for Release of Wastewater to Battle River," news release, December 7, 2011.

6 "Charlottetown Gets Order from Feds to Clean Up Harbour," CBC News, November 4, 2011.

7 Dianne Saxe, "Canada: Farmer Goes To Jail," *Mondaq*, November 14, 2011, http://www.mondaq.com.

8   Lynne Heustis, *Policing Pollution: The Prosecution of Environmental Offences* (Ottawa: Law Reform Commission of Canada, 1984).

9   *Enforcing Canada's Pollution Laws: The Public Must Come First!* (Ottawa: Standing Committee on Environment and Sustainable Development, 1998).

10   *The Canadian Environmental Protection Act, 1999—Five Year Review: Closing the Gaps* (Ottawa: Report of the Standing Committee on the Environment and Sustainable Development, 2007).

11   *2001 Report of the Commissioner of the Environment and Sustainable Development* (Ottawa: Office of the Auditor General, 2001).

12   Scott Vaughan, *December 2009 Report of the Commissioner of the Environment and Sustainable Development to the House of Commons* (Ottawa: Office of the Auditor General, 2009).

13   Scott Vaughan, *December 2011 Report of the Commissioner of the Environment and Sustainable Development* (Ottawa: Office of the Auditor General, 2011).

14   "Tetrachloroethylene," *Wikipedia,* http://en.wikipedia.org/wiki/Tetrachloroethylene.

15   William Amos et al., *Getting Tough on Environmental Crime? Holding the Government of Canada to Account on Environmental Enforcement* (Vancouver: Ecojustice, 2011).

16   Federal spending on research and development was $5.6 billion in 2008, compared with $5.1 billion from universities (the next biggest public-sector investor) and $14.5 billion from private businesses. "Domestic Spending on Research and Development (GERD), Funding Sector, by Province," Statistics Canada, http://www40.statcan.ca.

17   *A Guide to Understanding the Canadian Environmental Protection Act, 1999,* Environment Canada, July 15, 2011.

18   Tim Morris et al. (Gordon Water Group of Concerned Scientists and Citizens), *Changing the Flow: A Blueprint for Federal Action on Freshwater* (Toronto: Walter and Duncan Gordon Foundation, 2007).

19   Scott Vaughan, evidence given to the Standing Committee on Environment and Sustainable Development, fortieth Parliament, third session, December 8, 2010.

20 Ibid.

21 Scott Vaughan, *December 2010, Report of the Environment Commissioner* (Ottawa: Office of the Auditor General, 2010).

22 Mike De Souza, "No 'Credible Information' to Support Claims Oil Sands Are Green, Says Environment Canada," *Postmedia News*, December 9, 2011.

23 "Canadian Climate Research Funding Drying Up," CBC News, November 23, 2010.

24 James Bruce et al. (expert panel on groundwater), *The Sustainable Management of Groundwater in Canada* (Ottawa: Council of Canadian Academies, 2009).

25 Steve E. Hrudey, *Safe Drinking Water Policy for Canada: Turning Hindsight into Foresight* (Toronto: C.D. Howe Institute, 2011).

26 Ibid.

27 Bruce Campion-Smith, "700 Environment Canada Jobs on the Chopping Block," *Toronto Star*, August 3, 2011.

28 "Federal Government Job Cuts: The Story So Far," CBC News, August 9, 2011.

29 Mitchell Anderson, "Feds Undercut B.C.'s Oil Spill Prevention Panel," *The Tyee*, May 31, 2010.

30 Margo McDiarmid, "Environmental Network Forced to Close Doors," CBC News, October 14, 2011.

31 "Parliament Passes Amendments to Environmental Assessment Act," GLOBE-Net, July 13, 2010, http://www.globe-net.com.

32 Robert Sandford, *Canadian Water Security: The Critical Role of Science, Conference Summary, May 27th & 28th, 2010* (Ottawa: Canadian Foundation for Climate and Atmospheric Science, 2010).

33 "Canada Renews Investment in Water Research: CWN Receives $15 Million," Canadian Water Network, accessed December 14, 2011, http://www.cwn-rce.ca.

34 "Fed Deal with Charitable Group Scuttled after Enbridge Pressure," *The Canadian Press*, March 4, 2012.

35 *New Report Details Government Actions that Undermine Research into the Science of Climate Change* (Ottawa: Climate Action Network, March 15, 2010).

36 Mike De Souza, "Politicians Cancel Probe of Oil Sands,"
    Canwest News Service, July 7, 2010.

37 *Parliamentary Review of Canadian Environmental Assessment
    Act Abruptly Terminated* (Vancouver: West Coast Environmental Law,
    November 29, 2011).

38 Shawn McCarthy, "Ottawa Wants to Streamline Environmental
    Reviews," *Globe and Mail*, November 29, 2011.

39 "Are You Ready for a New Environmental Assessment
    Act in Canada?" *Lake Ontario Waterkeeper*, December 6, 2011,
    http://www.Waterkeeper.ca.

40 Margo McDiarmid, "Environment Agency Says Cuts Will Limit
    Oversight," CBC News, October 20, 2011.

41 McCarthy, "Support for Climate Action Still Strong in Canada,
    Poll Finds," *Globe and Mail*, November 30, 2011.

42 Speech for the Honourable Peter Kent, Signing of the Amended
    Great Lakes Water Quality Agreement, Washington, DC,
    September 7, 2012, Environment Canada, September 7, 2012.

43 John Jackson, *Will the New Great Lakes Water Quality
    Agreement Be Cause for Celebration? Governments Need to
    Promise Real Action and Funding* (Ottawa: Great Lakes United,
    October 31, 2011).

44 Geoff Nixon, "Canadians Favour Tougher Eco-Enforcement,
    Kent Told," CTV News, July 6, 2011.

CHAPTER 7

1 Evan Lehmann, "Insurers Warn Government Officials to
   'Wake Up' and Prepare for Disasters," *E&E News*, March 9, 2012.

2 Stefan Ambec et al., *The Porter Hypothesis at 20: Can
   Environmental Regulation Enhance Innovation and
   Competitiveness?" Série scientifique* (Quebec: Cyrano, 2010).

3 Ibid.

4 Ibid.

5 Inger Weibust, *Green Leviathan: The Case for a Federal
   Role in Environmental Policy* (Burlington, VT: Ashgate Publishing,
   2009).

6   Jacques Leslie, "China's Pollution Nightmare is Now Everyone's Pollution Nightmare," *Christian Science Monitor*, March 19, 2008.

7   Robert Watson et al., *UK National Ecosystem Assessment: Understanding nature's value to society*, UNEP-WCMC, Cambridge, 2011.

8   L. Emerton and E. Bos, *Value: Counting Ecosystems as Water Infrastructure* (Gland, Switzerland: International Union for the Conservation of Nature, 2004), http://data.iucn.org.

9   Saqib Rahim, "Philadelphia uses tough love to overhaul its water and sewer system," *E&E News*, January 13, 2012.

10 ICF Marbek, *Assessing the Economic Value of Protecting the Great Lakes Ecosystems: A Cost-benefit Analysis of Habitat Protection and Restoration* (Toronto: Ontario Ministry of the Environment, November 2010).

11 Nicholas Muller et al., "Environmental Accounting for Pollution in the United States Economy," *American Economic Review* 101 (August 2011).

12 Jim Robbins, "The Ecology of Disease," *New York Times*, July 14, 2012.

13 Ibid.

14 Estimates derived by the authors from data reported in Janet Honey, *Crops in Manitoba, 2009–2010*, University of Manitoba, December 2010, http://www.umanitoba.ca.

15 Steven Renzetti et al., *Running Through Our Fingers: How Canada Fails to Capture the Full Value of its Water* (Toronto: Blue Economy Initiative, 2011).

16 Paul Quinlan, "Far from Impeding Growth, Restoration Will Create 230,000 Jobs—Report," *E&E News*, January 3, 2011.

17 Rena Steinzor, "The Truth About Regulation in America," *Harvard Law and Policy Review* 5 (October 28, 2011).

18 "REACH," European Commission, http://ec.europa.eu.

19 Hongjun Zhang, *International Experience With Toxic Chemicals Management* (Washington, DC: World Bank Analytical and Advisory Assistance Program, n.d.).

20 *Taking Stock: North American Pollutant Releases and Transfers* (Montreal: Commission for Environmental Cooperation, 1997).

21 Nancy Olewiler and K. Dawson, *Analysis of National Pollution Release Inventory Data and Toxic Emissions by Industry*, prepared for Department of Finance Canada, Ottawa, 1998.

22 Jeff Sallot, "Canada Lags on Air Pollution Cleanup Compared with U.S., Coalition Finds," *Globe and Mail*, October 13, 2005.

23 *Taking Stock: North American Pollutant Releases and Transfers* (Montreal: Commission for Environmental Cooperation, 2011).

24 Thomas Gunton and K.S. Calbick, *The Maple Leaf in the OECD: Comparing Progress Toward Sustainability* (Vancouver: David Suzuki Foundation, 2005).

25 Mike De Souza, "No 'Credible Information' to Support Claims Oil Sands Are Green, Says Environment Canada," *Postmedia News*, December 9, 2011.

26 Sandy Hansen, "Forums to Discuss Water Supply Project that Will Impact Lake Ashtabula," *Times-Record*, January 18, 2006, and "Hearing Discusses Red River Water Project," *Associated Press*, February 8, 2006.

27 "Flooding Ranked Top 2011 Headline in North Dakota," *Associated Press*, December 30, 2011.

28 Paul Quinlan, "Flood Fears Downstream Hinder Plans to Divert Red River of the North," *New York Times*, August 27, 2010.

29 Jim Chliboyko, "What Happens When the U.S. Drains Polluted Water into a Canadian Watershed?" *Canadian Geographic* (June 2011).

30 Tadzio Richards, "Scientists Warn B.C. Mining Rush Would Harm Alaska and B.C. Salmon, Clean Water," *Rivers Without Borders*, November 15, 2011, http://riverswithoutborders.org.

31 Prairie Provinces Water Board, http://www.ppwb.ca.

32 In 2010. Agriculture Canada, Ottawa.

33 David Schindler and William Donahue, "An Impending Water Crisis in Canada's Western Prairie Provinces," Proceedings of the National Academy of Sciences, April 2006, http://www.pnas.org.

34 Ibid.

35 Chris Wood, *Dry Spring: The Coming Water Crisis of North America* (Vancouver: Raincoast Books, 2008).

36 *Leaky Exports: A Portrait of the Virtual Water Trade in Canada* (Ottawa: Council of Canadians, 2011).

37 Alaa El-Sadek, "Virtual Water Trade as a Solution for Water Scarcity in Egypt (abstract)," *Water Resources Management* 24, no. 11 (2011).

38 Jasmine Coleman, "World's 'Seven Billionth Baby' is Born," *Guardian*, October 31, 2011.

39 *How to Feed the World in 2050* (Rome: Food and Agricultural Organization of the United Nations [FAO], 2009).

40 Renzetti et al., *Running Through Our Fingers*.

41 Ibid.

42 Shannon Dueck, "Record Breaking Year For Weather," PortageOnline, accessed January 8, 2012, http://www.portageonline.com.

CHAPTER 8

1 David Boyd, "No Taps, No Toilets: First Nations and the Constitutional Right to Water in Canada," *McGill Law Journal* 57, no. 1 (2011).

2 Quoted in Boyd, ibid.

3 Kazi Stastna, "Clean Running Water Still a Luxury on Many Native Reserves: About 39% of First Nations Water Systems Deemed 'High Risk,'" CBC News, November 30, 2011.

4 Boyd, "No Taps, No Toilets."

5 Ibid.

6 Neegan Burnside Ltd., *National Assessment of First Nations Water and Wastewater Systems, Ontario Regional Roll-Up Report*, prepared for Department of Indian and Northern Affairs Canada, Ottawa, January 2011.

7 Jennifer Ditchburn, "How Harper Seized Control of the Pipeline and Health-Care Debates," *Globe and Mail*, January 20, 2012.

8 Melody Peterson, "The Lost Boys of Aamjiwnaang," *Men's Health*, November 5, 2009.

9 Ibid.

10 David Stern, "The Environmental Kuznets Curve," *International Society for Ecological Economics* (June 2003).

11 Stéphane Hallegatte et al., *From Growth to Green Growth—a Framework* (Washington, DC: World Bank, December 7, 2011).

12 Ibid.

13 P.J. Huffstetter, "PepsiCo Finds Low Levels of Fungicide in Orange Juice," *Reuters*, January 14, 2012. Oddly, this report citing the U.S. FDA also notes that "three samples of Canadian orange juice" were not contaminated. Perhaps Canadian orange groves are too cold to support fungal growth.

14 T.A. Aire, "Short-Term Effects of Carbendazim on the Gross and Microscopic Features of the Testes of Japanese Quails (Coturnix Coturnix Japonica)," *Anatomy and Embryology* (August 2005).

15 "Carbendazim Use Banned on Fruit Crops," Australian Broadcasting Corporation, May 2, 2010.

16 Mary Clare Jalonick, "Fungicide In Orange Juice: FDA Steps Up Testing," *Huffington Post*, Jan 9, 2012.

17 "Flame Retardants in Inuit Breast Milk," CBC News, September 17, 2003.

18 Geoffrey Lean, "It's Official: Men Really Are the Weaker Sex," *Independent*, December 7, 2008.

19 Merih Otker Uslu et al., *Chemicals of Emerging Concern in the Great Lakes Region* (Washington, DC: International Joint Commission, August 2011).

20 Dene Moore, "Toxic Drug Traces Detected in River. St. Lawrence Samples Show Pharmacological Pollution," *The Canadian Press*, July 5, 2006.

21 Mark Hume, "Fraser River Sockeye Face Chemical Soup of 200 Contaminants," *Globe and Mail*, May 11, 2011.

22 Brian Handwerk, "Caffeinated Seas Found Off U.S. Pacific Northwest," *National Geographic News*, July 30, 2012.

23 Jeff Donn et al., "Drugs Found in Drinking Water," *Associated Press*, September 12, 2008.

24 Jeff Donn et al., "Pharmaceuticals Lurking in Drinking Water," AP-MSNBC, March 10, 2008.

25 Chris Richard, "Hexavalent Chromium: Chemical Found in Drinking Water of 31 U.S. Cities," *Christian Science Monitor*, December 20, 2010.

26 Andrew Martin, "Antibacterial Chemical Raises Safety Issues," *New York Times*, August 19, 2011.

27 Other names for the same group of pollutants and phenomenon include endocrine disrupting substances and endocrine mimicry.

28 "Benzene," American Cancer Society, http://www.cancer.org.

29 Abrahm Lustgarten, "EPA Finds Compound Used in Fracking in Wyoming Aquifer," *ProPublica*, November 10, 2011.

30 *Threats to Sources of Drinking Water and Aquatic Ecosystem Health in Canada*, Environment Canada—National Water Research Institute, 2001.

31 David Boyd and S. Scott Wallace, *Fireproof Whales and Contaminated Mother's Milk: The Inadequacy of Canada's Proposed PBDE Regulations* (Vancouver: David Suzuki Foundation, 2006).

32 "Endocrine Disrupting Compounds," National Institute of Environmental Health Sciences, National Institutes of Health, http://www.niehs.nih.gov.

33 Ibid.

34 "About TEDX: Our People," Endocrine Disruption Exchange, http://www.endocrinedisruption.com.

35 Theo Colborn and Lynn E. Carroll, "Pesticides, Sexual Development, Reproduction, and Fertility: Current Perspective and Future Direction," *Human and Ecological Risk Assessment* 13, no. 5 (2007).

36 Lean, "It's Official: Men Really Are the Weaker Sex."

37 Marla Cone, "Low Doses, Big Effects: Scientists Seek 'Fundamental Changes' in Testing, Regulation of Hormone-Like Chemicals," *Environmental Health News*, March 15, 2012.

38 Colborn and Carroll, "Pesticides, Sexual Development, Reproduction, and Fertility."

39 "Endocrine Disrupting Hormones May Affect Low
    Male Birth Rate," *Beyond Pesticides* (blog), April 12, 2007,
    www.beyondpesticides.org/dailynewsblog/?p=75.

40 J. Toppari et al., "Trends in the Incidence of Cryptorchidism
    and Hypospadias, and Methodological Limitations of
    Registry-Based Data," *Human Reproduction Update* 7, no. 3 (2001).

41 Gwynne Lyons, *Men Under Threat: The Decline in
    Male Reproductive Health and the Potential Role of Exposure
    to Chemicals during In-Utero Development* (Somerset, UK:
    CHEM Trust, May 2009).

42 "Prostate Cancer May Be Linked to Birth Control Pills in Water Supply,"
    My Health News Daily, November 15, 2011.

43 Hannah Seligson, "The Pre-teen Girl Mystery," *The Daily Beast*,
    May 22, 2009, http://www.thedailybeast.com.

44 James Brophy et al., "Occupation and Breast Cancer:
    A Canadian Case–Control Study," *Annals of the New York Academy
    of Sciences* 1076 (2006).

45 Health Canada, Ottawa.

46 "Chemicals 'May Reduce Fertility,'" BBC News, January 29, 2009.

47 Lean, "It's Official: Men Really Are the Weaker Sex."

48 Chris Wood, "NAFTA and the Unmanning of North America,"
    Miller-McCune (March 2009).

49 Gwynne Lyons, *Effects of Pollutants on the Reproductive
    Health of Male Vertebrate Wildlife* (Somerset, UK: CHEM Trust,
    December 2008).

50 *Taking Stock: North American Pollutant Releases and Transfers*
    (Montreal: Commission for Environmental Cooperation, 2011).

51 Derek Muir et al., "Persistent Organic Pollutants and Mercury"
    in *Threats to Sources of Drinking Water*, 2001.

52 Ibid.

53 *The Great Lakes Water Quality Agreement—Promises to Keep;
    Challenges to Meet*, Alliance for the Great Lakes Biodiversity Project,
    Canadian Law Association and Great Lakes United, 2007.

54 Ibid.

55 Chris Wood, "The Last Great Water Fight," *The Walrus* (October 2010) and *Dry Spring: The Coming Water Crisis of North America* (Vancouver: Raincoast Books, 2008).

56 Personal communication from Guy Thacker, May 2010.

57 Ibid.

58 Rock Smith and Bruce Lourie, *Slow Death by Rubber Duck* (Toronto: Knopf Canada, 2009).

59 "Biographical Note," National Institute of Environmental Health Sciences, National Institutes of Health, http://www.niehs.nih.gov.

60 Linda Birnbaum, "Biology's Clock Interrupted: Endocrine Disrupting Chemicals in Drinking Water," Statement to the Subcommittee on Energy and the Environment, Committee on Energy and Commerce, U.S. House of Representatives, February 25, 2010.

61 Ibid.

62 Rebecca Klaper and Lyman C. Welch, *Emerging Contaminant Threats and the Great Lakes: Existing Science, Estimating Relative Risk and Determining Policies* (Chicago: Alliance for the Great Lakes, 2011).

63 *Taking Stock: North American Pollutant Releases and Transfers*, 2011.

64 *State of the Great Lakes Highlight Report* (Washington, DC: Environmental Protection Agency and Ottawa: Environment Canada, 2009).

65 *Economic Plan Supporting the Canada-wide Strategy for the Management of Municipal Wastewater Effluent* (Winnipeg, MB: Canadian Council of Ministers of the Environment, 2008).

66 Ibid.

67 *Taking Stock: North American Pollutant Releases and Transfers*, 2011.

68 Ian R. Falconer, "Are Endocrine Disrupting Compounds a Health Risk in Drinking Water?" *International Journal of Environmental Research and Public Health* (2006).

69 *The Great Lakes Sewage Report Card* (Vancouver: Sierra Legal Defence Fund, November 2006).

70 Wood, *Dry Spring.*

71 Gord Miller, *Engaging Solutions: Annual Report 2010/2011* (Toronto: Environmental Commissioner of Ontario, November 2011).

72 Personal communication from the director of the Iona Island Water Treatment Plant, Vancouver, 2006.

73 Steven Renzetti et al., *Running Through Our Fingers: How Canada Fails to Capture the Full Value of its Water* (Toronto: Blue Economy Initiative, 2011).

74 *A Review of the Current Canadian Legislative Framework for Wastewater Biosolids* (Winnipeg, MB: Canadian Council of Ministers of the Environment, 2010).

75 U.S. figures do not include upstream oil and gas industry. *Taking Stock: North American Pollutant Releases and Transfers*, 2011.

76 Sandra Hines, "Nitrogen 'Double Whammy' Could Alter Lakes," Futurity.org, accessed December 21, 2011, http://www.futurity.org/ earth-environment/nitrogen-'double-%20whammy'-could-alter-lakes.

77 *Threats to Sources of Drinking Water and Aquatic Ecosystem Health in Canada*, Environment Canada—National Water Research Institute, 2001.

78 Private communication.

79 "Algae Smother Chinese Lake, Millions Panic," *Associated Press*, May 31, 2007, http://www.msnbc.msn.com/id/18959222/ns/ world_news-world_environment/t/algae-smother-chinese-lake-millions-panic/#.TYR3CBxg-jQ.

80 "Canada's Sickest Lake," Canadian Parks and Wilderness Society, Manitoba Chapter, 2009, http://cpawsmb.org/news/ canadas-sickest-lake.

81 Julia Pyper, "Fate of the Great Lakes is Tied to Climate Change," *E&E News*, October 17, 2011.

82 Janet Honey, *Manitoba Pig and Pork Industry 2010* (Winnipeg, MB: Department of Agribusiness and Agricultural Economics, University of Manitoba, 2011).

83 Chris Wood, "The Business of Saving the Earth," *The Walrus* (October 2008).

84 Maureen Salamon, "Pediatricians Urge Better Protection From Chemicals," *HealthDay*, April 25, 2011, http://www.healthday.com.

85 "Precautionary Principle," *Wikipedia*, http://en.wikipedia.org/wiki/ Precautionary_Principle.

86 "Human Health Risk Assessment for Priority Substances," Health Canada, http://www.hc-sc.gc.ca/ewh-semt/pubs/contaminants/approach/intro-eng.php.

87 Peter Boyer et al., eds., *Expert Consultation on Emerging Issues of the Great Lakes in the 21st Century* (Washington, DC: International Joint Commission, November 2006).

88 Leonard Ritter et al., *Integrating Emerging Technologies into Chemical Safety Assessment: Report in Focus* (Ottawa: Council of Canadian Academies, 2012).

89 Ibid.

90 Andrew MacLeod, "Bias Built into Feds' Pesticide Use Review: B.C. Doctor," *The Tyee*, October 2011.

91 Cone, "Low Doses, Big Effects."

92 Louise Egan, "Canada declares BPA Toxic, Sets Stage for More Bans," *Reuters*, October 14, 2010.

93 David Boyd, *Dodging the Toxic Bullet* (Vancouver: Greystone Books, Vancouver, 2010).

94 Decamethylcyclopentasiloxane. Sarah Stiner, "Canada: Scientific Panel Disagrees With Government Assessment Of Environmental Danger Posed By Chemical Compound," http://Mondaq.com, January 25, 2012.

95 Ibid.

96 Nathan Vanderklippe, "Federal Documents Spark Outcry by Oil Sands Critics," *Globe and Mail*, January 26, 2012.

97 *Government of Canada Concludes Silozane D5 is Not Harmful to the Environment*, Environment Canada, February 29, 2012.

CHAPTER 9

1 Personal local knowledge. The remains of some of these works are preserved at several sites on the creek.

2 "Wetland Inventory for Research and Education Network, McMaster," McMaster University, http://wirenet.mcmaster.ca/casestudies/Cootes/cootesthree.php; Royal Botanical Gardens "Project Paradise," http://www.rbg.ca/Page.aspx?pid=312.

3 "Living Water Policy Project," the POLIS Project on Ecological Governance, University of Victoria, http://www.waterpolicy.ca.

4 *Navigating the Shoals: Assessing Water Governance and Management in Canada* (Ottawa: Conference Board of Canada, April 2007).

5 Tim Morris et al. (Gordon Water Group of Concerned Scientists and Citizens), *Changing the Flow: A Blueprint for Federal Action on Freshwate*r (Toronto: Walter and Duncan Gordon Foundation, 2007).

6 Peggy Holroyd and Terra Simieritsch, *The Waters That Bind Us: Transboundary Implications of Oil Sands Development* (Calgary: Pembina Institute, February 2009).

7 Morris et al., *Changing the Flow.*

8 *Moving to Action: Setting Priorities from NRT's Charting a Course Recommendations* (Ottawa: National Round Table on the Environment and the Economy, 2012).

9 Robert Sandford et al., *Climate Change Adaptation and Water Governance: Summary Report* (Burnaby, BC: ACT: Adaptation to Climate Change Team, Simon Fraser University, October 2011).

10 Chris Wood, "Water House Rules," *Alternatives Journal* (December 7, 2010).

11 Holroyd and Simieritsch, *The Waters That Bind Us.*

12 The Sustainable Planning Research Group, Simon Fraser University, *Canada's Environmental Record: An Assessment* (Vancouver: David Suzuki Foundation, 2005).

13 *Human Activity and the Environment: Economy and the Environment,* (Ottawa: Statistics Canada, 2011), http://www.statcan.gc.ca.

14 Amy Mannix and Vic Adamowicz, *Economic Instruments for Water Management: Selected Australian and Canadian Case Studies, and Issues for Application in Canada* (Ottawa: Sustainable Prosperity, October 2011).

15 Holroyd and Simieritsch, *The Waters That Bind Us.*

16 Morris et al., *Changing the Flow.*

17 Chris Wood, *Dry Spring: The Coming Water Crisis of North America* (Vancouver: Raincoast Books, 2008).

18 Randy Christensen, *Waterproof 2: Canada's Drinking Water Report Card* (Vancouver: Sierra Legal Defence Fund, 2006).

19 Jeremy Schmidt, *Alternative Water Futures in Alberta* (Edmonton: Parkland Institute, University of Alberta, December 2011).

20 Deborah Peterson et al., *Modelling Water Trade in the Southern Murray-Darling Basin: Staff Working Paper* (Melbourne: Australian Government Productivity Commission, November 2004).

21 Noah Garrison and Karen Hobbs, *Rooftops to Rivers II: Green Strategies for Controlling Stormwater and Combined Sewer Overflows* (New York: Natural Resources Defense Council, November 2011).

22 "Eight Toxics Proposed for Elimination from European Waters," *Environmental News Service*, February 1, 2012, http://ens-newswire.com.

23 Brandon H. Barnes et al., *United States: Broad Scope and Impact of California 'Green Chemistry' Regulations* (Chicago: McDermott Will & Emery, January 4, 2012).

24 Stefan Ambec et al., *The Porter Hypothesis at 20: Can Environmental Regulation Enhance Innovation and Competitiveness?" Série scientifique* (Quebec: Cyrano, 2010).

25 Neil Gunningham and Darren Sinclair, *Leaders and Laggards: Next Generation Environmental Regulation* (Sheffield, UK: Greenleaf Publishing, 2002).

26 Émilie Lagacé, *Shared Water, One Framework: What Canada Can Learn from EU Water Governance* (Toronto: FLOW [Forum for Leadership on Water], 2011).

27 Ralph Pentland and Oliver M. Brandes, "Chronology—Attempts at a Federal Water Strategy" in "Activity but No Action: Failed Attempts at Implementing a Federal Water Strategy in Canada," *Flow Monitor* 1 (Fall 2009).

28 Steven Renzetti et al., *Running Through Our Fingers: How Canada Fails to Capture the Full Value of its Water* (Toronto: Blue Economy Initiative, 2011).

29 Alexander Wood, "Why We Need to Measure Our 'Natural Capital,'"
    Globe and Mail (blog), April 19, 2012, www.theglobeandmail.com/
    report-on-business/economy-labwhy-we-need-to-measure-
    our-natural-capital/article4170695.

30 Jared Diamond, *Collapse: How Societies Choose to Fail or Succeed*
    (New York: Viking, 2005).

31 "Land and Weather," Citizenship and Immigration Canada,
    http://www.cic.gc.ca. Other sources rank Canada in fourth place for
    land area, after Russia, China, and the Unites States: see, for example,
    "Land Area of the World" at http://www world.bymap.org.

32 Giles Sheldrick, "EU Says Water Is Not Healthy," *Express*,
    November 18, 2011, http://www.express.co.uk.

33 "Illicit Sewage Spills Foul Baltimore Harbor," *E&E News*,
    December 12, 2011.

34 News conference, *c.* 1976.

35 *Northern Voices, Northern Waters: NWT Water Stewardship Strategy*
    (Yellowknife: Government of the NWT/Indian and Northern Affairs
    Canada, 2010).

36 *CIELAP's Call to Action for a Green Economy* (Toronto: Canadian
    Institute for Environmental Law and Policy [CIELAP], April 12, 2011).

37 Owen Saunders and Michael Weng, "Whose Water? Canadian
    Management and the Challenge of Jurisdictional Fragmentation"
    in *Eau Canada: The Future of Canada's Water* (Vancouver:
    UBC Press, 2006).

CHAPTER 10

 1 "Canada's Top Baby Names for 2010," Babycenter,
    http://www.babycenter.ca.

 2 *Human Development Report 1994* (Oxford, UK:
    Oxford University Press, 1994).

 3 Owen Saunders, *Managing Water in a Federal State:
    The Canadian Experience* (Ottawa: Forum of Federations, 2008).

 4 Peter Ross, "Opinion: Canada's Mass Firing of Ocean Scientists
    Brings 'Silent Summer,'" *Environmental Health News*, n.d.,
    http://www.environmentalhealthnews.org.

5   Peter O'Neil, "Fisheries Act Changes Introduced Amid Debate
     Over New Law's Intent," *Vancouver Sun*, April 26, 2012.

6   *The Great Lakes Water Quality Review: Synthesis of
     Public Comment* (Washington, DC: International Joint
     Commission, n.d.).

7   "Canadians Want More Action on the Environment,"
     Angus Reid Global Monitor, July 20, 2010.

8   *2011 Canadian Water Attitudes Study* (Toronto: RBC and
     Unilever Canada, 2011).

9   *Army 2040: First Look, Trends, Challenges and Implications
     for Canada's Army* (Kingston, ON: Directorate of Land Concepts
     and Designs, 2011).

10 *Global Trends 2025: A Transformed World* (Washington, DC: U.S.
     National Intelligence Council, November 2008).

11 Colin Sullivan, "Could Investors, Not Regulators, Better Solve the
     Climate Problem?" *E&e News*, January 13, 2012.

12 Lord Mansfield in *R. v. Bembridge* (1783), quoted in Evan
     Fox-Decent, *Sovereignty's Promise: The State as Fiduciary*
     (New York: Oxford University Press, 2011).

13 "Evan Fox-Decent Book Shortlisted for MacPherson Prize,"
     McGill University, http://www.mcgill.ca/law/node/3507.

14 Evan Fox-Decent, "The Fiduciary Nature of State Legal Authority,"
     Queen's Law Journal 31 (2005).

15 Cited in Fox-Decent, ibid.

16 "Brief for *Amicus Curiae* Law Professors-Exhibit A" in *Alec L. et al.,
     Plaintiffs, v. Lisa Jackson et al., Defendants*, in United States District
     Court for the Northern District of California, San Francisco Division,
     December 7, 2011.

17 Michael Blumm and Thea Schwartz, "Mono Lake and the
     Evolving Public Trust in Western Water," *Arizona Law Review* 37,
     no. 3 (1995).

18 Cited at paragraph 80 in *British Columbia v. Canadian Forest
     Products Ltd.*, Supreme Court of Canada, 2004.

19 "Complaint for Declaratory and Injunctive Relief,"
     in *Alec L. et al v. Jackson et al.*

20 Evan Fox-Decent, "From Fiduciary States to Joint Trusteeship of the Atmosphere: The Right to a Healthy Environment Through a Fiduciary Prism," *Social Science Research Network*, December 15, 2010, http://ssrn.com.

21 *Prescott v. Birmingham Corp.* (1954), *Bromley London Borough Council v. Greater London Council* (1983). Cited in Fox-Decent, *Sovereignty's Promise.*

22 "*M.C. Mehta v. Kamal Nath*," *Wikipedia,* en.wikipedia.org/wiki/M.C._Mehta_v._Kamal_Nath.

23 "Standing in Public Interest Cases," Queensland Public Interest Law Clearing House, July 2005.

24 *British Columbia v. Canadian Forest Products Ltd.*

25 Colin Freeze, "Top Mountie Delivers Candid, Scathing View of Force at the Brink," *Globe and Mail,* December 19, 2011.

26 "Section 324.1701," Natural Resources and Environmental Protection Act, 1994, Michigan Compiled Laws, http://www.legislature.mi.gov.

CHAPTER 11

1 Interview with Danny Gaudet, May 2010.

2 *Northern Voices, Northern Waters: NWT Water Stewardship Strategy,* (Yellowknife: Government of the NWT/Indian and Northern Affairs Canada, 2010).

3 Interview with Michael Miltenberger, May 2010.

INDEX